MW00608445

Investment Real Estate
FINANCE&ASSET MANAGEMENT

Fred W. Prassas CPM®

PROFESSIONAL REVIEW

Howard Campbell, CPM®

Ken Goodacre, CPM®

Enis Hartz, CPM®

IREM EDUCATION PUBLISHING

Nancye Kirk
Chief Strategy Officer / Education, Outreach, Advocacy

Nadia Geagea Pupa
Managing Editor, Publications

Dawn Brent
Editor, Content and Curriculum Development

Suzanne Hill
Editor, Content and Curriculum Development

INSTITUTE OF REAL ESTATE MANAGEMENT

Investment Real Estate
FINANCE&ASSET
MANAGEMENT

Fred W. Prassas CPM®

© 2013 by the Institute of Real Estate Management
of the NATIONAL ASSOCIATION OF REALTORS®
All rights reserved. First Edition.

Printed in the United States of America
10 9 8 7 6 5 4 3 2

SKU: 717
ISBN-13 978-1-57203-173-9

This book or any part thereof may not be reproduced, stored in a retrieval system, or transmitted, in any form
or by any means, electronic, mechanical, photocopying, recording, or otherwise, without the prior written
permission of the publisher. Inquiries should be directed to:

Publishing Department
Institute of Real Estate Management
430 North Michigan Avenue
Chicago, IL 60611-4090.

This publication is designed to provide accurate and authoritative information in regard to the subject matter
covered. Forms or other documents included in this book are intended as samples only. Because of changing
and varying state and local laws, competent professional advice should be sought prior to the use of any
document, form, exhibit, or the like. This publication is sold with the understanding that the publisher is
not engaged in rendering legal, accounting, or any other professional service. If legal advice or other expert
assistance is required, the services of a competent professional should be sought.

Cover Photo © Jon Boyes

Graphic Design: Maria Loxas

IREM® practices diversity. We are an inclusive organization that embraces and values differences and
welcomes individuals of all races, genders, creeds, ages, sexual orientations, gender identities, and national
origins, and individuals with disabilities, providing an equal opportunity environment among its members,
vendors, and staff.

Library of Congress Cataloging-in-Publication Data

Prassas, Fred.
  Investment real estate : finance and asset management / by Fred Prassas, CPM, DSA.
      pages cm
  Includes bibliographical references and index.
  ISBN-13: 978-1-57203-173-9 (pbk. : alk. paper)
  ISBN-10: 1-57203-173-5 (pbk. : alk. paper) 1. Real estate investment. 2. Real estate
investment--Finance. 3. Real estate business. I. Title.
  HD1382.5.P73 2013
  332.63'24--dc23
                                                                                    2013008445

Preface

ABOUT THIS BOOK

Investment Real Estate: Finance and Asset Management differs from other real estate investment and financial analysis publications in that it focuses on the real estate manager's role in ensuring that the real estate management company's clients realize their investment goals for any given property. Real estate managers today are more than property overseers who must manage the day-to-day operations of their clients' properties; they also often are asset managers. Even if a real estate manager is not actively performing the analysis and management of a portfolio of investment real estate, he or she must have a basic understanding of the impact various decisions about a property have on the cash flow and value of a property. This book provides insight into the real estate management company and manager's role in the financial analysis and asset management of a property. It also looks in detail at how to budget, forecast, and analyze cash flow.

HOW TO USE THIS BOOK

This book flows from an overview and historical perspective of real estate finance and investment to accounting basics to valuation and financial analysis. Each chapter in this book provides detailed information about the chapter topic and may include the following additional content.

Useful Information

Tips

TIPS

Various tips are provided throughout the book that point out key, or often overlooked, information.

Sidebars

> **Sidebar Information Boxes**
>
> Additional and background information that is related to the content is presented in sidebar boxes such as this one.

Real-Life Consideration

Interspersed within the text are lists of questions that illustrate how a real estate manager may consider the concepts being discussed in real-life situations.

Exhibits and Examples

> **Exhibit and Example Information Boxes**
>
> - Exhibits illustrate concepts in the text, show examples of documents, or provide screen shots of software being discussed.
> - Examples apply calculations, steps, and concepts to property-based scenarios.

Review Questions

Each chapter ends with a list of review questions that you can answer to test your understanding of the content presented.

Acknowlegements

Special thanks to David Domres, CPM®, architect of the IREM Financial Analysis Spreadsheet, a generous contributor, friend, and advisor.

Also many thanks to the subject-matter experts of the IREM finance and asset management series for their expertise, input, and contributions including: Steve Cary, CPM®; Howard Campbell, CPM® Emeritus; Bob Demson, CPM®; Len Frenkil, CPM®; Ken Goodacre, CPM®; Enis Hartz, CPM®; Yvonne Jones, CPM®; Steve Kerens, CPM®; Eric Storey, CPM®; Pedro Vermales, CPM®; and Kathy Whitman, CPM®.

Thank you to the following individuals who contributed forms, data, information and feedback: Lori Berger, CPM®; Joe Greenblatt, CPM®; Mark Jossart, CPM®; Nancye Kirk, Chief Strategy Officer/Vice President, Global Services IREM®; Pamela Monroe, CPM®; Richard Muhlebach, CPM®; Regina Mullins, CPM®; Peter Ogden, CPM®; Marjean Pountain, CPM®; and Robert Toothaker, CPM®.

The content and curriculum development staff and editors at IREM including: Dawn Brent, Suzanne Hausknecht, and Nadia Geagea Pupa.

Fred Prassas, CPM®

About the Author

Fred Prassas, CPM® is the Associate Professor and Program Director for the B.S. degree program in Property Management at the University of Wisconsin–Stout.

He is a founding member of the PMC Management Group based in La Crosse, Wisconsin, which specializes in multi-family property management throughout western Wisconsin and eastern Minnesota. He has been in the real estate business since 1973 and is a licensed real estate broker.

Prassas was the 2006 president of the Institute of Real Estate Management where he is also an instructor of the finance and asset management credentialing courses.

In addition to volunteer leadership positions with IREM, Prassas has held leadership positions with the National Association of Realtors. In 2010, he was presented with the NAR Distinguished Service Award, the highest honor bestowed upon a member by this organization of over 1,300,000 members.

Prassas is a member of the Board of Advisors of the James A. Graaskamp Center for Real Estate at the University of Wisconsin–Madison. He was president of the La Crosse Area REALTORS Association in 1985, president of the Wisconsin REALTORS Association in 1992, and was named REALTOR of the year by both organizations.

Prassas earned a Bachelor of Science degree in Communications from Southern Illinois University and a Master of Business Administration from the University of Wisconsin, La Crosse.

Table of Contents

Why Real Estate Finance?

Investment Real Estate: Finance and Asset Management explores the major topics of financial analysis and asset management from the perspective of the professional real manager. Many successful real estate managers consider "financial analysis" to be a process that begins and ends with the ***annual budget.*** Budgets are indeed a critical component of the real estate manager's role, and they will be explored in detail. However, the role of the real estate manager continues to evolve and become more complex. Real estate managers today work in widely varying business environments. Within those environments, client needs have changed, and the sophistication of owners continues to grow as knowledge and information become more readily available through experience, technology, and networking channels.

Today, owners have high expectations of their real estate management professionals, and a strong knowledge of finance is an advantage that can enhance a real estate manager's relationships with clients and the professionals that turn to them for their expertise. A steadily growing number of information resources are available to the real estate investor, including accountants, attorneys, ***appraisers,*** mortgage bankers, ***mortgage brokers,*** and real estate brokers, all with varying levels of expertise in real estate finance. The real estate manager must have the knowledge to participate in conversation and analysis with other real estate professionals that the client is likely to encounter. Further, real estate management software has evolved—from single-purpose, single-user accounting programs to comprehensive multi-user suites that allow for input of data, full marketing and financial analyses, and centralized data processing. Failing to understand a property from the perspective of investors and lenders will reduce the real estate manager to an operational specialist, unlikely to be granted a seat at the table with the decision makers. Therefore, the real estate manager plays a key role in preserving and enhancing the earning power of a real estate investment, and ultimately the investment's value. Experience, knowledge, and skills that are kept up to date are critical to being competitive and respected.

"How you perform as a real estate manager—NOI increases, vacancy decreases, and really looking at your budget fundamentals—has a direct impact on the value of your property. I would rather take a mediocre property and a top notch manager (preferably a CPM®) than a top notch property and a mediocre manager any day." –John D. Clayton, CPM®, Little Rock, Arkansas

OWNER'S GOALS AND OBJECTIVES

While most investment property owners seek to make a profit from their investment, each owner will have specific goals they wish to attain during the term of his or her investment. It is the real estate manager's responsibility to learn the owner's goals. During conversations and interviews, the real estate manager gathers the information needed to identify the owner's goals and objectives for a property.

Investors purchase income-producing real estate for two primary reasons: *speculation* and *investment.* Real estate speculation offers an investor an opportunity to take high risk and potentially receive high reward during a relatively short holding period. The return is typically achieved at the time of sale from the profit made in selling the property. Real estate investment, on the other hand, typically extends for a longer period. The five fundamental investment objectives can be summarized by the acronym "SPLAT":

S   **Safety** *(capital preservation)* An owner may want to protect a principal investment by acquiring high quality real estate that will hold its value over time. The property may not provide a strong return but should retain its initial value. Some properties may appreciate in value, even where the owner makes no further investment in the property, due to superior location.

P   **Periodic Return** *(cash flow)* An owner may purchase or develop real estate to obtain a steady source of income over a specific period. The cash flow will provide a rate of return that can be compared to other investments and is enhanced by the tax shelter effects of the real estate, such as *depreciation*. The strength of a rent roll or market greatly affects the quality of the cash flow received.

L   **Leverage** *(using borrowed funds)* The assumption with leverage is that the return on the real estate investment exceeds the cost of borrowed funds. So by using leverage, the owner can control and increase the value of a property with minimal capital.

A   **Appreciation of Capital Appreciation** *(hedge against inflation)* During inflationary times, when wages are increasing, residents and tenants leasing real estate expect their rents to increase as well. This in turn creates a higher rent value and a higher value to the property.

T   **Tax Shelter** *(income tax advantage)* An owner may want to defer recognition of income through a deduction of **cost recovery** (once more commonly called depreciation), which allows the owner to pay less income tax each year than might be true with alternative investments.

In addition to these fundamental financial reasons for real estate investment, many investors also enjoy pride of ownership from their income-producing properties.

What distinguishes speculation from investment? Though the answer is not always clear, one factor is **cash flow.** A property with a negative cash flow could be one used for speculation. This is the case when an investor buys a rental building with negative cash flow, in anticipation of rehabbing or retenanting to provide higher returns. An effective real estate manager understands the mix of the various relevant elements as they relate to the individual investor's risk tolerance.

Once the owner's goals are known, the real estate manager uses financial tools to make decisions or recommend courses of action that best meet the goals of the real estate owner. What improvements will result in the highest rents? Can operating costs be reduced? Should an owner pay cash for improvements to a property or finance them? Is it a good time to consider refinancing a loan? How can the vision of the developer best be realized? What will next year's **operating expenses** be? These examples are but a small sampling of the counsel a real estate manager may be asked to provide.

Many property owners, especially investors with small **portfolios** or those who purchase real estate as an alternative investment, have difficulty articulating their goals. It is not uncommon for such owners to express goals that are difficult to quantify, such as "I want to make money," "I want full occupancy," or "I don't want to fund negative cash flows." While remarks like these may give some guidance, it would be difficult for either the real estate manager or the owner to measure performance based on this type of statement. Therefore, the real estate manager should attempt to obtain measurable financial goals from a property owner by asking specific questions related to investment objectives. The real estate manager must then be able to transform these expectations into quantifiable measurable goals and understand how these impact the value equation. Once the goals are quantified, the manager has the data needed to measure property performance and make operational refinements to best achieve the goals and reassure the ownership of his or her ability to build, maintain, and enhance the value of a real estate asset.

. . . when considering owner's goals and objectives:

- What types of owner objectives exist for properties I am currently managing?
- If an owner's goals conflict, how do I, as a manager, reconcile these differences?

THE ROLE OF THE REAL ESTATE MANAGER

The expert real estate manager not only analyzes data but is the source of operational data. The real estate manager oversees the receipt and accounting of rents, budget development, maintenance arrangements, payment of operating expenses, and preparation of financial reports of the property's operation. Thus, the ability to prepare long-term operational and financial plans for a property requires a strong, working knowledge of real estate finance.

Someone considering a real estate investment analyzes every financial package with a fundamental assumption—that the property is or will be under prudent management. All other projections and assumptions rely on this premise. The profession of real estate management is often taken for granted and treated as a commodity. Prudent real estate management, however, is far more than a commodity—it is skills and knowledge, stewardship of resources, awareness of the market, understanding of buildings, and familiarity with the overall real estate market and economy. Most of all, it is knowing the impact of various decisions on the income and value of the investor's property.

Operating properties with sound budgeting skills is a key component of success. The actions real estate managers take in implementing market-rate rents, attending carefully to operating expenses, and maintaining properties at market standards significantly influence outcomes. Effectiveness requires a working knowledge of financial management, because the end result of a real estate manager's work is building, maintaining, and enhancing the value of a real estate asset. That work also is a critical component of the long-term **management plan,** with analytical skills being used to make recommendations for a property's future success. Real estate management is more than analysis—it is analysis put into action at the property level.

Principles of real estate finance, which are examined in detail in this book, provide a common language for analysis. Understanding the language of real estate finance not only makes communication among colleagues possible, it also has a benefit to students and persons starting or expanding a career in real estate management. The skills used for financial analysis are transferable among disciplines. A person with a solid understanding of financial principles of real estate and land economics can, with some additional training, be well suited to practice in any of the related real estate professions.

REVIEW QUESTIONS

- What are the two reasons why investors purchase income-producing real estate?
- When purchasing properties for investment purposes, what are the five fundamental objectives that the owner expects to satisfy?
- Why is it important to know the owner's goals and objectives for a property?
- What is the typical role of the real estate manager?

Economics of Real Estate Investment

The first step in understanding real estate finance is knowing where it fits in the bigger picture of the economics of real estate investment. Real estate, like other industries, is cyclical in nature, the result of imbalances between supply and demand and a reaction to the general business economy. Economic cycles in business are typically triggered by multiple influences, including variations in international money exchange, trade deficits, government debt, and monetary and fiscal policies.

BUSINESS AND REAL ESTATE CYCLES

In Exhibit 2.1, the solid line indicates the business cycle and the broken line shows the real estate cycle, which responds to the cycle of business and has more pronounced peaks and valleys.

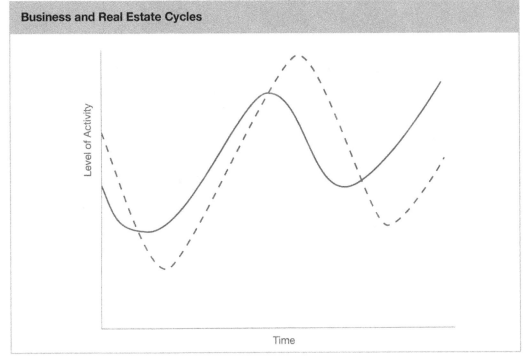

Business and Real Estate Cycles   *Exhibit 2.1*

— *Business Cycle*   --- *Real Estate Cycle*

The business cycle has four stages: *recession, depression, recovery,* and *prosperity.*

Stage	Description
Recession	• Slowdown in business activity • Competition increases as businesses vie for their share of a dwindling customer base • Banks become less willing to lend money and tighten credit lines • Businesses begin failing, banks cannot collect on loans, aneventually even financial institutions can fail, leading to a full-fledged depression
Depression	• Widespread reduction in business activity, increased unemployment rates, lower wages, and a decline in stock values • Prices decrease in response to low consumer demand, and the weakest businesses are eliminated • Leads to a reduction in business expenses because the cost of goods and wages has gone down • Capital that was not maintained during the depression will have to be replaced, creating a demand in the market—an early sign of recovery
Recovery	• Unemployment rates fall and wages increase again • Consumer demand returns, and prices climb • When prices rise faster than the cost of production, businesses begin to see higher profits—a sign of prosperity
Prosperity	• Production is increased, banks are willing to lend funds, and consumer demand and prices are high • The cycle completes itself as the expansion of the economy during prosperity leads to the recession caused by the contraction of the economy • These periods of growth and depression may be short-lived, or they may go on for many years • Sometimes a certain region or industry is more affected than others

In response to the business cycle, the real estate market rises and falls in four major phases that lag behind the business cycle. The peaks and valleys of the real estate cycle are typically more pronounced and can be characterized as the following phases: **overbuilding, adjustment, stabilization,** and **development.**

Phase	Description
Overbuilding	• Overbuilding easily occurs during periods of prosperity in the business cycle. • As businesses expand to meet consumer demand, new constructionis triggered. • Developers perceive a need for new construction and new building occurs. • At the peak of the business cycle, demand begins to fall off, yet there are still a number of construction projects already under way. Because permits, financing, and construction contracts are in place at this point, these projects are typically completed, leaving an oversupply of real estate in the market.
Adjustment	• Because the real estate market lags behind the general business economy, construction finally slows as business activity wanes during a recession. • The real estate market then undergoes a period of adjustment as demand decreases, vacancy rates increase, and rent concessions become common.
Stabilization	• At this point, the real estate market "hits bottom" and a period of stabilization begins. • As recovery begins in the general economy, rental rates start to increase.
Development	• As prosperity returns, occupancy rates and absorption levels rise and rents again reach a level that justifies new construction. At this point, a period of development begins.

TIPS

During a period of stabilization, excess supply may still be on the market, and rental rates may lag when prices begin to climb in other sectors of the economy.

During the 2007 to 2009 recession, the real estate cycle followed a slightly different path. At that time, high vacancy rates, rent declines, and the ensuing pullback in new construction were caused by a down economy rather than excess new development. In general, property performance is typically the driver of the real estate cycle. In discussing the impact of the recession in a Mortgage Banking Report article, *Viva El Cycle,* Jamie Woodwell suggested that "the effects of the economic declines on commercial real estate were just as pronounced as overbuilding would be." Just as the declines had an impact on the real estate cycle, economic growth starting in 2010 (even though slow) started to reduce vacancy rates and stabilize asking rents for every major type of property. Property values like property performance tend to react to the real estate cycle. Property values plummeted in reaction to the recession. Continuing economic growth created greater optimism among investors, which helped stabilize property values.

Questions
real estate
managers
may ask

. . . when considering the real estate cycle's impact on his or her business:

- What phase is the real estate market currently in? What information do I need to analyze to find out?
- What effect is the current real estate market phase having on my company's business? How am I responding?

MACROECONOMIC EFFECTS ON REAL ESTATE

Many economic factors, both domestic and international, affect the financial performance of real estate in the United States. Real estate managers must monitor macroeconomic influences, including inflation, **interest rates,** macroeconomic trends, and foreign investment.

Inflation

An important consideration for real estate managers is the value of money, or its "purchasing power." Consider $200 spent today on cleaning supplies for a property. Will $200 buy the same amount of supplies one year from now? That depends on the rate of inflation, which is the increase in the average level of prices, or equivalently, the decrease in the value of money. This can be compared to appreciation, which is the increase in value resulting from an excess of demand over supply. Investors are anticipating that properties will appreciate at a rate greater than the inflation rate.

Consumer Price Index (CPI)

A consistent **price index** is used to measure changes in the average level of prices reliably. A price index traces the change in prices for a select, representative group of commodities over a specified period.

When working with commercial leases, it is not unusual to see specific lease language governing how the rental rate may be escalated during the lease period. The most commonly used method of rate escalation other than negotiated increases established at lease inception is the Consumer Price Index (CPI). This index is monitored by the U.S. Bureau of Labor Statistics (BLS) and published along with other indices at its website, *www. bls.gov.*

The CPI has subindexes for various categories, including the *Consumer Price Index for Urban Wage Earners and Clerical Workers (CPI-W)* and the *Consumer Price Index for All Urban Consumers (CPI-U).* In real estate management, the index that is most commonly used is the *CPI-U, U.S. All Items.* This index attempts to measure the cost for a "market basket of goods" and the change in that cost over time. This can be a somewhat imprecise measurement because there is a weighting given to the products within the "market basket" and some of the products in the "market basket" disappear from the market while new ones are introduced into the market. However, it's generally considered to be among the most reliable measurements of inflation. Note that data takes about 45 to 60 days to be published. Some leases specify an adjustment month that is 60 days prior to the lease anniversary date.

All indices rely upon a starting point for reference. In using these indices, the starting point of measurement that equals 100 is from 1982 to 1984. You can measure the amount of inflation that has occurred by comparing the appropriate index for the most recent time period to that of the initially referenced time period. Remember the simple formula "NOON" for calculating a new rental rate.

New Rental Rate = (Old Rental Rate ÷ Old CPI) × New CPI

Example 2.1

Suppose it is the lease anniversary date for one of your tenants. Last anniversary, the applicable CPI was 190.7. This anniversary, the applicable CPI is 198.3. If the monthly rent paid by the tenant during the last year is $7,453, what will the new rent be?

New rental rate = ($7,453 ÷ 190.7) x 198.3 = $7,750

Interest Rates

An **interest rate** is a percentage charged for the use of borrowing money. It represents the "price" of borrowing money. When consumers have more money than they need for daily use, many choose the safety of a government-insured bank account. A bank pays consumers for the use of this money at a rate that is determined by market factors. In the reverse direction, a consumer who needs to borrow money for goods and services or to purchase a home pays interest to the lending institution. The behavior of interest rates is closely related to inflation—interest rates go up and down in the same direction as the inflation rate.

Several important money market investments indicate key interest rates:

- **Discount Rate:** the rate commercial banks pay to borrow funds from their regional Federal Reserve Banks in order to maintain overnight reserve requirements; because these loans are rare, this rate is largely symbolic

- **Federal Funds Rate:** the rate charged on short-term loans made between financial institutions (e.g., between mortgage bankers and commercial banks); the Federal Reserve sets this rate by buying and selling government securities until a target level is achieved, usually around .5% above the discount rate

- **Prime Rate:** a base rate or index rate commercial banks charge on short-term loans to business customers that have the highest credit ratings

- **Treasury Bill (T-Bill) Rate:** the rate paid by the U.S. Treasury on 90-day securities issued to finance government debt; investors follow the T-Bill rates because they trigger movements in commercial mortgage rates

- **10-Year Treasury Note:** the primary base rate for long-term commercial loans

- **Mortgage Rate:** the rate paid by those borrowing funds to purchase property

- **LIBOR (London Inter Bank Offer Rate):** international index that averages rate quotes from five major banks: Bank of America, Barclays, Bank of Tokyo, Deutsche Bank, and Swiss Bank

The 10-year treasury rate is particularly significant as commercial loans are typically indexed against this rate. Also, the prime rate runs approximately 300 basis points (or 3 percentage points) above the Federal Funds Rate, the interest rate that banks charge to each other for overnight loans.

Federal Funds Rate + 3% = Prime Rate

Prime rate data is maintained by the Wall Street Journal *at* www.online.wsj.com.

In a stabilized market, when interest rates are low or moderate, real estate value is greater relative to income, as illustrated in Exhibit 2.2. This is because borrowing money to buy, build, or improve property costs less. Debt payments are lower, so cash flow is greater. Consequently, real estate investors are willing to pay higher prices for real estate.

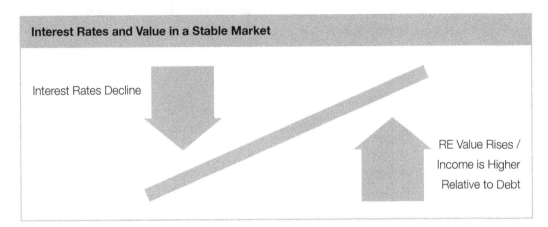

Interest Rates and Value in a Stable Market

Interest Rates Decline

RE Value Rises /
Income is Higher
Relative to Debt

Exhibit 2.2

However, in an unstable market, this relationship may not always be true. For example, as a result of the depression beginning in 2007, interest rates dropped to record lows, but real estate values did not increase. In fact, real estate values dropped dramatically. In late 2012, as economic growth slowly began to take hold, real estate values slowly began to stabilize, and as the economy continues to grow it seems that values are slowly increasing. Although property values differ dramatically from region to region, increasing in some regions while staying low in others even though interest rates remain low across all regions.

Macroeconomic Trends

Macroeconomic trends also affect the financial performance of real estate. These trends can be related to social or environmental movements, changes in technology, or government taxation and regulation.

Unemployment & Foreclosures

As we have seen in the recessionary cycle of recent years, the demand for real estate is affected by the strength of employment:

- If unemployment is high, demand for office space may decrease as companies downsize.
- High unemployment also means a reduction in consumer spending, which may impact retailers.
- Finally, the rise in foreclosures of single-family homes affects both the demand for renting, and the supply, as some foreclosed homes may be introduced into the market as rental property.

Environment

The demand for real estate is affected by environmental concerns that range from mold in buildings to wetlands preservation. Environmental issues regarding air quality, water quality, and waste disposal (especially hazardous wastes) all influence real estate desirability and sometimes result in government restrictions on land use. In fact, environmental audits might be a required element in the feasibility report of a loan package in an application for a mortgage loan on a property.

Technology

The transformation of business systems is likely to affect the demand for real estate space.
For example:

- Demand for retail space is or has been adversely affected due to virtual (e.g., online, television, etc.) shopping alternatives.

- Demand for office space may be reduced with technological advances such as wireless access that make telecommuting more viable.

- Computer-based manufacturing is expected to drive renovation in industrial space.

Government Policy and Currency

Our Federal Government attempts to manage economic activity in order to maintain stable or moderately increasing prices as well as relatively high employment levels. It has two primary methods or tools available to it in order to do so:

- **Fiscal Policy:** its method as well as level of taxation and spending

- **Monetary Policy:** its control of money supply and interest rates through the Federal Reserve Bank

The Fed is governed by a board of governors that is comprised of seven members, each of whom is appointed by the president to serve staggered 14-year terms. It maintains budgetary self-sufficiency by charging fees for services and generating investment income to offset its operating expenses. Although it must periodically report to Congress, it conducts its most important policy discussions in private and the board of governors function independently from it as well as from the president.

The Fed has three primary methods for controlling money supply and credit in our economy:

1. The first method is specifying what amount of reserves member banks must set aside as deposits at their regional reserve banks or physical currency in their vaults. By raising reserve requirements, the Fed can reduce the money supply. Conversely, by lowering requirements, the Fed can increase it. To meet Fed reserve requirements, banks often lend one another money over night. The rate on such loans, known as the Federal Funds Rate, is considered a key measurement of how "tight" or "loose" monetary policy is at a given point in time.

2. The second method by which the Fed controls the economy is increasing or decreasing the interest rate (known as the discount rate) that commercial banks pay to borrow funds from it. Increasing this rate will typically result in less borrowing, while decreasing it will typically result in greater borrowing.

3. The third and most important method used by the Fed, known as open-market operations, is the buying and selling of government securities. When it wishes to increase the supply of money, the Federal Reserve buys government securities from banks or other businesses and pays for them with a check. When those checks are deposited, they create new reserves for the depository bank. In turn, the bank can now lend or invest a portion of those funds, which increases the monetary supply. Conversely, by selling government securities to member banks, the Fed reduces the money supply.

Using any or all of these methods, the Fed can expand or contract the money supply (amount of money and credit in the economy). If the money supply increases ("loose" money), interest rates tend to drop, causing new business and consumer spending. This results in an increase in employment. Conversely, when the Fed contracts money supply, interest rates rise, causing businesses and consumers to reduce spending. The Fed continually uses these tools to keep inflation in check without negatively impacting employment levels. Too much money can lead to inflation; too little money can result in rising unemployment.

When the Fed reduces money supply or increases the discount rate, mortgage interest rates tend to increase. When it increases money supply or reduces the discount rate, mortgage interest rates tend to fall. So, although properties that have existing mortgage loans are minimally impacted by the Fed's actions, to-be-built properties or existing properties seeking refinancing can be significantly impacted by its actions.

The strength of the U.S. dollar influences real estate in this country as well. When the dollar declines against other currencies, real estate investment in the United States might become inexpensive.

Foreign Investment

Foreign investment in U.S. real estate increases yearly, as foreign investors earmark a large percentage of their cross-border allocations for U.S. real estate. Despite the decline in real estate values in the U.S., a recent survey of global investors concluded that the U.S. is still considered among the most stable and secure countries for real estate investing.

Major foreign players in U.S. real estate include Australia, Germany, the United Kingdom, the Netherlands, and other European and Asian investors. Up-to-date information regarding foreign real estate investment can be found through the Association of Foreign Investors in Real Estate (AFIRE) website at *www.afire.org.*

The global financial environment has direct impact on investors and managers in real estate. It is imperative to keep up with the fast-changing marketplace in order to understand the availability of funds and the cost of borrowing.

<table>
<tr><td>

Questions
real estate
managers
may ask

</td><td>

. . . when considering macroeconomic trends:

- Is there one or more macroeconomic trend(s) I need to start monitoring (e.g., inflation, interest rates, trends in the marketplace, foreign investment)?
- What can I share with my owner about the economic and market indicators for my area?

</td></tr>
</table>

● ●

REVIEW QUESTIONS

- How does the real estate cycle typically respond to the business cycle?
- What are the two most common price indexes used to measure inflation?
- How does the strength of the U.S. dollar affect foreign investment in this country?

The Finance Function

Today, one cannot try to identify a single business model for a real estate management office and its finance function. Rather, three or four general business models are refined into nearly as many permutations as there are companies in a given market. This provides for great flexibility as well as for market differentiation in terms of levels and costs of service.

REAL ESTATE MANAGEMENT COMPANY STRUCTURES

A real estate firm may have a management division, or a business may be established to engage solely in real estate management services to real estate clients. Both types of business are referred to as *fee management firms*—they charge clients a fee to manage their properties. In other situations, owners of sizable real estate holdings may have their own management divisions. Instead of being a client of a fee management firm, the property owner employs the real estate management staff, either directly or through a subsidiary company. These are referred to as *in-house managers.*

While real estate management offers great flexibility in terms of organizational structure, the profession is regulated through standards based on ethical principles in the real estate brokerage, securities, and accounting professions. In some cases, standards are clearly defined by legislation; others, while not legally binding, are defined by local practice. Operational standards are sometimes set by company policy and sometimes by legal requirements. Properties that are financed by securities or owned by publicly traded companies may be subject to additional regulations set by federal law. Some standards are established by the real estate brokerage laws where the office or property is located. These laws may include accounting and financial reporting requirements. States may regulate the manner in which bank accounts are established along with establishing timelines for financial reporting. Real estate trust accounts are usually governed by state law. State laws also dictate some policies that must be followed in landlord–tenant relationships. Other standards are necessitated by financial reporting requirements in the ever-changing environment of securities and financial integrity regulations. The real estate manager must stay informed about all standards of the profession. Violations of any federal, state, or local laws and regulations are both illegal and unethical.

One important role of a real estate management company is to be a **fiduciary,** with the real estate manager acting as agent for the owner in handling the financial affairs for a given property. Being a fiduciary places obligation on the agent to report all funds that come into its possession on behalf of a real estate owner and to further report all expenditures. The manner in which this reporting is handled may vary among companies, but timely, accurate reporting is an ethical obligation and in many states a legal requirement. While there are no specific written industry standards for real estate managers, successful practitioners strive to operate their companies according to industry-identified **best practices**—norms for operation used by ethical and honest companies. Wherever possible, this text will address real estate finance and financial reporting consistent with defined best practices of the industry. An excellent tool for defining standard procedures for your company is *Best Practices: Real Estate Management Service,* published by the Institute of Real Estate Management (IREM®). IREM is a worldwide society of professional real estate managers and an affiliate of the National Association of REALTORS. The profession of real estate management, in addition to having identified best practices, is self-regulated. Standards of ethical conduct have been articulated by IREM, which confers the well-respected CERTIFIED PROPERTY MANAGER® (CPM®) designation to members who meet its educational requirements and subscribe to its Code of Professional Ethics. Other organizations, including but not limited to BOMI International, National Association of REALTORS® (NAR), and National Association of Residential Property Mangers (NARPM), also confer designations that require adherence to strict standards of ethical conduct.

THE ACCOUNTING FUNCTION

A real estate management company's success hinges on the strength of its major components, which can be compromised if the accounting department produces substandard work. Ineffective accounting can jeopardize a company's earning ability as well as expose it to serious legal consequences. A successful and efficient accounting department generates quality financial statements, but it must do much more—it must carry out activities that support every aspect of the real estate management environment. Providing meaningful, understandable, and timely financial statements to property investment stakeholders month after month confirms a management company's value.

It is imperative that the real estate management company establish, maintain, and update as needed an accounting system that supports company operation, is consistent with client directives, and complies with accepted accounting and financial reporting principles. The handling of client funds is accomplished through an accounting system that accommodates both the management company and the properties under its care. Accounting is generally defined as the practice of classifying, recording, and summarizing financial transactions. It is largely concerned with monitoring the flow of income and expenses in a business, accomplished through categories of debits and credits. In a further refinement, short-term movements in accounts are monitored through accounts payable and accounts receivable. **Financial accounting** is a system of classifying financial transactions that documents the financial position of a given entity—either the management company or the properties under its management—in the form of a **balance sheet** and an income statement.

Client directives with respect to accounting systems can vary widely: Some institutional owners may provide the management company with an accounting procedures manual that sets forth all of the institution's requirements; other clients may have less stringent, though no less important, accounting expectations. Any accounting system should support both cash and accrual accounting (see Chapter 4: Accounting Basics) to the extent that client reporting requirements dictate.

An accounting system can be provided through an in-house accounting department, or the accounting function can be outsourced. In either case, the management company is responsible for that system and its adherence to all accepted accounting and financial reporting principles.

In-House or Outsource

As mentioned, within a real estate management company, the accounting function can be handled in several ways. Depending on the firm's size and in-house capabilities and the client's needs, the company may handle all accounting functions on its own or may outsource to meet some or all of its accounting requirements. While use of an outside accounting firm might be prudent, many clients want the accounting function to be tightly controlled by the real estate manager. It is also common for real estate management companies to hire accounting firms or other management companies that have in-house accounting personnel to handle their accounting function. Examples 3.1 and 3.2 compare in-house and combination accounting approaches.

In-House Approach to Accounting	*Example 3.1*

Multi-State Management is a regional real estate management firm that handles properties of all types in three states. Their in-house accounting department handles or supervises all functions, including accounts receivable, accounts payable, and preparing monthly statements for owners.

Multi-State Management also has a roving team of maintenance technicians who are invoiced to the properties they manage on a time and materials basis. The company maintains a separate maintenance billing department to invoice clients for maintenance services. While all functions are supervised by Multi-State's accounting department, certain tasks are performed onsite at the offices of the managed properties.

Example 3.2	**Combination Approach to Accounting**

Bark River Company, a real estate management firm operating 1,000 residential apartment units for three separate clients, uses its computer system to track occupancy and delinquency. The Bark River employees deposit rent checks into the bank and record them in the software. Invoices for property operating expenses are approved by the real estate manager and forwarded to the in-house accounts payable clerk for processing and payment. By handling check processing, the real estate managers can monitor and enforce collections on a timely basis, and by paying the invoices in-house, the firm can track cash flow effectively.

However, Bark River contracts with Mid City Accounting to prepare the monthly statement of operations for each of its three clients. Mid City Accounting accesses the records from Bark River's computer system, reconciles the bank statements, and prepares and mails the monthly statements. Bark River feels this approach allows it to focus on the operational side of real estate management while giving its clients high-quality and timely operating statements.

In many ways, a real estate management company operates several businesses. It operates each property as a business entity separate from other properties and from the management company. The company itself must also be managed as a profitable business. Its accounting department must be organized to service all of these business entities. The management firm may have several departments, including real estate management and administrative services, as well as centralized maintenance in lieu of property-based maintenance personnel. In addition to the company's general bookkeeping of the firm, there may be a billing department that invoices properties for management and ancillary services. Whatever the permutation, each real estate management company must put in place a financial management strategy supported by knowledgeable personnel to handle accounting, budgeting, and financial management.

ACCOUNTING PERSONNEL

The number of employees who have accounting responsibilities will depend on the size of the management company's portfolio and the degree of reporting required by its property owners. If a single bookkeeper focuses solely on accounting work, it is a good practice to train one or more others to perform that work as a backup. Other staff members may be assigned to specific accounting tasks on a part-time basis, but the costs of these personnel should be considered. Establishing a professional connection with an accounting firm or a Certified Public Accountant (CPA) who understands the management firm's operations is one option for providing backup resources as needed.

Important accounting functions include full-charge bookkeeper, accounts payable, accounts receivable, and rent collection as described in the following chart.

Position	Description
Full-Charge Bookkeeper	In a small company, the accounting "department" may be a single full-charge bookkeeper who performs all of the accounting functions necessary to operate the managed properties in addition to keeping the books for the management company. One of the advantages to hiring a full-charge bookkeeper is that at least one employee generally knows the accounting system's capabilities and fully understands the owner's requirements for each property.
	A disadvantage is that this exclusive knowledge may place the employee in a position to manipulate the system dishonestly. This possibility can be averted by instituting a system of checks and balances; the bookkeeper's work should be reviewed periodically to catch inadvertent errors and discourage dishonesty. If the bookkeeper writes checks, someone else in a position of authority, such as the company executive, should sign them. Invoices should be reviewed and approved by someone other than the bookkeeper, with no exceptions. On a regular basis, someone in authority should also review the bank account reconciliations and verify income items and compare them to the tenant records.
Accounts Payable	The accounts payable function should be assigned to an employee who can evaluate invoices, analyze them for accuracy, and make sure bills are not duplicated. An invoice should always be submitted for preapproval, along with the account to be charged, by the person ordering the product or service. Accounts payable personnel also check approved invoices for accuracy, **discounts,** and merchandise not delivered and prepare invoice payments.

Position	Description *(continued)*
Accounts Receivable	Accounts receivable personnel are responsible for receiving and recording the company's income from management fees and other sources and for the income received directly from the managed properties. An employee responsible for the accounts received usually maintains the tenant records, works with lease summaries, and sends out monthly invoices for rent collection. She or he also logs in rent checks and ensures that residents and tenants have paid the correct amounts, monitors rent increases, tracks **percentage rents,** and prepares **delinquency reports.** Accounts receivable employees are generally responsible for making sure that all accounts are balanced and in agreement with the bank statements.
Rent Collection	In many companies that manage commercial properties, real estate managers are ultimately responsible for rent collection. The professional relationships they have established with tenants lay the foundation for them to assume this responsibility. For residential properties, the onsite manager typically collects rents. If a situation develops requiring legal action (such as an eviction), it is handled by other management company personnel. For smaller properties without onsite management, the real estate manager who supervises the property's operations assumes responsibility for rent collections. Residents might also be given the option to mail rent payments to the management office, leave them in a secure drop box, or submit them electronically. Whichever option is used to collect rent, the collections should be the responsibility of one person to ensure that rent payments are handled properly, including immediately stamping checks "For Deposit Only" and ensuring they are promptly deposited.

ACCOUNTING DEPARTMENTS IN SMALL AND LARGE OFFICES

Technology has blurred some of the traditional divisions among administrative duties, and each real estate management company decides how to organize itself. Many companies have an operations division responsible for some administrative tasks while others are concentrated in the accounting department. The term **front office functions** is commonly used to refer to the real-time accounting functions that require interaction with tenants, residents, and vendors—including lease administration, enforcement, and rent collection. These functions largely take place during an accounting period rather than after it is closed, and in a multifamily property or a large office building, at a property's onsite office rather than the real estate management company's office. Computer technology makes it possible to enter data at its most logical point of entry. Where front office staff are working directly at a property, the cost becomes a property expense, which helps prevent the confusion often associated with allocating and invoicing employee time when front office duties are performed in a central office.

The term **back office functions,** on the other hand, typically refers to accounting functions that do not require interaction with residents or tenants; they primarily address preparation of historical operating data after an accounting period is closed, payment of operating expenses for properties, and carrying out the operation of the management company. Even in cases where the front office accounting is performed onsite, the chief financial officer or accounting supervisor—each considered a member of the back office—is responsible for assuring that internal controls are being met and verifying all input data prepared at the front office.

Note that while there may not be a physical front and back office, especially in smaller offices, these terms are used to highlight the different types of functions within an account department.

Though probably no two real estate management companies organize their accounting departments identically, most handle basic functions in the same way. Large firms may have multiple employees that work together to serve single functions, while smaller firms likely combine functions under management of a single individual. Some departments may be easily scaled down to meet the needs of a smaller firm by combining duties, but real estate managers should be aware that scaling down too much may prohibit adequate internal controls, which, among other objectives, require certain duties be performed by separate individuals.

Centralized vs. Decentralized Input and Processing

Centralized input and processing occurs when a site manager at a residential property, for example, would fax or e-mail a completed tenant application to the *home office* where the credit screening would be done and the lease prepared. Then, in all likelihood, the tenant would have to mail their check to the home office where it would be processed and applied to the property owner account. The site manager would receive daily or weekly reports of "who lived where" and also lists of delinquencies—all of which would be generated by a central office. Additionally, paying invoices usually requires an invoice go to the central office, then sent to the site office for initial approval, and finally back to the central office for processing and payment.

Centralized vs. Decentralized Input and Processing *(continued)*

A totally decentralized system begins when the site manager enters the tenant's information into a module of the computer system. That same information would transfer to partially fill out the application form, which could automatically generate the credit report. If approved, the same data would be automatically entered into the lease document where it would be printed out onsite— obviously with some approval levels from a regional manager. In addition, the site manager may accept and process checks even to the extent of scanning the check and handing it back to the tenant. The site manager can print their own reports of occupancy and delinquency as well as mail/email notices to tenants where appropriate. Accounts payable could be 'routed' from the site through the approval process.

From a financial perspective, what this does is push the cost of all this processing from the *central office* (which is usually paid for as part of the management fee) to the *site office* (which is usually paid for by the property owner). It is also considerably more efficient if the proper internal controls are in place.

ACCOUNTING REQUIREMENTS BY PROPERTY TYPES

The type of property under real estate management influences the specific needs for accounting services. For example, rental apartments and condominiums may have many of the same accounting needs, but offices, industrial parks, and retail properties present new considerations and challenges.

Rental Apartments

Rental apartments have fairly simple requirements for accounting. Differently from commercial properties, apartment owners are generally responsible for maintaining apartment interiors as well as the building as a whole, so operating expenses are usually higher as a percent of income. The major source of property income is normally monthly rents; often owners also charge separate fees for swimming pool, fitness center, or parking, such income items must be tracked separately.

Condominiums

Condominiums likewise have fairly simple accounting needs. The income consists almost entirely of monthly assessments collected from the owners, and these usually change only once a year. Because owners maintain their individual homes and pay their own property taxes, the only expenses are for maintenance of common areas and operations (e.g., laundry, internet services). An office condominium might account separately for pass-through of some building operating costs to the occupants, but this situation is rare.

Office Buildings and Industrial Parks

Accounting requirements for office buildings and industrial parks are a little more complex than for residential space, in that building operating costs, known as *Common Area Maintenance (CAM)* expenses, are almost always passed through (billed back) to the tenants. This requires preparing a budget each year, billing tenants an estimated amount each month, reconciling the estimated amounts with actual figures at year's end, and billing or crediting tenants for the difference. Examples of other additional charges that may be incurred by a tenant through the normal course of their occupancy include air conditioning, parking, or office maintenance services. If an office building includes ground-floor retail tenants, their leases may require payment of percentage rent, an amount that varies from month to month.

Shopping Centers

Shopping centers have the most complex accounting needs of managed properties. In addition to pass-through charges—including operating costs, common area maintenance expenses, property taxes, and insurance—there is the added element of percentage rent. Charging percentage rent requires collecting and analyzing sales reports and billing tenants accordingly. A shopping center may also have marketing funds for which they must account, such as holiday events.

. . . when considering the accounting function and requirements for his or her company:

- How is the accounting function handled in my company? Is this effective?
- Are there ways the accounting function can be improved?
- How better might my company staff its accounting department to ensure efficient and effective processes?

Questions real estate managers may ask

ESTABLISHING FINANCIAL POLICIES AND PROCEDURES

Much of the success of a real estate management firm is rooted in the policies and procedures established by the accounting department, under the supervision of the real estate manager: dependable administrative procedures, timely reporting to owners, safeguarding client funds, accurate billing, and supervising all staff administrative procedures. Accounting departments that practice disciplined administrative procedures allow real estate managers to focus on the operational issues impacting the success of their properties.

Among the many functions of the accounting department, none is more important than handling funds. Because monies belonging to clients are received and paid in the name of the managed property or its ownership, specific policies and procedures for handling receipts and disbursements are imperative. Supervision of any personnel who handle funds is a primary safeguard. This especially may be needed in smaller companies that have a single bookkeeper. Financial responsibilities are generally assigned so that one person collects funds, but another makes up the bank deposit. Payments are approached similarly: When an invoice is received, one person approves the payment and another prepares the check. A third person often actually signs the check, and when possible, yet another puts the check in the envelope to be mailed.

Once established, the internal controls must be applied to the handling of the company's financial transactions as well as those of its clients. Strict adherence not only minimizes problems within the accounting function, it also helps assure that very few problems will be uncovered in any performance audits clients may request.

Internal checks and balances reduce the possibility of theft or misappropriation of funds and minimize the potential for accounting errors. Most management companies institute an internal audit system in which a supervisor reviews prior transactions for irregularities. For example, if an unusual charge shows up, the supervisor questions those who approved the expense and may even contact the vendor to determine what product or service was provided (and, when applicable, how it applies to a specific property). If the staff's answers are satisfactory, the audit is considered closed. If not, the supervisor continues investigating until satisfaction is achieved or the problem has been corrected or eliminated.

In most companies, authorization to sign checks for the business is limited to the principal (the business owner), the executive responsible for accounting and finance (the controller), and an accounting supervisor. Authorizations to sign, as well as dollar limitations and situations requiring more than one signature, are on record at the bank holding the account. (Typically, checks exceeding a particular amount require two signatures; this reduces the chance for error and averts the potential for misdirection of funds.)

If the real estate management company establishes accounts for clients, checks may require the signature of a company executive or, in some cases, a representative of the client. Accounting personnel need to know who is authorized to sign checks for company and client accounts and to understand the limitations on individuals' signatory authority. Many real estate management companies and owners now use accounting software and online banking features that allow for electronic signature authorization, online payments, direct ach (automatic clearing house) payments, and other electronic banking functions. In addition, owners may own and pay for accounting systems used by the real estate management company. With the increased use of these electronic and virtual tools and functions, it becomes more difficult for the real estate management company to monitor controls. However, it is still imperative that controls be put in place to ensure ethical management and protection of funds.

ETHICAL MANAGEMENT AND PROTECTION OF FUNDS

Handling clients' funds requires insurance to protect them. Most **management agreements** oblige the real estate management company to provide a **fidelity bond** in an amount sufficient to cover the largest balance of client funds that the company is likely to have on hand at any time. Regular electronic transfers of money to clients can reduce the funds on hand and lower the amount of the fidelity bond needed. A large management company may employ an internal auditor as an added safeguard.

Real estate management firms must maintain strict separation of the accounting duties required for property management and those needed by the firm. Special care must be taken to avoid **commingling,** which is the deliberate or accidental combining of funds of several real estate owners or of property owner funds and the management company's funds. Commingling of funds is illegal in many states, and it is a violation of IREM's Code of Professional Ethics, which requires real estate managers to hold propriety information in confidence, to maintain accurate financial and business records for the managed property, and to protect owners' funds. Note, in those jurisdictions where it is *not* illegal to commingle accounts, real estate management companies must disclose to their clients that all funds are in a single account. Also, cash in and cash out must be accounted for by owner or property and disclosed accordingly. In areas where commingling is *not* illegal, real estate management firms may be tempted to commingle client funds to earn interest or credits because the recipient of these would be the real estate management firm. However, even in jurisdictions where commingling of funds is allowed, it is illegal for a real estate management firm to make money from the commingling of funds unless the situation is disclosed to and approved by the client. At *no* time should a management company's funds be commingled with the property owner's funds.

The client will almost always designate the types of bank accounts to be maintained, although the choice of institution may be left to the manager. This issue is typically addressed in the management agreement. Usually two bank accounts are maintained by the accounting department for each property or each client. One is a **disbursement account,** from which expenses are paid; the other, which bears interest, is a **deposit account,** used as the repository for all income. Typical procedure is for a batch of invoices to be collected periodically, such as once a week, and money transferred from the client's deposit account to the disbursement account, against which payment checks are written. Sometimes a client retains the right to remove excess funds from the deposit account electronically.

Whatever the details of the client arrangement, a real estate manager is likely to work with two other basic types of accounts: *trust accounts* and *agency accounts.*

Trust Accounts

The typical trust account is set up by the real estate broker or real estate manager on behalf of its clients. The **broker** and/or the broker's designated personnel are the only signatories on the account, which is subject to very strict state regulation. Clients sometimes ask to be signatories on trust accounts, but such an arrangement should not be allowed, as it might jeopardize the broker's standing with state agencies. A client's funds should not be commingled with any others. Any interest earned belongs to the client (unless specified otherwise in the real estate management agreement), and all funds must be fully accounted for at all times—funds cannot be held outside the account or borrowed by the real estate manager against future fees without client approval.

In most states, a state representative audits trust accounts routinely, and disciplinary action can be taken if discrepancies are discovered. Depending on the severity of an infraction, the action may be only a letter demanding compliance with account requirements, or it could be as severe as suspension or a loss of license for the broker. Each real estate manager taking on responsibility for a trust account must determine state-specific requirements, which may be more exacting than the client's.

Agency Accounts

An agency account serves a similar purpose as a trust account, without the same state requirements. The real estate manager still has a fiduciary responsibility to the client to handle funds prudently. An agency account is generally set up with the same stipulations as a trust account, except that the client is often an additional signatory. While the client can withdraw funds from the account at will, typically this is not done without consulting the real estate manager about the operational funds required.

. . . when considering his or her company's financial policies and procedures:

- Does my company have financial policies and procedures in place to ensure ethical financial management and protection of funds?

Questions
real estate
managers
may ask

● ●

REVIEW QUESTIONS

- Describe one important role of the real estate management company.

- Describe some factors that differentiate fee management companies from in-house management?

- What are the key accounting functions within a real estate management company?

- What is the difference between centralized and decentralized input and processing?

- How might accounting requirements differ by property?

- Why is establishing financial policies and procedures imperative?

- What is commingling of funds and why is it considered unethical?

- What are two ways to protect funds from being commingled?

Accounting Basics

Accounting terms and concepts are the basis of the language of real estate finance. The top reasons why real estate managers need to understand and speak this language are:

1. Setting the operating goals of the property to meet the owner's expected return.

2. Showing the performance of properties under management through financial statements.

3. Interpreting financial data that comes from other companies when soliciting new business.

4. Gathering and interpreting market financial data for comparison with a subject property's operation.

5. Performing budget analysis.

6. Communicating with brokers, appraisers, and other real estate professionals.

TYPES OF ACCOUNTING

Accountants and the Internal Revenue Service (IRS) recognize three methods of financial reporting: *cash-basis accounting, accrual-basis accounting,* and *modified accrual accounting.* The basic distinctions center on when income and expenses are declared.

Cash-basis Accounting

Cash-basis accounting recognizes income when it is actually received and expenses when they are paid. This accounting method, the easiest one to understand, utilizes a simplified bookkeeping system. Cash-basis accounting mirrors the effect of looking at a check register—all rents and other money collected are stated as inflow, and all checks written to pay invoices are reflected as outflow. The remaining balance reflects cash in the bank account or profit for a particular period. Most individual tax payers and many companies also elect cash-basis accounting for tax purposes.

Although easy to understand, cash-basis accounting can fail to report the true earning power of a property. Serious consequences can result from analyzing a cash-basis statement without inquiry into unpaid invoices and unpaid rents, because cash-basis accounting ignores both. Income can be understated if rents are delinquent, and, more importantly, expenses can be understated if the property is experiencing cash problems and all invoices are not paid promptly each month. A real estate manager analyzing a property that reports on a cash basis should obtain both current and historical schedules of accounts payable and accounts receivable to be factored into the analysis.

Accrual-basis Accounting

Accrual-basis accounting recognizes income when it is due and expenses when they are incurred, but the records may not reflect actual receipts and disbursements. It increases the comparability of financial statements between periods. In contrast with cash-basis accounting, rents are recognized as income when the rent is due, whether or not it has been paid. Similarly, expenses are realized when they are incurred, even if the invoice has not yet been paid.

So, for example, if in June two tenants did not pay their rent of $1,000 each, the income statement reflects $2,000 of revenue that month from their rents, even though the money was not paid. To reflect the unpaid rents, an **account receivable** is created to show what money is still owed. From an operational standpoint, the real estate manager may begin actions to evict the delinquent tenants, but the rent continues to **accrue** to the property and the accounts receivable continues to increase. At some point, the real estate manager needs to determine if the unpaid rents will ever be collected; rents that appear uncollectable are written off from accounts receivable to a bad debt account. Conversely, if the tenants pay the rent late, the account receivable is liquidated when the cash is received.

Accounting principles suggest two methods of addressing doubtful accounts: **direct write-off** and **allowance for doubtful accounts.** The direct write-off arguably reflects the relationship to operational real estate management most clearly, as tenants are evicted when their debt becomes uncollectable. However, the allowance method is used for budget forecasting because there is no way to know which accounts will become delinquent. There is no set period for writing off rents to bad debt, but the determination is often made based on the assumption of aged-tenant balances. The older the receivable, the less likely it is to be collected. For example, 100% of 120+-day-old money is in the account, 80% of 90+-day-old money, 50% of 60+-day-old money, and so on. It is a way of recording what is owed before it is written off. The real estate manager must use prudent judgment to reflect the realistic value of receivables when using accrual-basis accounting to report income.

Under the accrual method, operating expenses are reflected on a financial statement when they are incurred. Consider the real estate manager who orders $1,000 of cleaning supplies that are delivered in June. Even if the invoice is not due for 30 days—meaning the vendor does not expect payment until July—the $1,000 cost is reflected in the operating expenses of the property in June, and an **account payable** is reflected on the books showing a debt to the supplier. If the invoice is paid in July, no new expense is incurred. Instead, cash is reduced to reflect payment of the invoice, and the account payable is liquidated. However, if the property has financial issues that prevent the invoice from being paid, the unpaid invoice and any other unpaid invoices are reflected on the balance sheet as accounts payable until paid in full.

When analyzing a property on an accrual basis, the real estate manager must review accounts receivable to determine the effectiveness in collecting delinquencies and must analyze accounts payable to understand whether the property can generate the cash necessary to meet operating expenses. Accrual accounting has many advantages because everything is disclosed on the income statement, which can be analyzed to determine profitability. Accrual-basis accounting can be time-consuming, so strong internal controls are necessary to check that all expenses are reflected on the income statement when they are incurred.

Modified Accrual Accounting

Under modified accrual accounting methods (sometimes called modified cash-basis accounting), some income categories and expense categories are declared on a cash basis and some are declared on an accrual basis. For example, taxes and insurance may be treated as accrual expenses rather than as cash expenses. Small companies, especially those with smaller budgets, may choose to keep their books on a modified accrual basis. They may record small transactions (say, under $100) on a cash basis but larger transactions and withheld payroll taxes, which may be paid out annually or semi-annually, on an accrual basis; alternatively, they may record income on a cash basis and expenses on an accrual basis.

When a resident or tenant is behind more than a month in rent, the likelihood of payment declines with every day the resident or tenant remains on the property. This is why residential real estate managers are quick to evict nonpaying residents. From the perspective of a financial statement, this methodology recognizes there is no point in accruing income that will likely have to be written off in a future accounting period.

Another use of modified accrual accounting occurs as a modification to a cash-basis statement. Even though cash-basis accounting expenses are not realized until they are paid, some categories of expense may be accrued to present a clearer picture of the property's operations. For example, real estate taxes are an accrued *lien* on every income-producing property and must be paid. Even a property in bankruptcy cannot discharge payment of real estate taxes. The following chart demonstrates reported income and expenses under each of the three accounting methods.

Accounting Type	Income	Expenses
Cash-basis *Examples:* Yearly income; small business; self-employed person	Recognized when cash is received *Example:* Rent payments are recognized in the accounting period in which they are actually deposited	Recognized when cash is paid out *Example:* Utilities are recorded as expenses when they are actually paid
Accrual *Examples:* Real estate firm with rentals; mid-sized and larger corporations	Recognized when income is earned *Example:* Rent payments are recognized in the accounting period in which they are due	Recognized when expenses are incurred *Example:* Supplies are recorded when they are ordered
Modified Accrual *Examples:* Mixed method; items that repeat at regular intervals are accounted on a cash basis; items requiring accumulation of funds toward a large dollar payout are accounted on an accrual basis	Recognized when income becomes available and measurable to pay for the current period's liabilities	Recognized when the associated liability is incurred (that is, when the transaction or event is expected to draw upon current spendable resources rather than future resources)

Example 4.1 provides a scenario of cash-basis accounting wherein expenses are not realized until they are paid.

Cash-Basis Accounting *Example 4.1*

Suburban Flats, a small office property, has the following rent roll for April:

Suite A	$2,416
Suite B	$1,055
Suite C	$ 861
Suite D	$3,000
Total Rents	$7,332

Operating expenses for April in the Repairs and Maintenance category include the following:

Cleaning supplies	$ 425
Janitor service	$ 775
Plumbing repairs	$1,217
HVAC spring tune-up	$ 887

The property's remaining operating expenses are $2,050 per month, and the invoices are paid on time each month. At the start of April, the real estate manager received all rents except for Suite B, whose tenant has been having financial difficulty. The real estate manager has monitored this tenant carefully and has been assured the rent will be caught up in May.

All operating expenses are paid on a timely basis; however, the invoice for plumbing repairs was received too late in the month for it to be processed in the final accounts-payable batch. The invoice was paid early in May.

GENRALLY ACCEPTED ACCOUNTING PRINCIPLES (GAAP)

The IREM standards of practice state that the real estate manager must report finances consistent with accepted accounting methodology that meets the requirements of the owner as expressed in the management contract. In addition, tax returns and full-accrual financial statements for public companies follow strict guidelines set by an independent agency as a form of professional self-regulation. The standards for the United States are commonly known as *Generally Accepted Accounting Principles (GAAP).* These guidelines are set by the Financial Accounting Standards Board, an agency independent of any industry or government. The standards are well respected and are accepted by the Federal Government as well as by the Securities and Exchange Commission

(SEC). GAAP standards change as necessary to meet public accounting needs. For example, the Sarbanes-Oxley Act of 2002 passed as a result of financial crises in the wake of the Enron auditing scandal, and other acts of alleged corporate malfeasance have reshaped the way publicly traded companies report their income.

GAAP standards are the most restrictive accounting standards, and many real estate management firms have changed from cash-basis to accrual-basis GAAP accounting. A real estate management firm whose accounting practices meet GAAP standards can prepare almost any other type of financial report requested by an owner or any operating report needed by a real estate manager.

USING AND CREATING A CHART OF ACCOUNTS

Whatever accounting practices are in place, a **chart of accounts** is needed to organize the financial data that is collected in the **general ledger,** which is the basis for creating the primary financial statements—the income statement and balance sheet—as well as managerial reports. (See Chapter 7: Financial Reporting.) Every financial transaction is recorded somewhere in the general ledger. (See the sidebar for more information on general ledgers.)

General Ledger

An essential financial report is the general ledger. In real estate management, a general ledger is a formal record of all the financial transactions of the business or property. Accounts are transferred as final entries from the various journals to the general ledger, where they are posted as debits and credits in a double-entry accounting system and thus show the accumulated effects of transactions. Financial statements are built from the general ledger and become part of the periodic management reporting.

- A *Journal* is a registry of accounting entries.

- A *Debit* is one of two values in a double-entry accounting system (left side). For every debit there is an equal and offsetting credit. At least one component of every accounting transaction (journal entry) is a debit amount. Debits increase assets and decrease liabilities and equity.

- A *Credit* is one of the two values in a double-entry accounting system (right side). At least one component of every accounting transaction (journal entry) is a credit amount. For every credit there is an equal and offsetting debit. Credits increase liabilities and equity and decrease assets. The sum of all general ledger debit balances should always equal the sum of all general ledger credit balances.

The general ledger tells the story of the property. The main reason for the general ledger is to provide a tracking of all transactions. Ownership dictates how often general ledgers should be provided (monthly, yearly, etc.).

No standard chart of accounts exists across all companies, or even within particular industries; each company customizes a chart of accounts to meet its financial reporting needs. Most real estate management companies actually use at least two charts of accounts: one tailored to the real estate management firm as a professional service company and a second geared to the type of property under management. Some integrated accounting software may have a shared chart incorporating the real estate management company and the property.

The property-type chart of accounts for a company specializing in retail is likely to look very different from the one for a company that manages multi-family properties or condominiums. Some companies use a different chart of accounts for each type of property they manage, while others use a single format for all income properties. Occasionally, a large-property owner may dictate the chart of accounts to be used so that reports from all the company's real estate managers provide data in an identical format. Therefore, when developing a chart of accounts, it's important to consider not only the real estate management company's reporting needs, but also the reporting requirements of the real estate owner. Sample charts of accounts are available from many organizations in real estate management.

The chart of accounts is used at every level of the company. The creator must decide on potential tradeoffs between simplicity and the ability to use accounting data for historical comparisons. For example, a maintenance technician may have several service calls regarding repair and replacement of locks. For maximum simplicity, the maintenance supervisor may prefer to code all of the expenses to general repairs and maintenance. This level of detail, while probably sufficient for a tax return, would do little to inform the real estate manager of specific tasks being performed in the field. A very detail-oriented real estate manager might want all expenses relating to keys and locks separated into four categories: lock replacement, lock repair, keys, and lock preventive maintenance. A less detail-oriented manager might want a single category: keys and locks. While the maintenance supervisor may consider looking up every category in a detailed chart of accounts a poor use of time, other members of the organization may find this level of detail necessary to making long-term decisions, such as whether to charge residents or tenants for keys or whether to make a capital improvement to replace all lock sets.

Every chart of accounts needs categories that support financial and **managerial reporting.** Most use a numbering system with a description of the specific category. Exhibit 4.1 shows a commercial property management firm's chart of accounts listed numerically. These accounts would have to be modified for use with residential properties, which would include account numbers for items such as rental income, including pet fees, laundry facilities, parking fees, storage fees, washer and dryer rental, and so on.

Exhibit 4.1	Chart of Accounts—Numerical List

Administrative—71000

71100	Advertising
71101	Merchants assoc. contributions
71105	Entertainment & promotion
71110	Contributions
74105	Automobile lease expense
74108	Parking/ferry tolls
74110	Automobile repairs & maintenance
74810	Management fees
74875	Management fees—cash
75510	Insurance expense
76100	Air freight
76105	Bank charges
76110	Dues and subscriptions
76115	Office equipment rental
76120	Office supplies
76125	Postage
76130	Repairs and maintenance
76135	Telephone expenses
76140	Miscellaneous expense
77100	Accounting fees
77105	Consulting fees
77110	Legal fees
77115	Architect fees
77120	Leasing commissions
78100	Business tax
78105	Licenses
78110	Permits
78115	Personal property tax
78120	Real estate tax
78125	Sales tax on capital additions
79100	Air fare
79105	Car rental
79110	Lodging
79115	Meals
80100	Salaries
80105	Payroll taxes
80110	Profit sharing expenses
80115	Insurance—life
80120	Insurance—medical/dental
80130	Gasoline
80135	Management training

Utilities—81000

81100	Electricity
81200	Gas
81300	Oil
81400	Water
81500	Sewer
81900	Other utilities

Building supplies—83000

83100	Licenses & permits
83150	Alarm
83200	Music
83300	Signs
83350	Supplies
83400	Tools/equipment/uniform
83450	Rentals
83500	Trash removal

Repairs, maintenance & contract service—84000

84110	Salaries
84120	Payroll taxes
84130	Employee benefits
85100	Building repairs/ maintenance
85200	Flooring
85300	Ceilings
85400	Landscaping
85410	Window maintenance
85500	Roof
85600	Elevator/escalator
85700	Plumbing/sprinklers
85800	Parking lot
85900	Security
86000	Janitorial
86100	Painting
86200	Sweeping/snow removal
86300	Electrical
86400	HVAC
86500	Insurance damage
86600	Reserve account

Tenant costs—89000

89100	Tenant repairs
89200	Tenant improvements
89220	Landlord improvements
90000	Rent expenses
96000	Federal income tax expense

When setting up a chart of accounts, the real estate manager must decide the level of detail needed for efficient operation. Similar to the earlier example about keys and locks, some owners might want a single category of grounds maintenance to include lawn mowing, snow removal, salt, fertilizer, and landscape lighting. While lumping all of these expenses into one category makes for a briefer operating statement, a real estate manager might question its usefulness for budgeting purposes. For example, if expenses in the grounds maintenance category started to escalate, the manager would need to go through individual invoices to ascertain which costs were the source of the increase. On the other hand, a very detailed chart could break out the same expenses. However, financial reporting that is too detailed could result in too much information and potential confusion for the property owner.

Most financial software can handle a very detailed chart of accounts by combining categories for financial reporting. For example, a real estate manager could use a detailed report of the repairs and maintenance category to track various expenses within it. He or she might find for owner-reporting purposes that grounds maintenance is too broad, but that 12 categories of expenses is too detailed. Categories could be combined for reporting purposes into just four line items, such as lawn care, snow removal, grounds supplies, and grounds maintenance labor.

The real estate manager should create a chart of accounts with the detail she or he anticipates needing for the properties being managed. It is much easier to alter the chart by combining or subtotaling accounts that end up not being needed than to add accounts when it is found that more detail is needed. Any categories required by the IRS for tax purposes should not be overlooked.

TIPS

*Many companies also have a **manual of accounts** (sometimes called an **explanation of accounts**) that details which category to use for every cash inflow, cash outflow, and expense accrual. For example, the manual would specify whether an invoice for snow removal is coded to the category of grounds maintenance, road maintenance, snow removal. Some companies do not actively use all categories that are included in their chart of accounts, so a manual helps eliminate confusion (for example, between sidewalk snow removal or parking lot snow removal) and extensive recategorization by the accounting department.*

. . . when considering general accounting practices:

- Which accounting methods are used in my company? Are they being used in the appropriate manner to ensure effective, ethical accounting?

- Is my company's chart of accounts detailed enough? Too detailed? How may it be used more effectively?

REVIEW QUESTIONS

- What are the three main accounting methods used to produce financial reports? How do they differ?

- What the Generally Accepted Accounting Principles (GAAP)?

- What is the purpose of a chart of accounts?

Understanding and Implementing Budgets

Mastering sophisticated financial analysis and its impact on property value is likely to chart the course of a real estate manager's professional future. Budgets—itemized projections of income and expenses over specific periods for particular properties—are a tool used by real estate managers to plan and control a property's operations. Learning and applying the skills to develop budgets is essential for all real estate managers; few at any level will enjoy a satisfying career if they rely on others to create budgets and only operate properties according to someone else's specifications.

The adage "If you don't know where you are going, you can't know when you've arrived" applies to a discussion of budgets. The most fundamental purpose of any real estate management budget is to measure the steps needed to accomplish the goals of the property owner and to monitor progress toward those goals. The owner may have both long-term and short-term financial goals for a property, and the short-term goals may change each time the budget is prepared. Market conditions, especially in a tough economy, may alter an owner's willingness to fund improvements or may demonstrate a need for increased cash flow.

How does a real estate manager learn the goals of a property owner? The prudent real estate manager will schedule a focused interview about budget and goals with the property owner every year. Some goals are determined by the type of ownership or the financing in place on a particular property. For example, a property utilizing HUD financing will likely have a goal to meet the requirements of the regulatory agreement. The owner of an office building whose tenants participate in operating expenses will want to forecast costs accurately so that annual adjustments are minimal and timely. A condominium homeowner association may establish a goal of keeping assessments reasonable, while building a reserve account capable of replacing physical assets. The results of these annual focused interviews will reveal the owner's current goals and will lay the foundation on which the budget can be built.

Hence, budgets are the basis for setting measurable goals, planning to accomplish those goals, and assessing how well goals have been achieved. Budgeting is not a clerical task. It is an information-gathering and information-monitoring process that helps managers achieve goals by easing decision making, allowing daily operations to be managed more closely, controlling costs and expenditures, and planning for future goals, including the amounts of cash flow and periodic income.

Top 4 Purposes of a Budget

1. Budgets serve as a foundation of the overall management plan and are the guidelines for operating a property. They can be used in competition with actual amounts from previous years' experience or from a similar property to analyze opportunity to increase efficiency.

2. Budgets, when compared to actuals, become a measure of the manager's and management company's performance. If projections are routinely wrong, this could be a sign that the property is not adhering to the budget (or being used correctly as a monitoring tool for the property).

3. Budgets give owners and managers a method to project, measure, and monitor cash flow (income and expenses).

4. Budgets forecast future income and expenses. While they do not see into the future, they can be used to make fairly accurate projections. These projections become the basis for decision making.

TYPES OF BUDGETS

Different budgets serve specific purposes and monitor distinct types of finances. Most have the same basic elements (see sidebar, "Elements of a Budget").

Elements of a Budget

- *Income (Revenues):* includes rent, fees, and other sources
- *Expenses (Disbursements, Expenditures):* include operating expenses such as maintenance, utilities, payroll, advertising, and taxes
- *Net Operating Income (NOI):* total collections *less* operating expenses; NOI represents a property's earning power and serves as a gauge of the financial strength of a property
- *Financing Expenses:* property loan(s), loans for equipment, rehab, or furniture
- *Capital Expenditures:* include major improvements, large equipment, additions to buildings, buildings themselves, and land
- *Cash Flow Requirements:* include the rate of return on the investment, equity, and the owner's other specific financial objectives

---

Budgets can be divided into three categories: short-term, long-term, and other.

Short-Term Budgets

Type	Description	Period Reviewed	Preperation & Updates
Annual Operating	Plans and forecasts all income and expenses to determine the projected NOI for managing a property.	One year	Prepare: annually Update: monthly or quarterly
Cash Flow	Projects the cash position of the property. It accounts for all sources of income and expected expenditures over the next budget period, which often is as short as a month. Ensures funds are available in the month they are paid out.	12 individual months	Prepare: once *operating budget* is complete Update: monthly

A Word About Short-Term Budgets

The purpose of budgeting for cash flow is to determine how much actual cash will be generated during the next budget period and how much cash will be needed for operations and debt service. The operating budget, including rents, vacancies, and operating expenses for the year, must be projected before the cash flow can be forecast.

The cash flow budget has the same line items as the operating budget, but it forecasts actual cash inflows and outflows. The operating budget may show, for example, the total fee for window washing as $12,000 a year. The cash budget would reflect when the money is actually paid to the window washing contractor (for example, $6,000 in April and $6,000 in October).

The cash flow budget can show budgeted and actual cash flows (both in and out) for operating, investing, and financing activities. See Exhibit 5.1 for a sample monthly *cash flow budget.*

Exhibit 5.1	**Sample Monthly Cash Flow Budget**			

January	February March			
Income				
1.	Rental Collections	$93,058	$96,558	$100,233
2.	Other Collections	500	500	500
3.	**Total**	93,558	97,058	100,733
Expenses *(Conform to Spreadsheet Categories)*				
4.	Payroll & Management	6,833	6,833	6,833
5.	Decorating	1,250	900	1,300
6.	Maintenance	833	670	920
7.	Supplies	833	750	810
8.	Trash Removal	425	475	500
9.	Electricity	500	450	525
10.	Gas	7,000	6,800	6,500
11.	Water & Sewer	2,500	2,400	2,450
12.	Legal & Accounting	792	800	825
13.	Miscellaneous	666	600	550
14.	Administration	2,000	2,000	2,000
15.	**Total Expenses**	23,632	22,678	23,213
16.	**NOI**	69,926	74,380	77,520
17.	**Debt Service**	26,616	26,616	26,616
18.	**OTHER (CAPX, etc.)**	0	15,000	0

Long-Term Budgets

Type	Description	Period Reviewed	Prep & Updates
Long-range	Long-term projection that estimates future expenditures and the return period. It is used to improve decision making related to use, capital improvements, financing, when to sell a property, etc.	Two to five years	Prepare: as needed Update: as needed
Capital	Projection that describes the sources of funds for building up capital reserves for capital improvements. Describes how and when reserves will be used. Can be a component of the operating budget or kept as a separate budget.	One month to five or more years	Prepare: annually or as needed Update: as needed

A Word About Long-Term Budgets

Every building has a life cycle. Over time, the fixtures, appliances, decor, and the building itself become obsolete or wear out. Eventually, replacement is needed, and replacing and renovating parts of a building often entail large outlays of cash, which means cash reserves are needed.

When setting aside cash reserves, a long-term view is best. A real estate manager should consider planning for at least five years. Some owners request that cash reserves be deducted from the property's cash flow and set aside for future capital expenses. If the owner does not want to set aside reserves, capital expenditures must come from the property's cash flow at the time of the expenditure, advances from the owner, new equity from the owner, refinancing, or additional financing. Some lenders may require reserve account, such as HUD-insured loans.

A Word About Long-Term Budgets *(Continued)*

Capital budgets must consider the life cycle of the components of a building. The complexity of the property components, the ownership structure, and the lending and legal environments may all influence the detail to which the capital budget is produced.

For example, a capital budget for a large apartment community may break down expenses by individual unit. Such a property may have no capital reserves, so a request for owner funding would accompany the budget. On the other hand, a capital budget for a large homeowner association would be accompanied by a complete reserve analysis performed by a third-party company. Such a study would break down every component of the property by its useful life and develop a replacement schedule for each. When compared to reserves on hand, this information would indicate to the manager if additional contributions are required to fund necessary capital improvements.

Absent state or local laws, regulatory agreements, or lender requirements to the contrary, funding proportions for capital improvements are largely an owner decision. If the estimated capital requirement for the next 10 years is known, such as with the large homeowner association example above, the real estate manager may decide to collect 100% of the estimated funds needed each year or may collect a smaller portion with the hope that the replacements are not needed as quickly as projected. A shopping center owner may choose to reserve no funds and instead to fund capital improvements as the items are needed. In the case of the apartment community, with no funds available, the real estate manager asked the owner to fund certain needed capital items.

Payback Period

Sometimes a real estate manager wants to isolate the increased revenue that would result from a capital improvement. For example, a real estate manager in a residential setting may be considering replacement of appliances and want to know how long it will take to recover the cost with increased rents. Or a real estate manager in an office building may consider installing an improved energy management system and wants to determine how long it will take for the energy savings to pay for the cost of the new system. In both cases this period of time being determined is called the payback period, which is a meaningful measure for budgeting that isolates a single variable.

Other Types of Budgets

Type	Description	Period Reviewed	Prep & Updates
Rent-up/ Lease-up	Used for new buildings, rehab projects, and properties with abnormal vacancies. Estimates income and expenses for the first year of operation or until occupancy is stabilized. In that sense, it is a variation of an annual operating budget. Note that a major factor to consider is how long the building will take to reach normal (not necessarily full) occupancy. Reflects the monthly changes that occur as a building comes on the market. Reflects special costs that new buildings incur, such as extensive marketing programs and advertising.	Monthly	Prepare: monthly or as needed Update: monthly
Pro Forma	A projection that estimates the revenues and expenses of a future project under normal, stable market conditions. Analyzes the merits and drawbacks of real estate investments based on projected results as well as the effects of major changes on a property.	As needed	Prepare: as needed Update: as needed

A Word About Pro Forma Budgets

Besides outlining each category of expenses, a pro forma budget reflects factors like the cost of financing, the amount of space (or number of units, by type) likely to be leased over the course of a year, and income projections. For proposed new construction, the real estate manager, owner, architect, and contractor may compile a pro forma budget covering a number of variables, such as different floor sizes, occupancy rates, amenities, and staffing. The scenarios in the budget can be adjusted until the right mix emerges. In this sense, a pro forma budget highlights the use of the budget as a plan.

Budget Timelines

With the exception of lease-up and cash flow budgets, most budgets are prepared on an annual basis. However, some detailed budgeting requires analyzing income and expenses on a monthly basis, and most property management software can break the annual budget into monthly components to provide meaningful reports for monitoring purposes. Software typically also allows for entries to be weighted so that seasonal expenses, such as landscaping and snow removal, are reflected in the periods when the expenses are incurred.

Current-year projections can pose challenges in budget preparation. A budget that follows a calendar year will first be drafted in August or September of the current year, so estimates of current-year data will be needed for the remaining months. (Often a budget will have several drafts before the owner gives final approval.) After all information is gathered, and current-year figures are projected, the detailed analysis begins.

Since the budget will likely become the operating plan for the coming year, it should be completed and approved no later than the end of November. Remember that a budget is not written in stone; if conditions change markedly during the year, it is appropriate to adjust the budget. This should always be done with the owner's knowledge and approval, especially if the change is necessitated by negative developments. Owners who will not be realizing their financial expectations need to be informed as quickly as possible so they have time to make their own adjustments. Positive developments must also be reported promptly. An owner often pays estimated taxes, and penalties are imposed when unreported income exceeds a certain percentage. Therefore, the owner must be notified of unexpected "windfalls" so that payment of estimated taxes can be adjusted accordingly to avoid any penalties.

Regardless of the type, preparing any budget requires gathering a significant amount of information. In a large organization, multiple individuals will be involved, including the real estate manager, site manager, maintenance supervisor, property accountant, and property owner.

- Which types of budgets are used in my company, and when?

- Are there any types of budgets that our company should be using that we are not currently using?

FORECASTING

Predicting a property's expenses and income is an essential step in creating a budget. After all, it is uncertainty about the future that makes budgeting necessary; forecasting techniques project current knowledge into future performance. Most of this section focuses on expenses, but first a few words about income, or revenue. Revenue forecasts must take into consideration multiple variables, including in-depth market analysis. Real estate managers need to consider occupancy, a realistic assessment of *gross potential rents,* vacancies—including possible concessions—and *collection losses.* This part of the budgeting process should involve marketing and leasing staff or brokers for the property as well as the real estate manager and accountant.

Methods for projecting revenue differ based on the property being analyzed. Shopping centers, for example, have complex leases that are usually long-term and include revenue from rents, percentage rent, participation in some operating expenses, expense caps, and offsets. Loss of income as a result of move-outs from lease expirations and business failures must be considered against the potential for quickly filling space with new tenants. For apartment buildings, on the other hand, revenue projections are based on an analysis of market rents and occupancy projections. When forecasting gross potential income, the real estate manager should be careful to consider demographic trends in the property's neighborhood and competing property rents. Miscellaneous income, such as parking, vending, and advertising, is included for every type of property.

Forecasting techniques help to produce accurate figures for a budget. Forecasting income and expenses is an essential step in creating a budget. Forecasting expenses involves thinking about how costs arise and classifying them accordingly.

- *Fixed costs* do not change as occupancy rates change and are generally stable during the budget period. Insurance and real estate taxes can be considered fixed costs.

- *Variable costs* change with usage. Electricity and water are typical variable costs.

Fixed and variable costs are concepts commonly used in accounting. They may be further separated into *controllable expenses* and *uncontrollable expenses* as illustrated in Exhibit 5.2.

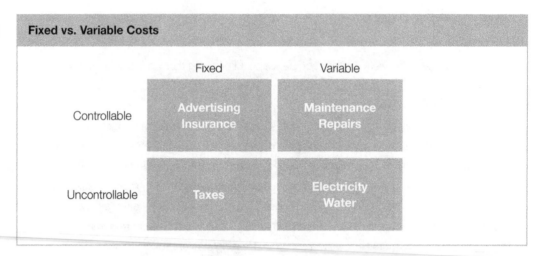

Exhibit 5.2 **Fixed vs. Variable Costs**

	Fixed	Variable
Controllable	Advertising Insurance	Maintenance Repairs
Uncontrollable	Taxes	Electricity Water

History-Based Forecasting

Forecasting future expenses usually begins with gathering information about past actual expenses, which is helpful for budget items that change by predictable amounts from year to year. While budget items controlled by the real estate manager are usually fairly predictable, it should not simply be assumed that any budget item will change predictably. Special attention should be paid to the current year and the last full year of operations for emerging trends.

Examining the past three years of actual expenses, with an emphasis on the current year, gives a good basis for a forecast. Invoices for operating expenses of the past year should be pulled and available for review along with the general ledger and inventory reports. Averaging is a common technique for arriving at realistic numbers for a forecast. If the previous winter was severe, for example, those heating bills may be unusually high and could skew the budget being prepared.

Interpreting averages is important to working with budgets. (See "Arithmetic Mean," "Weighted Mean," and "Median and Mode" in Chapter 12: Property Valuation for detailed information about calculating averages.) Averaging past years' figures usually gives a reasonable estimate of future years' performance, but no figures should be followed blindly. Averages are sensitive to unusual numbers and can easily be distorted.

It is uncertainty about the future that makes budgeting necessary; forecasting techniques project current knowledge into future performance.

As mentioned, the real estate manager whenever possible should consider expenses from at least the prior three years to reasonably forecast future costs. Two basic techniques are used for forecasting expenses: 1) percentage increase and 2) consumption × rate.

Percentage Increase

Say a property had landscaping costs of $10,000 last year. Using a percentage increase technique, next year's expense might be forecast at $10,500, $10,366, or $10,085, depending on the method used to arrive at the amount of increase. The first method applies a percentage increase derived from the economic environment, industry trends, or the real estate manager's own experience. In this case, an increase of 5% is determined to be reasonable, so last year's cost of $10,000 would become $10,500 in next year's budget.

The second method averages the percentage increases of the past three years to arrive at the new percentage increase. If the increases for landscaping over the last three years were 2%, 6%, and 3%, averaging them would result in an increase for next year of 3.66%. Applying that factor to the $10,000 historical figure would yield a budget forecast of $10,366.

The third technique applies the chosen percentage increase to an average of the actual costs for the last three years. If those costs for landscaping were $9,116, $9,700, and $10,000, averaging these expenses would create a base figure of $9,605. This base is then multiplied by the determined percentage increase—in this case, 5%—to arrive at a forecast of $10,085.

Whichever method is used to arrive at the increases using the percentage increase technique, the real estate manager should be careful to choose an *inflation* rate that is meaningful for the line item under consideration.

Energy costs, for example, may increase or decrease at rates different than labor rates for a given market. Each line item should be considered independently when forecasting expense trends.

Consumption × Rate

This technique still uses historical data, but it breaks expenses down into the components of consumption and rate. Continuing the landscaping example, last year's (y–1) cost of $10,000 was based on 286 hours of labor billed at a rate of $35 per hour. If there is no reason to project additional hours of labor, then a reasonable forecast would multiply 286 hours by the landscaping company's expected rate per hour next year. If that rate is $37 per hour, the figure for next year would be 286 × $37, or $10,582.

The consumption × rate method is especially useful when forecasting utility expenses. Consider the cost of heating a building. If last year's heat cost was $50,000, and the utility company expects energy costs to go up 10%, is it appropriate to simply multiply last year's cost by the projected increase? The answer requires a more careful look, both at the utility bills and at other circumstances.

Assume the building is heated by natural gas. The gas bills indicate a cost per therm of 48 cents, indicating consumption last year of 104,168 therms ($50,000 ÷ 48). A 10% increase in energy costs would result in a cost per therm of 53 cents. Multiplying last year's consumption by the projected cost per therm would yield a forecast of $55,000, exactly 10% more than last year. But often it is not appropriate to assume consumption will remain identical.

Was last winter typical in terms of temperature? Was the building occupancy the same last year as is expected next year? If the answer to either question is no, the expected consumption should be projected, either by averaging consumption figures for several prior years or by comparing the severity of the weather in terms of heating degree days.

Though it is fairly common practice for real estate managers to simply use the percentage increase approach to forecast many expense categories, accurate forecasting may warrant breaking a general ledger item down into its components for examination. The real estate manager's first step is using historical data, then, deciding whether a percentage increase is sufficient for a given expense or if analysis of the components is warranted. For small expenses, detailed analysis may not be worth the time it would require, and certain expenses, including human resource costs (if stable), might be fixed by long-term contracts.

Where the real estate manager decides that detailed analysis of consumption and rate are in order, the first task is to obtain at least three years of historical data for each line item. This information should come from actual invoices, not simply from earlier operating statements. Each line item is then broken down into its components so that both consumption and rate are apparent. In the examples already given, this may be less difficult than costs of perhaps an elevator contract or trash removal. These contracts may have inflationary cost adjustments in addition to consumption and rate costs.

Zero-Based Budgeting

Another forecasting technique is ***zero-based budgeting.*** Zero-based budgeting de-emphasizes the historical role of income and expenses in creating the current budget and emphasizes the development of a management plan. Past numbers may be inaccurate or may not reflect the current economic situation and that can cause them to distort the budgeting process.

Zero-based budgeting prevents expenses from being inserted automatically (and unthinkingly) into budgets year after year. Normally, when using zero-based budgeting, a real estate manager incorporates current information from sources like contractors, vendors, utility companies, and other sources instead of plugging in historical expenses. For example, both expense scenarios used earlier—landscaping and heating costs—could be estimated from sources independent of the property's historical data.

The real estate manager should exercise caution using historical data, especially when taking on **foreclosure** or receivership properties, as any data supplied may be inaccurate or provided on a cash basis. Even at properties where historical data is reliable, preparing a zero-based budget on an occasional basis can serve as a check on the historical budget.

TIPS

The IREM® Income/Expense Analysis Reports are published for five property types: conventional apartments; office buildings; federally assisted apartments; shopping centers; and condominiums, cooperatives, and planned unit developments. The reports can be purchased at www.irem.org.

CHOOSING A FORECASTING METHOD

So which forecasting technique should a real estate manager use for a given situation? There are no specific rules, but good judgment is required. One common approach is to use a percentage increase on line items below a predetermined dollar figure and those with a history of predictability or fixed by contract. After that, one can use historical analysis based on available information. Certain line items may lend themselves to a historical method in some years but zero-based analysis in others. For example, elevator contracts, insurance, and refuse removal may not require zero-based forecasting every year, but it is a good idea to obtain competitive bids periodically, perhaps every two or three years. It also is important to check fixed contracts for escalation clauses, which may be included in boilerplate language in the agreement. It is not necessary to use the same technique for each line item in the budget, but the methodology used should be justifiable and documented.

When to Use Zero-Based Budgeting

Four factors indicate that zero-based budgeting may be the best course of action:

1. If historical information is not available, such as for new buildings or new accounts, the budget necessarily begins at zero.

2. When projections from past expenses are likely to be unreliable, for example when expenses are highly variable from period to period, zero-based budgeting smoothes out the variation and consequent uncertainty.

3. When records are inaccurate or nonexistent, zero-based budgeting is preferable because it avoids bringing mistakes into the budget cycle.

4. As a balance against expenses forecast by another method, zero-based budgeting removes financial preconceptions from the budget cycle.

Forecasting Tools

Financial spreadsheets with built in formulas, such as the *IREM® Financial Analysis Spreadsheet,* and financial software are available to assist in budget forecasting. However, these tools must be completed using accurate data compiled using one of the forecasting methods discussed.

CHECKLIST: FORECASTING TIPS

❑ Use zero-based budgeting to determine payroll expenses. This technique allows you to analyze salaries during each budget cycle.

❑ Collect information on utility use. Use averages of past years' monthly utility expenses to estimate heating and cooling costs for each month.

❑ Determine how the expenses have changed in the past to forecast future expenses. Analyze what factors may have produced the change. Use weighted averages where one-year anomalies may exist (e.g., in years with severe weather requiring greater expenses).

❑ Examine all potential risk factors that may produce expenses. Risk factors include a wide array of events, from bad weather to nonpaying residents or tenants to insurance settlements.

❑ Factor in inflation, even in low-inflation times. Over time, inflation has an enormous effect on costs and expenses.

❑ Talk to insurance companies to anticipate trends in insurance premiums. In recent years, with natural disasters and other risks increasing, insurance premiums have been adjusted upward dramatically. Communicating with the insurance company may enable property management to be aware of looming industry-wide increases so that it can forecast the increase.

❑ Know the current economic conditions of the neighborhood and region of the subject property's marketplace.

❑ Know real estate tax rates in your area—and keep up with changes in tax laws, tax rates, and the cycles for assessing local property taxes. Also know real estate reappraisal schedules as observed by taxing entities.

Questions real estate managers may ask

. . . when considering forecasting methods:

• Which forecasting methods should be used for my properties, and why?

• From where do should I be gathering historical data?

VARIANCE ANALYSIS

Budget variance analysis is another important technique in monitoring existing budgets and preparing new budgets. It is most often used when working with the operating and cash flow budgets. A budget **variance** is the difference between the amount forecast for an account in a budget and the actual amount spent or earned in the account. Variance analysis and reporting are used to determine the causes of differences between actual and forecast amounts and to revise budgets, goals, and plans.

Budget variances can be favorable or unfavorable. (See Exhibit 5.3.)

- A **favorable** variance raises NOI (more income to owner).

- An **unfavorable** variance lowers NOI (less income to owner).

Note that some real estate managers use the terms positive and negative or over-budget and under-budget instead of favorable and unfavorable.

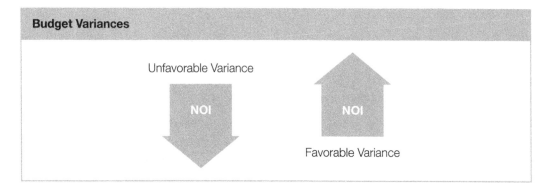

Budget Variances   *Exhibit 5.3*

Unfavorable Variance

NOI

NOI

Favorable Variance

Favorable and unfavorable variances have different meanings depending on whether the variance is in income or expenses. For example, if you project that the electric bill next month will be $2,100 and the actual bill is $2,450, the variance is $350, or 17% ($350/$2,100). Since the actual bill (expense) is $350 over what was forecast, the variance is *unfavorable*. It has decreased NOI. Keep in mind that the operating budget predicts NOI for the year and favorable or unfavorable variances will also change the corresponding cash flow.

Amount Projected	Amount Spent on Electric Bill	Variance	Description
$2,100	$2,450	+17%	Unfavorable

Now, consider this example. If monthly rental income is projected at $104,000, and the actual figure for the month is $120,000, the variance of $16,000 or 15% is *favorable.* The variance has increased NOI.

Amount Projected	Annual Income Earned	Variance	Description
$104,000	$120,000	+15%	Favorable

To determine the total variance, find the difference between the total unfavorable variances and the total favorable variances. This is called the *net total variance.*

Total unfavorable variances **〈** Total favorable variances ⇨ *favorable* net total variance

Total unfavorable variances **〉** Total favorable variances ⇨ *unfavorable* net total variance

BUDGETING ETHICS AND DECISION-MAKING

A real estate manager must act with honesty and integrity when preparing budgets, attempting to achieve the owner's goals but realizing that property operation is largely a market-based business. Under competent management, both revenue and expenses are market driven. Real estate managers must always budget based on their best professional judgment of a property's ability to perform, realizing that no method of forecasting can be 100% accurate.

Competitive forces in real estate management can create pressures to budget unrealistically in the effort to keep a client's business. While there is nothing inherently wrong with budgeting either aggressively or conservatively, the real estate manager must always use her or his best efforts to budget accurately and in the best interests of the owner. If the marketplace is volatile, consider creating several budgets: an expected budget, a worst-case budget, and a best-case budget.

A variety of valuable resources are available to real estate managers for help in determining market trends and making ethical budgeting decisions as shown in the chart that follows.

Resource	Description
Industry Reports	Both IREM and the Building Owners and Managers Association (BOMA) publish reports with operating statistics and trend analysis by city. The BOMA publication, **Experience Exchange Report**, is available for office buildings only. IREM publishes *Income/Expense Analysis Reports* for specific property types: conventional apartments, office buildings, federally assisted apartments, shopping centers, and condominiums, cooperatives, and planned unit developments. Reports like these can be particularly useful for zero-based budgeting because the information is verified from actual buildings in the market under consideration. Units of measure are determined by the property type but include costs per square foot and percent of gross potential income.
Comparable Properties	A real estate manager preparing a zero-based budget for a property may want to consider comparable buildings in his or her management portfolio as a guide. Costs for many line items will be similar per unit or per square foot, and these indicators can be prudently applied to the property in question.
Professional Estimates	For some expenses, an appropriate professional can provide information to support budget projections. For example, a mechanical engineer could be engaged to estimate a building's heat loss and apply seasonal temperature variances to project fuel usage. The real estate manager could then apply the usage estimate to projected fuel rates in order to budget for heat costs.
Competitive Bidding	Many real estate managers work with the same contractors or suppliers year after year, often for good reasons. When using zero-based budgeting, however, it is prudent to develop specifications outlining the scope of work and obtain competitive bids. For example, a competitive bid, or request for proposal (RFP), for snow removal at a property in a northern climate may spell out the accumulation of snow that must be present before plowing, the need for spreading de-icing compound, and the frequency of hauling accumulated snow. The contractor may respond with a cost "per push" for each snowfall or may offer a price for the season. With variables substituted as appropriate, competitive bids can be solicited for almost any product or service.

Budgets and Accounting Choices When Forecasting

With the exception of the cash flow budget, all budget forecasts for expenses should be done on an accrual basis. That means that all expenses should be accounted for, whether the property is capable of paying them on time or not. Failure to use accrual accounting when forecasting expenses and monitoring budget performance could have serious financial consequences.

Accounting decisions for forecasting revenue should be based on the real estate manager's best judgment of revenue reliability. For example, an office building leased to a government entity is very likely to have a reliable income stream, while income for the same building with spaces leased to several small businesses may be less reliable and may be better forecast using cash-basis accounting. Apartment properties almost always use cash-basis for projecting revenue.

TOOLS AND CONVENTIONS FOR BUDGETING

The real estate manager may be responsible for working with the accountant to create the annual operating budget for the properties he or she manages. Much software is available to assist in budget preparation and analysis. Most of the popular programs for property management accommodate inputting an annual operating budget and producing budget reports. Many real estate managers find a spreadsheet program to be very effective for annual budgeting. Using spreadsheet formulas in the budgeting process is highly recommended and expected. It eliminates errors and provides a tool to see the "logic" behind the formula created. Different areas of an operating budget demand the use of more complex formulas, but most are simple to understand and use. Multi-year budgets may warrant more sophisticated software, to forecast over longer periods using more complex economic variables.

There are many resources available for preparing budgets. For example, IREM includes the following two tools in the *IREM® Financial Analysis Spreadsheet;* note that these types of budget can be built into any spreadsheet.

- Pro Forma Statement, which has two components: historical data and "pro forma," or forecasted data. The tool provides three columns for entering historical data. It also allows forecasting of up to 10 years of income and expenses by using a percentage increase per year or by entering specific figures for each year.

- 12-Month Operating Budget, which can be used to forecast income and expenses for the *next* year, using expected income and expenses for each month. The 12-month budget tool can be used in conjunction with the pro forma data, or it can stand alone. This tool is helpful in creating a projection for the first year of the analysis.

The IREM® Financial Analysis Spreadsheet is free to all IREM Members and can be purchased by non-members at www.irem.org.

The following conventions are used in this book with regard to current and historical budget data:

Year	Description
Time Point Zero	A snapshot of one specific point in time; one specific day
Current Year	The current year of operations
Year −1	The year before the current year (or previous year)
Year −2	Two years before Year 0 (or two years ago)
Year −3	Three years before Year 0 (or three years ago)
Year 1	One year after Year 0 (or next year)
Year 2 through 11	Two to 11 years after Year 0 (or subsequent years)

BUDGETING EXCEPTIONS

Because the methodology used depends somewhat on the reliability of historical data and the volatility of the market for a particular good or service, the budgeting process cannot be fully automated. Real estate managers must pay special attention to line items that change more than once per year. Some line items should be zero-based every year, while others can be done with cautious automation. Documenting the methodology used along with any other justifications will be helpful if questions are raised during budget reviews. Line items of common concern are addressed in the following sections.

Real Estate Tax Valuation

Formulas for calculating real estate taxes vary by state and sometimes even by municipality. The most basic formula is the tax rate multiplied by the assessed valuation. The assessed valuation is set, usually by the taxing entity, on each property, based supposedly on its **market value.** It is called "assessed value" rather than market value because not every municipality reviews property values every year, and some states regulate the assessment process. Some, for example, will set the assessed value at a percentage of a property's market value. Others may not review assessments for several years, and newer properties may be assessed at a lower percentage to equalize their value in light of the older appraisals. In other states, the assessed value may depend on a property's use.

For example, a single-family home might be assessed at 75% of its value, low-income housing at 5%, and shopping centers at 100%. Take the state of Wisconsin, for example, where a typical real estate tax bill includes five different taxing authorities that are funded by real estate taxes: the state, county, municipality, school board, and technical school system. In essence, each taxing authority calculates the money it needs to operate and divides it by the total assessed valuation of the property tax base.

This aspect of the taxation process is technically fair, since every property owner is charged based on property value. Potentially unfair, however, is the assessed value of a property. Property owners should be alert to the assessed value of their property compared with similar properties. This information is public record. If an assessment seems out of line, an expert can be engaged to protest unfair valuation on behalf of the property owner; compensation is a fee based on the tax savings. Some firms perform this service as a specialty, and some professionals, such as attorneys and real estate appraisers, handle tax appeals as part of their regular practice. Real estate managers may want to consider using such professionals to track valuations of their properties rather than try to develop expertise in an arena with such wide variations.

Real Estate Tax Timing

Just like real estate managers, taxing authorities must prepare budgets and submit them by a specific date. Estimating real estate taxes can be especially problematic when the underlying rate (known as the "mill rate") is not established until late October or November. Some taxing authorities may have estimates of the mill rate they expect to be approved, which the real estate manager can use for estimating upcoming taxes. Final tax estimating may require some late adjustments to the budget. Remember that in most states the real estate tax bill received at the end of the year is the current year of real estate tax. The real estate manager must forecast the expected tax for the following year from that cost.

Insurance

Insurance pricing can change rapidly based on a company's experiences with real estate–related risks. For example, a company may decide that it no longer wants to encourage apartment building risks, so it prices itself out of that market. A real estate manager must be alert to price changes from individual companies and not simply interpret an increase as an industry-wide change.

Similarly, there can be opportunities for value when a company well respected in one line of insurance decides to break into another. For example, a well-regarded auto and home insurer recently decided to take on insuring apartment buildings. Since they had to compete with established insurers, they underbid everyone in the market to gain business.

After the first year of service, an insurance carrier typically offers a renewal premium for the next year. Renewal premiums are not always the best rate a company has to offer; a real estate manager may need to rebid insurance coverage to obtain the best pricing. If many properties are covered by a single policy, the premium cost needs to be properly allocated among them.

Contracts

A real estate manager should exercise care when entering into a contract with a vendor. Some vendors will offer strong incentives to sign contracts for longer than one year, which may be beneficial to the property owner as well. These incentives might freeze price increases for the term of the contract. Long-term contracts are common for services such as trash hauling and elevator maintenance. Take note of any automatic renewal clauses, and adjust budget timing where appropriate to prevent an unwanted renewal. Also, be alert for contracts that appear to be fixed-price but have escalation clauses for factors such as fuel costs or collective bargaining labor rate increases.

Utilities

Costs for fuel and electric services should be analyzed regularly. In some states, deregulation allows some flexibility in selecting a provider. Even where this is not the case, the real estate manager should periodically review invoices or have them reviewed by a specialist. Utilities may make errors in billing, usually by charging an incorrect rate for a building. For example, a high-volume user of natural gas may be entitled to a reduced rate but be billed at a rate designed for consumer use.

For utilities owned by municipalities, a covert method of increasing revenue as budget pressures increase has been to charge more for utility services. Be alert to any sudden increases in a rate structure, and do not automatically apply a percentage increase. Check with the utility regarding rates for the coming year when preparing a budget. Also be aware that a municipal utility may have the right to apply unpaid utility bills against the property's real estate taxes.

Payroll

Labor costs warrant special attention when preparing budgets. It might be a good idea to use zero-base budgeting for wage costs based on current pay rates. At the very least, pay special attention to labor costs for the previous two or three months, and be sure to factor in any automatic increases, planned bonuses, and expected staff increases or decreases. Remember to include the costs of all employer-related expenses, such as benefits and employment taxes.

Collective Bargaining Agreements

If a property uses union labor, be sure to review applicable collective bargaining agreements. They typically span more than a single year and have built-in escalations of wages and benefits.

Capital Expenditure vs. Operating Expense

Some costs may be capital expenditures in one situation but operating expenses in another. For example, parking lot sealing may be a capital expenditure in an apartment building, but in an office building or shopping center it would be an operating expense charged back to the tenants as common area maintenance.

Budgeting is clearly a complex process that requires the expertise of several members on a property management team. Collecting meaningful data is critical, as is intelligent use of forecasting techniques. In many companies, the budget process starts well before the start of the fiscal year, but it should always start no later than the end of the third quarter. The risks associated with making errors in forecasting the fourth quarter are minimal compared to starting the process too late.

· ·

REVIEW QUESTIONS

- How does budgeting contribute to planning for profit and positive cash flow?
- What time period does the operating budget normally cover and what are its purposes?
- Which type of budget does a real estate management company use to plan and forecast all income and expenses to determine the projected net operating income for managing a property?
- Which type of budget does a real estate management company use to project the cash position of a property?
- Which type of budget is a long-term budget used to project sources of funds available for property improvements?
- Describe the two main types of forecasting techniques.
- Define budget variance analysis and list it purposes.
- What effect does an unfavorable variance have on NOI?
- What effect does a favorable variance have on NOI?
- When comparing historical operations to future budgets, what is the designation given to the current year? What is Year -1? What is Year +2?

Cash Flow Analysis

The data gathered in financial reports during the real estate management company's accounting and budgeting efforts is the basis of the real estate manager's financial analysis. **Cash flow statements** are commonly used to organize financial analyses. Cash flow describes a stream of money and is typical of how a business operates: payments come into a business (income) and payments are made by the business (expenses). Thus, cash flow is the amount of remaining income from a real estate investment; it is the amount of cash available after all expenses and debts have been paid.

Real estate managers use cash flow data to analyze the property. There are two broad categories of analysis: (1) valuation analysis, which is maximizing the earning power of the property by studying income and expenses, leading to net operating income (NOI); (2) investment analysis, which meets the goals of the owner through studying financing and taxes, leading to **before-tax cash flow (BTCF)** and **after-tax cash flow (ATCF):**

- NOI represents a property's earning power. The elements of NOI are factors independent of any particular owner or investor. Any owner should be able to achieve the NOI that is calculated. When used for valuation purposes, NOI should be a stable amount, remaining relatively constant from year to year. This is the reason why NOI is a determinant of a property's market value. [Note that, if the NOI is not likely to be stable, another technique, known as **discounted cash flow (DCF)** analysis, can be used. DCF is discussed in detail later in this book.]

- BTCF refers to the amount of money remaining after operating expenses (including real estate taxes) and debt service have been paid but before income taxes are considered.

- ATCF is the money remaining after income taxes have been deducted; it is the real estate owner's **net profit.** Projections of ATCF for the life of an investment can be made to demonstrate the overall value of a property meeting its goals, including tax savings.

The key tool for analysis is the cash flow statement. Cash flow statements can have different titles, such as annual operating data and multi-year operating data. A format referred to as the **pro forma statement** of cash flow is commonly used in the industry. It is an annual statement that lists income and expenses for the property. It includes revenue and operating expenses through NOI and before-tax cash flow BTCF. The basic pro forma statement is shown in Exhibit 6.1.

Exhibit 6.1

Pro Forma Statement of Cash Flow

Gross Potential Income *(GPI)*

– Loss to Lease

– Vacancy and Collection Loss

= Net Rent Revenue

+ Miscellaneous Income

+ Expense Reimbursements

= Effective Gross Income *(EGI)*

– Operating Expenses

= Net Operating Income *(NOI)*

– Annual Debt Service (ADS)

– Blank (CAPX, Reserves, etc.)

= Before-Tax Cash Flow *(BTCF)*

Market Forces

Investor Decisions

The pro forma statement illustrates some important financial measurements used in real estate. It shows that **gross potential income (GPI)** is adjusted to give **effective gross income (EGI),** which in turn is adjusted by operating expenses to produce NOI. As mentioned previously, NOI is a commonly used measure of financial health in real estate.

Note that this overview statement is sufficient when analyzing an overall investment return. However, as you've seen, for a budget, operating expenses are broken down into detailed categories that can be examined more closely. Also note how changes in the market and the investor decisions may influence BTCF.

This chapter examines how a pro forma statement "works down" to BTCF. Management of BTCF may determine whether a company will remain in business over time and how solvent the property will be. The process of preparing a cash flow budget affords the real estate manager the opportunity to plan for the future; the uses of cash need to be monitored.

Some owners will require the accounting practices for a property to show certain expenditures such as capital expenditures, **tenant improvements,** and leasing commissions *above* the BTCF line. These expenses do not impact NOI but, in many cases, have a material impact on cash flow.

See "Pro Forma at a Glance" in the sidebar for an overview of the elements of the statement.

Pro Forma Statement of Cash at a Glance	
Gross Potential Income (GPI)	Maximum amount of rental income a property can produce when 100% of the property is leased 100% of the time at full-market rents
– Loss to Lease	Amount of money lost due to contract or leased (actual) rents being less than the maximum market rents, or GPI
– Vacancy and Collection Loss	• PHYSICAL VACANCY: available but unoccupied space • ECONOMIC VACANCY: loss from concessions or space not available for lease (e.g., if used for models or offices) • COLLECTION LOSS: delinquent and/or uncollectible rent
= Net Rent Revenue	Difference between GPI and losses due to below-market rents, vacancy, and delinquencies
+ Miscellaneous Income	Income from any source other than rent (e.g., parking, coin-operated laundry)
+ Expense Reimbursements	Funds collected from tenants in addition to rent to pay for tenants' pro rata share of property operating expenses such as real estate taxes, insurance, or common area maintenance
= Effective Gross Income (EGI)	Net rent revenue plus miscellaneous income and reimbursement for expenses
– Operating Expenses	Costs associated with operating the property (e.g., real estate taxes, salaries, insurance, maintenance, utilities, and administrative costs)
= Net Operating Income (NOI)	EGI less operating expenses
– Annual Debt Service (ADS)	Annual payments of principal and interest on a loan
– BLANK (CAPX, Reserves, etc.)	The property may be required to add reserves for replacement, leasing commissions, and tenant improvements expenses, or capital improvements expenses above the before-tax cash flow line
= Before-Tax Cash Flow (BTCF)	NOI less ADS

SIGNIFICANCE OF NOI AND BTCF

Although the revenue and expenditures detailed on a pro forma statement are for a specific property, there is an important relationship between any property's NOI and the overall marketplace. Assuming prudent management, similar properties in the same market should have similar NOIs. This same reasoning applies to properties of a similar type, even if they are configured different or different sizes.

For example, Central Business District Class A office buildings in a given city should have similar rents and similar operating expenses on a square footage basis. Analysis of subject property should include a review of revenues, vacancies, and expenses for similar properties to assure consistency with the marketplace. In preparing a stabilized NOI, careful consideration of market expenses could reveal issues with the property's management. Unusually low expenses could be the result of **deferred maintenance** and signal much higher future expenses. Unusually high expenses, on the other hand, could be the result of earlier deferred maintenance, favoritism in selecting vendors, or a failure to bid projects effectively. IREM's *Income/Expense Analysis Reports,* a real estate manager's own historical records on similar properties, and other reliable market resources can help with estimating the most reliable NOI for a given property. Because NOI by definition is market-based, no prudent real estate manager would pay more for operating expenses than can be found generally in the marketplace, nor would she or he rent space for less than the appropriate market rent.

Beyond NOI, cash flow calculations (i.e., BTCF) are not market-based. Instead, they take into account many factors specific to an individual owner, such as financing details or specific owner requirements. Thus, analysis of the same property for two different owners will reveal the same NOI, but potentially completely different cash flows.

For the purposes of investment analysis, the nine elements of NOI outlined in the pro forma statement in this book are sufficient for evaluating the fundamental merits or drawbacks of a property, and they may reveal major trends. For example, historical presentation of data at this level of detail might reveal if overall operating expenses were increasing at an unusual rate or if rent revenue were dropping. An investor often uses this type of format when selecting a property for further analysis. Basic ratio analysis can be performed that, when compared to asking price, gives a would-be investor enough data to eliminate a property from consideration or highlight if for further analysis.

The cash flow budget determines how much cash will be generated and how much cash will be needed for operations and debt service during the next budget period. Even though a property may have a positive cash position at year-end, the position may be negative for periods during the year. Those periods must be anticipated and accounted for. As will be seen, forecasts of cash flow can also be used in evaluating the viability of a project.

COMPONENTS OF THE PRO FORMA STATEMENT

In order to calculate the figures that measure a property's financial performance, it is important to understand the components of the pro forma statement of cash flow.

Gross Potential Income (GPI)

Cash flow is not just money in movement; it involves planning and some calculation. The first step in computing cash flow is **gross potential income (GPI).** Also known as potential gross income and potential rental income, GPI is the maximum rent that can be derived from 100% occupancy at market rent over the course of a financial period (normally, a year). To determine GPI, assume that all space/units are occupied, all rents are paid in full, and all payments are received on time.

GPI is usually calculated as the total of all rents under existing leases at the **contract rent** plus all vacant space at the **market rent** for that type of space. This method is based on the concept that in the current year the maximum revenue the property could produce is limited by the leases in place on the property. Vacant space has the potential of being rented at market rates.

Note that, when 100% of the space in a building (or all apartments in a property) is reported at market rent, the result shows what *could* be achieved if all space or all units were generating market rent. This number is seldom achieved, of course, largely because some space is subject to existing leases. For example, an office building may have several leases with, say, five years to maturity that were negotiated when rents were lower. Even though the owner will not likely receive market rent for this space for five years, in the calculation for GPI the figure is reported at market rent and then modified by a deduction known as **loss to lease,** which is the next line item in the pro forma statement of cash flow.

Example 6.1 | **GPI**

Consider the rent roll for a 40,000-square-foot office building with 75% of the space rented and 25% vacant. In the rented space are three tenants with leases expiring over the next three years; their current rents are $590,000. A recent survey of rents revealed that the vacant space is worth $27 per square foot, or $270,000 a year. Adding that figure to the existing rents yields a GPI of $860,000. However, when GPI is used in a pro forma for long-term projections, it is often calculated using market rent for all space, irrespective of existing leases. This stipulation would increase the GPI to $1,080,000. When the figure is used properly in the larger analysis, either is acceptable, and the final analysis is likely to elicit the same result.

A critical first step in determining GPI is a thorough lease analysis (see Chapter 15). The lease identifies the rent structure as well as the operating expenses paid for by the tenant. In commercial leases, especially for large national tenants, the tenant dictates the format of the lease. Lease provisions can vary widely, so the real estate manager must be alert to key elements, including rent, escalations, and percentage rent, as well as some less obvious provisions like early cancellation, renewal options, and amortization costs of improvements.

Leases on commercial properties are often analyzed in detail in the process of calculating NOI. Part of the leasing process includes preparation of an **abstract** of the key lease provisions for each tenant to help the real estate management company be aware of key obligations of both parties. Residential leases typically pose less concern than commercial leases, because they are short-term in nature (seldom more than one year) and because the landlord dictates the lease format and its key provisions.

Loss to Lease

Loss to lease is the income that is lost as a result of contract (actual) rents being less than maximum market rents. This figure is most important when evaluating a property in a rising market and projecting future rent increases.

Example 6.2 | **Loss to Lease**

Using the example of the 40,000-square-foot office building, the loss to lease would be represented as the difference between the actual leases of $590,000 and the market value of that space, or $810,000 (30,000 square feet at $27). The loss to lease is $220,000 (the larger figure minus the smaller.)

In a rising market, knowing the value lost on space leased earlier can help the real estate manager plan for future leasing activities. In a declining market, where existing leases are higher than current market rents, the pro forma may reveal a *gain to lease.* This figure may also be used to plan future leasing and operational activities, with a planned reduction of revenue. In a declining market, the real estate manager should be prepared to negotiate rent reductions when leases are renewed, or even earlier than the renewal date in an attempt to keep tenants who might be tempted to move to a building with more attractive rent.

A loss to lease can occur in any type of property. Even a multi-family property, where rents can be raised more easily, can experience a loss to lease due to a site manager's unwillingness to raise rents (on long-time tenants, for example). Analysts sometimes calculate loss to lease to monitor lost market potential and, in the case of office or retail tenants, to terminate leases when the loss is considered too great.

Vacancy and Collection Loss

In the real world, all space/units are not rented all of the time. GPI has to be adjusted down to reflect market conditions. Coming up with an accurate adjustment for vacancy and collection loss will depend in part on the real estate manager's attention to these figures (i.e., good record keeping). There are two types of vacancies:

- *Physical Vacancy* consists of any space that is unoccupied.
- *Economic Vacancy* includes the physical vacancies plus:
  - Space that is leased but not producing rent
  - Space that cannot be rented as is
  - Apartments used as offices, models, or for storage
  - Apartments provided to staff as part of their compensation (and that do not produce rent)

Collection loss is made up of the following categories:

- *Bad Debts* are rents that may not be collected.
- *Concessions* are rent reductions given to attract tenants.

Net Rent Revenue

Net rent revenue is the difference between GPI and losses due to below-market rents, vacancy, and collection losses. This adjustment is the first part of the equation for calculating NOI.

Miscellaneous Income

GPI is limited to rent-related income. Many buildings have additional sources of miscellaneous income besides rent. Some sources of miscellaneous income include:

- Fees charged for parking
- Coin-operated laundry, vending machines, and/or washer/dryer rental
- Charges for use of a party room or other recreational facilities
- Forfeited portions of security deposits
- Late fees, legal charges, and fees assessed to tenants for returned checks
- Cable television, telephone and Internet service
- Roof-top rentals (cell phone antenna/satellite dishes, advertising)
- Storage fees
- Furniture rental
- Scaffolding advertising space

Expense Reimbursements

In addition to miscellaneous income, expense reimbursements are added to the net rent revenue. This revenue consists of amounts collected from the tenants in addition to rent. Examples of expense reimbursements are submetered utilities, real estate taxes, insurance, and **pass-throughs** (see following sections). In regards to their role in multi-year budgets of income, it is important to remember that expense reimbursements will vary by lease.

Net Leases

Some commercial leases, especially in the retail leasing sector, may pass costs from the building owner to the tenant. The definition of the costs needs to be clearly worded and defined as either maintenance or repair costs in the lease terms. Single and double net leases, for example, pass through the costs of taxes, and taxes and insurance, respectively. **Triple net** leases pass through the costs of taxes, insurance, and maintenance. Triple net leases should be considered carefully when budgeting for the property, as maintenance of the building exterior, roof, and even in some markets the management fee will be "passed through" to the tenant. The three "nets" refer to the "pass through" of the certain costs from the landlord to the leaseholder, as shown in Exhibit 6.2.

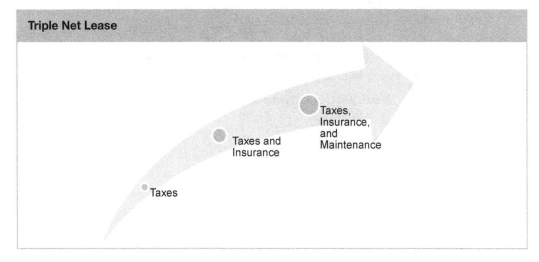

Pass-Throughs

Pass-throughs for commercial properties include operating expenses that are paid by the tenants usually on a pro rata basis in addition to base rent, including real e state taxes, insurance on the property, and common area maintenance (CAM) costs.

Pass-through expenses can be reimbursed 100% or some lesser amount and can be calculated using either a **base-year method** or an **expense-stop method.** The base-year method requires tenants to pay a particular percentage of operating costs above those incurred in the base year. The expense-stop method requires tenants to pay expenses that exceed a specified amount. Many times, the tenant is expected to pay his or her estimated share in equal monthly installments during the year, with a reconciliation made after year-end.

- In office buildings, **expense stops** obligate the property owner to pay operating costs up to a certain amount per square foot per year; tenants pay their pro rata share of any costs in excess of that amount.

- In retail properties, **expense caps** obligate the tenants to pay a pro rata share of operating expenses up to a certain amount per year; the owner pays any costs in excess of that amount.

It is important to recognize that expense-stop line items will be reduced for vacancy. The critical challenge in budgeting long-range income and expenses is in accounting for the balance of the leasable space.

Another form of expense reimbursements to consider when creating a **pro forma budget** is automatic rent increases. Sometimes owners increase rent in accordance with Consumer Price Index (CPI) increases in addition to or in lieu of other forms of expense reimbursements.

Example 6.3

Calculating Pass-Throughs

Base-year expenses are $100,000; the operating budget for the new year is $125,000. The tenant pays 10% of any cost escalation.

What is the expected monthly increase in expenses?

The expected increase is:

$$\$25,000 \times 0.10 = \$2,500 \text{ annually}$$

$$(\$25,000 \times 10\% = \$2,500)$$

$2,500 \div 12 = \$208.33 added to tenant's monthly rent at beginning of new lease year

---

Example 6.4

Calculating Pass-Throughs

A lease calls for tenant payment of most operating expenses above a "stop" of $4.50 per square foot (rentable area) per year. The tenant is leasing 3,000 square feet of rentable area. Typically adjustments are also made based on budgeted expenses for the following year and reconciled at the end of the period based on actual expenses.

Given the following facts, how much will the tenant pay in expenses?

Operating expenses	$203,000
Minus: Exclusions	
Management fees	(5,250)
Administrative costs	(27,650)
Total exclusions	(32,900)
Adjusted operating expense	&170,100
Rentable area (in building)	35,000 sq ft

Adjusted Cost = Adjusted Expenses ÷ Rentable Area

= $170,100 ÷ 35,000 sq. ft. = $4.86/sq. ft

Tenant pays $4.86 – $4.50 = $0.36/sq. ft.

Tenant's total payment = $0.36 × 3,000 sq. ft. = $1,080.00

$1,080.00 ÷ 12 = $90.00 added to tenant's monthly rent at beginning of new lease year

A retail tenant is required to pay its pro rata share of CAM expenses at $2.40 per square foot per year. The tenant is leasing 5,000 square feet of rentable area.

How much will the tenant pay in CAM costs for the year?

Tenant pays $2.40/sq. ft./yr. x 5,000 sq. ft. = $12,000/yr

Effective Gross Income (EGI)

Effective gross income, also known as total income, is the net rent revenue combined with miscellaneous income and expense reimbursements. EGI is the actual amount collected in all categories of income. Because EGI is the actual receipts, this figure becomes the source of funds used for the property's operating expenses.

Operating Expenses

The final component in calculating NOI is operating expenses. Operating expenses are all the normal, day-to-day expenses of running a property.

Operating Expenses	Non-Operating Expenses
• Management fees and administrative fees • Utilities • Payroll • Maintenance/repairs • Insurance • Real estate taxes • Other services (e.g., contracted services, administrative expenses)	• Capital expenditures • Debt service • Income taxes

Administrative expenses may include the management fee and office supplies. Categories of operating expenses can be customized to reflect the property's needs and plans. In some markets, leases may provide for pass-through of **capital expenditures** to reduce operating costs.

Understanding operating expenses as they relate to cash outflows is critical to properly formatting data for financial analysis. Expending funds is not equivalent to an operating expense. This concept is especially important regarding budgeting for long-term operational planning.

Expenditures made to operate a property on a daily basis are considered operating expenses, but costs of ownership and capital replacements are expenditures that should not be incorporated into the calculation of NOI, even though they may impact daily operations. For example, a roof in need of replacement certainly would impact the desirability of a property and the comfort of its tenants, but the replacement expense should not be included in calculating NOI because it represents an additional investment in the property that will be returned over time through rents and cost recovery. (See Chapter 7: Financial Reporting and Chapter 12: Property Valuation for additional discussions about cost recovery [also known as depreciation]).

Operating Expense Benchmarks

Operating expense benchmarks can be used to compare efficiencies across properties, assuming the properties have no deferred maintenance or curable functional obsolescence:

- **Deferred Maintenance** occurs when the ordinary maintenance of a building has not been performed, and the lack of maintenance negatively affects the use, occupancy, and value of the property.

- **Curable Functional Obsolesence** refers to reversible deterioration of a building that results from deferred maintenance and detracts from the building's value or marketability.

The operating expense ratio can be used as a benchmark to compare properties—the lower the ratio, the more efficient the operation.

$$\textit{Operating Expense Ratio = Operating Expenses} \div \textit{GPI}$$

There are different ratios depending on the property's use.

Office Buildings and Retail Properties: Operating Expenses ÷ Square Footage

Multifamily: Operating Expenses ÷ Number of Units

Property Taxes

Property taxes are considered an operating expense and are an entirely separate issue from an owner's income taxes.

TIPS

Property taxes are included in Before-Tax Cash Flow, but income taxes on the investment are not. Income taxes are accounted in After-Tax Cash Flow (see Chapter 16).

Taxation can have a significant impact on the cash return produced by investment real estate, both during ownership and at sale. A real estate manager is responsible for helping the property owner achieve his or her financial goals for the property. Thus, the real estate manager must be aware of the property tax laws that affect real estate.

Property taxes can be one of the largest expense categories for income-producing property. Local taxing authorities impose property taxes to pay for local government services. Taxes are one of the very few liens that have priority over mortgages. In case of default, taxes are usually paid first, then the mortgage. (In some areas, water and sewer payments take priority over mortgages in the lien hierarchy.) In many states, property taxes are the single largest operating expense.

Local governments collect property taxes. In most areas of the country, property taxes are paid on the assessed value of real estate multiplied by a local rate. Real estate managers can appeal the assessed value of the property based on market conditions and trends; the local rate, however, is set by the local government and is not negotiable.

Real estate managers should routinely examine how taxing bodies assess and value the property. While taxes often seem inexorable, there is some leeway with property taxes. A real estate manager's area of expertise is knowing the selling prices of properties in the area. This information aids in determining whether a property has been fairly appraised for tax purposes.

Differing "Values"

With real estate properties, three types of "values" must be distinguished as described in the following chart. Real estate managers should know the method for determining taxable value on the properties in their local jurisdictions.

Type of Value	Description
Market Value	As will be detailed in a later chapter, market value is the estimate of the most likely price that a seller can expect to command for a property from a typical buyer under normal conditions.
Assessed Value	Assessed value is the value of real property established by the local authority as the basis for taxation. The tax rate is applied to the assessed (or taxable) value to determine the amount of real estate tax.

Type of Value	Description *(continued)*
Taxable Value	The final taxable value may be different than the assessed value in certain jurisdictions. Some states have an assessed value, and then take a percentage of that amount as the taxable value. For example, taxable value may be set at 80% of the assessed value for residential properties and 85% for commercial properties.

Millage Rates

A millage rate is the property tax rate under which the assessment basis is one dollar for every one thousand dollars of assessed property value (1 mill = $1/$1,000). Thus, the owner of a property with an assessed valuation of $100,000 and property taxes assessed at a millage rate of 20 mills would pay $2,000 in property tax. Millage rates are set by government agencies and vary widely.

Improvements made by a tenant are sometimes double-taxed if the tenant's personal business property is taxed. The building's assessed valuation may be raised because the leasehold is considered a capital improvement.

Building managers should be aware that double taxation is possible and take steps accordingly. The lease should state who has responsibility for the tax payment and increases.

Appealing Property Taxes

Often a real estate manager participates in appealing property taxes. The key to a successful appeal is documentation: thorough analysis of market rental rates, occupancy levels, and operating expenses, and a history of the sales of comparable properties, including photos. Keep in mind that deadlines are critical. Appeals processes vary widely by jurisdiction.

A property tax assessment has two parts: the assessed value and the rate. When protesting tax values, only the amount of valuation can be disputed as the rates are not subject to protest (unless a jurisdiction-wide tax rollback is being voted upon). The millage rates are usually set annually by the respective taxing entities, which may include the city, the school district, county or state, hospital districts, community college district, a municipal utility district (MUD), and others.

Being aware of assessed value and sales prices of comparables is very important in weak markets because the assessed valuation can continue to increase even if the market value of the property declines.

Net Operating Income (NOI)

Net operating income (NOI) is an important gauge of financial strength. It is the primary determinant of a property's market value. NOI is:

- Used to measure a property's financial performance and also determines its value.

- Not the same as profit, but it is a widely used measure of financial health in real estate.

The formula for NOI is:

$$EGI - Operating\ Expenses = NOI$$

Annual Debt Service (ADS)

Annual debt service (ADS) is the total amount of money needed to pay all of a property's principal and interest each year. Debt service usually has two components: (1) paying off the mortgage loan (principal); and (2) paying the cost of the funds used (interest), according to the terms of the promissory note. At the beginning of the loan servicing period, the payment will be mostly interest. Each month, the interest will be slightly less as the amount of principal increases and the debt decreases, assuming a fixed interest rate.

BLANK (Capital Expenditures, Reserves, Etc.)

The property may be required to add reserves for replacement, leasing commissions, and tenant improvements expenses, or capital improvements expenses above the before-tax cash flow line.

Reserves for replacements are a form of savings that can be voluntary or lender-mandated. While reserves are a reduction in cash flow, the expense may not occur until a later year. Therefore, reserves may be considered cash flow in the year earned or deferred to a subsequent year. However, note that the Internal Revenue Service examines control of money. If reserves for replacements are mandated by the lender, they are considered financial expense paid to the lender and the owner must ask the lender to use the money. The interest earned on the money (assuming it is invested) is accrued to the owner, and he or she pays income tax on the interest earned.

The owner's accountant usually determines how to handle the capital improvements expenses in regards to BTCF. Some lenders, however, require that an amount be expensed above the NOI for routine replacements (e.g., carpets and appliances). The definition of what is a capital expense may vary according to the owners' goals and the accounting practice for the property. When large payouts of capital expenses are being planned over a multiyear period, a line in the BTCF may capture expenses incurred.

Before-Tax Cash Flow (BTCF)

Before-tax cash flow (BTCF) is an important measure of profit in real estate. It is an owner-specific amount that can be viewed different ways. For example, if a project involves 40 partners, each person will evaluate BTCF differently, depending upon his or her investment objectives. (See Chapter 14 for an example of a BTCF analysis.) BTCF can be derived by subtracting debt service (loan and interest payments) from NOI.

$$NOI - ADS = BTCF$$

Some points to keep in mind about BTCF:

- BTCF along with NOI is an indicator of financial health.
- BTCF shows that the property successfully meets its major obligations (operating expenses, debt service).
- The BTCF figure is the owner's income before taxes are considered. The owner can then decide whether to reallocate part of the cash flow to the property.

In many instances, increasing cash flow will be one of the real estate manager's goals. Because ADS is not likely to be altered easily, real estate managers are better off monitoring and controlling operating expenses, minimizing vacancy and collection loss, and carefully budgeting reserves for replacement and capital to meet the owners' financial goals and show management effectiveness.

CASH FLOW TRENDS

Actual income and expenses should be analyzed once they are known. One of the signs of effective management is the ability to spot a trend early and react to it appropriately. Trend analysis involves comparing current income and expenses with amounts from past periods to highlight increases and decreases. Besides analyzing increases and decreases in various income and expense categories, trend analysis focuses on changes in the NOI.

The cash flow budget and the operating budget are sources of information for trend analysis. Any trend analysis should have the same line items as the operating budget and cash budget. The results of the analysis can be entered on a form modeled after those budgets that includes columns for dollar and percentage changes. The analysis can be done yearly, although quarterly analyses would follow trends more closely. Exhibit 6.3 provides an example.

Cash Flow Trends

Exhibit 6.3

	(1) Year 1	(2) Year 2	(3) Year 3	(4) Year 4
GPI	$101,000	$115,000	$14,000	13.9%
Vacancy & Collection Loss	$9,290	$9,900	$610	6.6%
Net Rent Revenue	$91,710	$105,100	$13,390	14.6%
Misc. Income	$1,000	$700	$(300)	30.0%
EGI	$92,710	$105,800	$13,090	14.1%
Operating Expenses	$23,000	$22,300	$(700)	3.0%
NOI	$69,710	$83,500	$13,790	19.1%

Note that column 3 reports dollar changes, while column 4 reports the percentage changes. The dollar, or cash, figures can be used as a check on the percentages.

Calculating your cash flow trends as percentage changes may help reveal trends that might otherwise be disguised. For example, what if the percentages for a given three-year period showed that your NOI grew more slowly than EGI? That might mean your operating expenses have taken up a larger portion of property income in Year 2 than Year 1. This decline in growth calls for investigation.

Per square foot (or unit) analysis helps when comparing expenses for different properties, which is always important in dealing with costs. To calculate dollars per square foot, simply divide each income and expense item by the rentable area of the property.

. . . when considering cash flow analysis:

- Why is it so important that I have an accurate forecast of net operating income (NOI)?

- What are the cash flow trends for my properties telling me about how effectively the properties are being managed?

Questions
real estate
managers
may ask

DATA ANALYSIS AND ACCURACY

The financial data used to analyze a property, as you've seen, comes from many sources, and its presentation may vary with the needs of the party preparing it. The first step in readying financials for analysis is to scrutinize the quality of data under consideration. Sources of information may include real estate brokers' offering memoranda, accountant financial statements, and owner records as well as analyses by appraisers and real estate managers. Real estate professionals with different roles bring differing perspectives to data analysis, and their interpretations may be inconsistent with that of a real estate manager.

In the case of an investor considering the purchase of a property, one or more real estate brokers may present offering memoranda, typically including a disclaimer that the information cannot be relied on and should be verified independently. This disclaimer must be taken seriously. Often such documents minimize operating expenses by "capitalizing" many cash outflows (recategorizing operating expenses as capital ones). Deciding how to categorize cash outflow is a judgment call that requires verification from an operational perspective. Serious tax implication can result from inappropriate allocation between expense and capital items.

When preparing contracts to purchase property, investors specify a period during which they have access to all property records. The prospective buyer retains a team of professionals, including a real estate manager, to review and verify all financial data in a **due diligence** process. Data should be verified against the owner's records and through independent sources to determine if the property's performance is accurately represented. In addition, the data should be compared to market statistics to verify the income and expenses are consistent with market standards.

A real estate manager organizing data for analysis must likewise confirm the data's reliability. All income sources and expenses should be verified for accuracy, and actual expenses studied to determine if they are consistent with market expenses for similar properties.

• •

REVIEW QUESTIONS

- What is the purpose of a pro forma statement of cash flow?
- Define before-tax cash flow (BTCF) and after-tax cash flow (ATCF).
- How does BTCF relate to NOI?
- Of what is NOI an indicator?
- What is the purpose of analyzing cash flow trends?

Financial Reporting

To report accurately on budget income, expenses, and variance, the real estate management company must scrupulously record all financial transactions. Accurate information is the foundation of managerial decisions. Therefore, the real estate manager must be aware of the different criteria that apply to various financial reports.

REAL-TIME DATA AND REPORTING

While the organization of accounting departments and their extensions into the field may vary by company and property type, the accounting software will be the main source for generating both financial (external) and managerial (internal) reports, which will be examined in detail later in this chapter. Timely and accurate input of data has always been expected of real estate management companies. However, contemporary property management software has produced a change in expectations because the software makes possible the generation of real-time reports from multiple locations. It is now assumed that new data will be input immediately, and accuracy is expected on an up-to-the-minute basis. The features of such software make it possible for real estate managers, site managers, and company executives to have instant access to all permitted information.

In the past, when administrative staff controlled the flow of data, they also controlled the generation of reports. If data entry staff fell behind in entering payments, for example, they would just delay generating a delinquency report until everything was caught up and the deposits were in the bank. Such delays are no longer considered acceptable; those who can access information, even from thousands of miles away, expect all data to be collected and entered as it is received.

Property owners also access real-time data about their properties. Web-based access to property information can be granted as needed and desired to owners, their asset managers, and virtually any stakeholder in the investment. Some real estate management firms use this as a differentiating factor in promoting their business. A property owner's choice of a real estate management company may be influenced by the ability to generate instant reports or by having 24/7 access to data online.

Companies need to be cautious when structuring contracts with owners, disclosing limitations and specifying the schedule on which accurate external financial reports will be generated. Real-time access should apply only to generating managerial reports and monitoring key statistics. It is also important to note that real-time reports for a period not yet closed can give incomplete information.

FINANCIAL REPORTING REQUIREMENTS

Property owners have varying needs for financial reporting, and real estate managers must be flexible in generating financial statements to meet those needs. Similarly, the investment community has its own requirements for financial reporting and analysis.

In daily practice, real estate managers are exposed to financial reports from four general sources:

- External reports generated by a property owner's accounting professionals, including financial statements and tax returns
- Reports generated by another property management firm, by the owner of a property if it is self-managed, or sometimes by a court-appointed receiver or bank
- Reports generated by the real estate management firm, both for internal analysis and for reporting to the property owner
- Forecasts prepared by brokers for a property under management or under consideration for purchase by a potential or existing client

Typically real estate managers collect property-operating data in great detail. It is organized and categorized, and then reports are provided at the level of detail needed by the particular user. Whether historical data is intended for external financial reports or for internal managerial reporting, the collected data is the same—it is just organized differently based on the type of report being generated.

The accounting department in most real estate management firms is charged with preparing financial reports for the property owner—usually monthly or as agreed to between the owner and manager—to meet contractual requirements. The type of statements, methodology, and frequency are determined by the owner, along with whether reports are delivered directly to the owner or to the asset manager responsible for the account.

A real estate manager must be able to understand the differences in financial reporting from various sources and to modify the statements into a format that allows for analysis of the property. In general, the real estate manager plays two roles in financial reporting. He or she may:

- Analyze reports and draft a cover letter that explains salient factors of the period's operations, including variance explanations.

- Prepare supplemental managerial reports to include with the financial reports.

All entries into an accounting system are posted to accounts in the general ledger. At the end of an accounting period, any irregularities are corrected before a trial balance is run listing the balances in each account. The data may be adjusted for preparation of various financial statements, but all data remains in the general ledger, from which other forms of financial statements also may be produced.

FINANCIAL ACCOUNTING AND EXTERNAL REPORTING

Reports for external parties tend to give an overall financial picture, focusing on the figures themselves. They provide a historical representation of the performance of a business, describing how a property has performed in the past. Preparing financial reports for external use is part of financial accounting. Financial accounting is a system of classifying financial transactions that documents a company's financial position in the form of a balance sheet and an income statement (external reports). These condensed external reports are sent to the various stakeholders in the property, including lending institutions, the IRS for tax purposes, as well as stockholders and other types of owners.

They often include a narrative portion with a summary that describes how the owner's goals and objectives for the period have been addressed. The narrative report should be supported by any necessary financial monthly and/or annual reports or statements, including a summary of cash receipts and disbursements, a budget variance report, a capital improvements recap, and an income statement. The most fundamental financial statements shared with external stakeholders are the balance sheet and the income statement. The periodic management report also is often accompanied by a rent roll that provides details of lease arrangements with all tenants to date as well as vacancies. However, the content of these reports should always be tailored to satisfy the owner's requirements.

MANAGERIAL ACCOUNTING AND INTERNAL REPORTING

In general, reports for internal use include more detail about specific financial transactions and the manager's assumptions about a property. Internal reports use accounting data in a format that allows the user to arrange the data for specific analyses and to forecast performance. They are based on historical or forecasted information and address past performance, current data, or future expectations. That is, the real estate manager uses this information from the past, evaluates it in terms of current market conditions, and projects future performance.

Financial reports that are for internal use are part of **managerial accounting,** which is also concerned with the analysis of new investment proposals. Real estate managers are concerned mostly with managerial accounting. Managerial accounting, with its focus on the internal workings of a company, is increasingly seen as a way of providing information to internal managers and owners for decision making and planning. Most of the analytical tools addressed in this book are used for managerial reports, which show the results of projections and analyses, as opposed to financial accounting's external reports.

While the information in internal reports should be complete, they do not always have to follow a strict format. Some of the reports provided to external stakeholders are also commonly used internally as part of managerial accounting. Some common reports used internally are listed below and are sorted by property type.

Report	Residential	Office	Retail
Rent Rolls	✓	✓	✓
Vacancy Reports	✓	✓	✓
Delinquency Reports	✓	✓	✓
Accounts Payable, Accounts Receivable	✓	✓	✓
Percentage Rent Reports			✓
Tenant Sales Analysis Reports			✓

FINANCIAL REPORTS

The following section details some of the financial reports that owners commonly want to receive. Many of these also may be used internally in a more detailed form.

Balance Sheet

The balance sheet is a statement of the financial position of a property (or person or company) at a particular point in time, indicating assets, liabilities, and owner equity (or net worth). Balance sheets are prepared at the end of each accounting period. A balance sheet reports the **book value** of land and buildings as well as other assets, including the reserves for replacement account. The real estate manager must exercise caution when analyzing a balance sheet because the reported book value is based on accounting rules and tax code and may have little relationship to the market value of a property.

The detail to which assets and liabilities are portrayed depends on the level of service contracted with the real estate manager. Frequently the assets are limited to cash and accounts receivable (if accrual-basis accounting is used), and liabilities include accounts payable (if on accrual) and possibly the loan balance. The real estate manager must be careful to assure that the correct assets and liabilities are being reported and to avoid commentary on net worth unless the real estate management firm is keeping all records for the ownership entity. For example, the individual property may be adequately reported upon listing the accounts just noted, but the actual net worth of the business entity may be considerably more complex. Often the real estate management firm reports only on the assets and liabilities that it direct supervises, leaving the rest to the accounting firm representing the ownership entity. A sample balance sheet is shown in Exhibit 7.1.

Exhibit 7.1 **Balance Sheet**

Balance Sheet (Accrual)
Rawood/Golf Road Limited Partnership - (rawood)
Months: Sep 2010

ASSETS
CURRENT ASSETS

CASH

Cash in Bank-Checking	119,874.35
TOTAL CASH	119,874.35
R.E. Tax Insurance Escrow	103,636.88
Accounts Receivable	129,238.41
TOTAL CURRENT ASSETS	352,749.64

PROPERTY

FIXED ASSETS

Land	288,000.00
Buildings	1,238,830.06
Capital Improvements	21,503.00
Building Improvements	357,602.00
Personal Property	19,155.91
Less: Accumulated Depreciation	(883,473.67)
Sec. 743 Step-Up	13,795.40
Accum Deprn-Sec 743 Set-Up	(12,415.86)
TOTAL FIXED ASSETS	1,042,996.84

OTHER ASSETS

Lease Cost	21,434.00
Lease Cost Amortization	(10,945.70)
Loan Costs	34,106.78
Accum Amort-Loan Costs	(11,090.94)
TOTAL OTHER ASSETS	33,504.14
TOTAL ASSETS	1,429,250.62

LIABILITIES & EQUITY

LIABILITIES

Accounts Payable	12,893.34
Accrued Loan Interest	8,154.43
Mortgage/Loans Principal 1	1,381,384.06
Prepaid Rent	2.01
Security Deposits Held	6,170.00
Property Tax Payable	202,169.56
TOTAL LIABILITIES	1,610,773.40

EQUITY

Capital-RFLP	(113,887.30)
Capital-Alan Schwartz	(85,185.27)
Capital-AGS-I, Inc.	(2,234.33)
Capital-Kevera LP	(23,080.69)
Retained Earnings	42,864.81
Capital Accounts	(224,387.59)
TOTAL EQUITY	(181,522.78)
TOTAL LIABILITIES & EQUITY	1,429,250.62

Importance of Balance Sheet Ratios

Balance sheet ratios measure a property's financial strength. Working Capital and the Current Ratio both measure liquidity, which is the relative ease with which an asset can be disposed of or turned into cash and used to meet the company's financial obligations:

- **Working Capital:** the dollar difference between total current assets and total current liabilities. Because working capital involves a short-term turnover of money, long-term assets and liabilities are not included.

Current Assets – Current Liabilities = Working Capital

- **Current Ratio:** the ratio of total current assets to total current liabilities. It shows the ability to pay current bills with funds on hand; the higher the ratio, the greater the company's liquidity.

Current Assets ÷ Current Liabilities = Current Ratio

Net Worth and the Debt/Worth Ratio measure capitalization and leverage:

- **Net Worth:** the dollar difference between total assets and total liabilities. Net worth can be increased by the company's earnings or the raising of new equity; generally, an increasing net worth indicates the overall growth and general financial health of the company.

Total Assets – Total Liabilities = Net Worth (Owner's Equity)

- **Debt/Worth Ratio:** the ratio of total liabilities to net worth. Generally, the lower the ratio, the better capitalized the company is; however, the ratio needs to be considered in light of the company's business, quality of assets, and liquidity. For example, a financial institution would have a much higher ratio than a manufacturer.

Total Liabilities ÷ Net Worth (Owner's Equity) = Debt/Worth Ratio

Income Statement

The income statement, which reflects the operating history of a property, displays the income for a property and deducts all of the operating expenses to arrive at a net income. While this type of statement seems a logical starting point for analyzing a real estate investment, here also the manager must exercise caution. Income statements that are correct from an accounting perspective may not provide completely relevant data for financial analysis.

No matter what the form, the income statement will display revenue, expenses, and—in one form or another—a measure of net income. For internal property management analysis, the income statement will follow a pro forma statement of cash flow terminating in **net operating income (NOI),** such as the one provided in the *IREM® Financial Analysis Spreadsheet* used by many real estate management companies. But an income statement prepared for external reporting may very well include factors that are not part of NOI, such as cost recovery and interest. A sample income statement is shown in Exhibit 7.2.

Exhibit 7.2   **Income Statement (Accrual), Page 1**

	Month to Date	%	Year to Date	%
INCOME				
RENT INCOME				
Basic Rent	39,179.40	72.92	325,535.22	68.73
Less: Concessions	(2,111.11)	(3.93)	(8,444.44)	(1.78)
NET RENTAL INCOME	37,068.29	68.99	317,090.78	66.95
REIMBURSEMENT				
Property Tax Reimbursement	12,101.42	22.52	103,327.38	21.82
Property Tax Reimb-Prior	0.00	0.00	13,380.65	2.83
Insurance Reimbursement	224.19	0.42	1,914.23	0.40
CAM Reimbursement	4,335.10	8.07	36,791.80	7.77
CAM Reimb-Prior	0.00	0.00	1,138.87	0.24
TOTAL REIMBURSEMENT	16,660.71	31.01	156,552.93	33.05
GROSS INCOME	53,729.00	100.00	473,643.71	100.00
EXPENSES				
OPERATING EXPENSES				
UTILITIES				
Electricity	2,022.22	3.76	4,254.23	0.90
Water	2.41	0.00	21.34	0.00
Building Phone	72.58	0.14	642.84	0.14
TOTAL UTILITIES	2,097.21	3.90	4,918.41	1.04
Roof Repairs	300.00	0.56	1,835.50	0.39
Lighting Maintenance	99.00	0.18	1,371.50	0.29
Plumbing Repairs	0.00	0.00	800.00	0.17
Snow Removal	0.00	0.00	4,250.00	0.90
Keys & Locks	0.00	0.00	132.00	0.03
TOTAL REPAIRS & MAINTENANCE	399.00	0.74	8,389.00	1.77
BUILDING SERVICES				
Grounds Maintenance	454.00	0.84	4,490.00	0.95
Building Supplies	0.00	0.00	3,456.86	0.73
Parking Lot Sweeping	1,080.00	2.01	4,860.00	1.03
TOTAL BUILDING SERVICES	1,534.00	2.86	12,806.86	2.70
SECURITY				
Fire Security	390.00	0.73	1,170.00	0.25
TOTAL SECURITY	390.00	0.73	1,170.00	0.25
GENERAL & ADMINISTRATIVE				
Management Fees (Reimbursable)	1,512.85	2.82	16,732.49	3.53
Late Fees	30.16	0.06	42.08	0.01
Postage/Courier	0.00	0.00	81.69	0.02
Meals & Entertainment	0.00	0.00	20.00	0.00
TOTAL G & A EXPENSE	1,543.01	2.87	16,876.26	3.56
TAXES				
Real Estate Taxes	13,739.68	25.57	126,607.12	26.73
R.E. Tax Appeal	3,760.00	7.00	3,760.00	0.79
TOTAL TAXES	17,499.68	32.57	130,367.12	27.52
INSURANCE				
Property & Casualty	0.00	0.00	3,724.00	0.79
TOTAL INSURANCE	0.00	0.00	3,724.00	0.79
TOTAL OPERATING EXPENSES	23,462.90	43.67	178,251.65	37.63

Page 1

	Month to Date	%	Year to Date	%
NET OPERATING INCOME	*30,266.10*	*56.33*	*295,392.06*	*62.37*
NON OPERATING EXPENSE				
INTEREST				
Mortgage/Loan Interest 1	7,789.62	14.50	70,789.87	14.95
TOTAL INTEREST	*7,789.62*	*14.50*	*70,789.87*	*14.95*
Legal	1,622.95	3.02	5,397.55	1.14
Accounting/Corporate Compliance	0.00	0.00	250.00	0.05
Keys & Locks	165.00	0.31	165.00	0.03
Maintenance & Repairs	0.00	0.00	300.00	0.06
Sign Improvements	0.00	0.00	(216.07)	(0.05)
Parking Lot Sweeping	0.00	0.00	180.00	0.04
Sales/ Leasing Commissions				
Sales/Leasing Commissions	0.00	0.00	37,539.72	7.93
Total Sales/Leasing Commissions	*0.00*	*0.00*	*37,539.72*	*7.93*
Tenant Improvements	0.00	0.00	82,583.71	17.44
UTILITIES				
Water & Sewer	0.00	0.00	126.36	0.03
TOTAL UTILITIES	*0.00*	*0.00*	*126.36*	*0.03*
Corporate Licenses and Fees	0.00	0.00	100.00	0.02
TOTAL NONOPERATING EXPENSE	*9,577.57*	*17.83*	*197,216.14*	*41.64*
TOTAL NON OP INCOME/EXPENSE	*9,577.57*	*17.83*	*197,216.14*	*41.64*
NET INCOME	*20,688.53*	*38.51*	*98,175.92*	*20.73*

Income Statement Formats

An income statement may be formatted in different ways depending on the needs of the user. For example, various income statements can be prepared for the same property owner on the same date using different methodologies depending on who they are prepared for and what their purpose is. While they may differ, each one would be fully accurate. It is critical that real estate managers understand the methods used to prepare financial data so they can interpret it properly and accurately understand current operations and make future projections. Consider the example that follow.

Statement One

One statement as shown in Exhibit 7.3 could be generated for tax purposes. Most individuals are cash-basis taxpayers. The statement may be collapsed to include only the major categories of income and expense. Expenses likely will include those allowable for income tax purposes including cost recovery. Consider this scenario illustrated in Exhibit 7.3:

Molly Brennan owns several income properties. Her accountant uses the data collected from the property manager, but formats the data to include all expenses that may be deducted as expenses for income tax purposes. One property is a retail strip shopping center with one successful anchor and six spaces occupied by struggling local merchants. One space is vacant. The accrual-based statement from the property manager is reformatted for cash-basis accounting and certain cash outflows are not considered, such as principal on the mortgage since it does not impact taxes.

Further, some expenses are included, such as mortgage interest and cost recovery since they are allowable expenses for income tax purposes even though they do not impact the earning power of the property from a valuation perspective.

Exhibit 7.3	Cash-Basis Statement for Tax Purposes

Brennan Plaza December, 2012
Cash Basis (Formatted for Tax Purposes)

Rental Income	$ 299,090.75
Reimbursements	$ 156,552.93
Total Income	**$ 455,643.68**
Operating Expenses	
Utilities	$ 4,918.41
Maintenance	$ 8,389.00
Building Services	$ 12,806.86
Security	$ 1,170.00
Gen & Administrative	$ 16,876.76
Insurance	$ 3,721.00
Real Estate Tax	$ 130,367.12
Subtotal	**$ 178,249.15**
Interest	$ 70,789.82
Depreciation	$ 84,157.00
Net Income (loss)	**$ 122,447.71**

Statement Two

Another statement as shown in Exhibit 7.4 could be prepared by a real estate manager as part of a year-end report. In this type of statement, the "bottom line" profit on the report would be net operating income (NOI). Remember that NOI considers the earning power of a real estate asset from the market's perspective without regard to an owner's tax or financial positions. In such a statement, the loan payment may be displayed on two lines showing both the principal reduction and interest amount. Because these are not considered "property-based" figures, they are not included in NOI but are shown as a notation since the loan is a liability of the owner relating to this investment. Consider this scenario illustrated in Exhibit 7.4:

Tri-City Management operates Molly Brennan's retail center. The company supplies Molly with a monthly report of operations that includes a balance sheet and income statement. The report, showing year-end performance, is formatted to meet the needs of property owners and managers in displaying NOI, the key component of value from operation of the property. Molly gives this report, and similar reports from her other properties, to her accountant for tax and external reporting financial statements.

Brennan Plaza December, 2012

Accrual Basis

Rent Revenue	$ 325,535.22
Less: Concessions	$ (8,444.44)
Net Rental Income	**$ 317,090.78**
Utilities	
Heat	
Electric	$ 5,164.00
Water and Sewer	$ 21.34
Building Telephone	$ 642.84
Total Utilities	*$ 5,828.18*
Maintenance	
Roof Repairs	$ 1,835.00
Lighting Maintenance	$ 1,371.50
Keys & Locks	$ 132.00
Snow Removal	$ 4,250.00
Plumbing	$ 8,000.00
Total Repairs and Maintenance	*$ 15,588.50*
Building Services	
Grounds Maintenance	$ 6,972.00
Supplies	$ 3,456.86
Parking Lot Sweeping	$ 4,860.00
Total Building Services	*$ 15,288.86*
Security	
Fire Security	$ 1,170.00
Total Security	*$ 1,170.00*
General and Administrative	
Management Fees	$ 16,732.49
Late Fees	$ 42.08
Postage	$ 81.69
Meals & Entertainment	$ 20.00
Total G & A	*$ 16,876.26*
Taxes	
Real Estate Taxes	$ 130,367.12
Total Taxes	*$ 130,367.12*
Insurance	
Property & Casualty	$ 3,724.00
Total Insurance	*$ 3,724.00*
Total Expenses	**$ 188,842.92**
Net Operating Income (NOI)	**$ 128,247.86**

Statement Three

Finally, a third statement as shown in Exhibit 7.5 might report income and expenses based on different methodology, such as reporting income when received, but expenses when incurred. Consider this scenario illustrated in Exhibit 7.5:

Molly keeps in regular communication with the real estate brokerage community. Joyce Reynolds, a real estate broker with whom she has worked in the past, is consulting with Molly on whether this is a good time to list the shopping center for sale. The statements provided by the real estate management company as part of the year-end report are very useful for establishing a potential list price and projections for future owners. However, Joyce knows that shopping centers commonly have financial issues stemming from financially strapped tenants. She uses the information in the statement used for year-end reporting to be sure all costs of operation are included in her projections, and she also takes into account the late-paying retail tenants.

Exhibit 7.5	**Modified-Accrual Statement**

Brennan Plaza December, 2012
Modified Accrual Basis

Rental Income	$ 307,535.19
Less: Concessions	$ 8,444.44)
Total Rental Income	**$ 299,090.75**
Reimbursements	$ 156,552.93
Total Income	**$ 455,643.68**
Utilities	
Heat	
Electric	$ 5,164.00
Water and Sewer	$ 21.34
Building Telephone	$ 642.84
Total Utilities	**$ 5,828.18**
Maintenance	
Roof Repairs	$ 1,835.00
Lighting Maintenance	$ 1,371.50
Keys & Locks	$ 132.00
Snow Removal	$ 4,250.00
Plumbing	$ 8,000.00
Total Repairs and Maintenance	**$ 15,588.50**

Modified-Accrual Statement *(continued)*

Building Services

Grounds Maintenance	$ 6,972.00
Supplies	$ 3,456.86
Parking Lot Sweeping	$ 4,860.00
Total Building Services	*$ 15,288.86*

Security

Fire Security	$ 1,170.00
Total Security	*$ 1,170.00*

General and Administrative

Management Fees	$ 16,732.49
Late Fees	$ 42.08
Postage	$ 81.69
Meals & Entertainment	$ 20.00
Total G & A	*$ 16,876.26*

Taxes

Real Estate Taxes	$ 130,367.12
Total Taxes	*$ 130,367.12*

Insurance

Property & Casualty	$ 3,724.00
Total Insurance	*$ 3,724.00*

Total Expenses	**$ 188,842.92**
Net Operating Income (NOI)	**$ 266,800.76**

While each of these three operating statements is completely accurate, they have various purposes and different methods were used in their preparation. One method is known as accounting basis, or the way that the timing of income and expenses is realized. The second method relates to the classification of operating expenses. Real estate managers analyzing a property must first concentrate on the earning power of the property, and then they may enhance their analysis with characteristics of a particular investor. See the sidebar for a discussion of classifying operating expenses.

Classifying Operating Expenses

Real estate managers must also be aware that not all cash outflows are operating expenses. Sometimes cash is used for **capital expenditures,** which are items that have a "useful life," such as a roof replacement. An expenditure of this nature would not show on a normal profit and loss statement as an expense, where it would skew the actual cost of operations; it would appear instead on the balance sheet as a capital investment.

Interest, expressed as a percentage of the amount borrowed, represents the cost of borrowing money. From a real estate manager's perspective, while the use of borrowed funds, or **leverage,** is an important component of any real estate investment, it is not a component of a property's earning power. From an accounting perspective, interest is an operating expense, and it is expressed as a whole dollar amount actually paid in the financial period in financial statements customized for a particular owner.

Cost recovery is another important component of a real estate investment. One of the economic benefits an investor expects from any investment is both a **return _on_ investment** and a **return _of_ investment.** There are many ways an investor recovers capital investment, including cost recovery and eventual sale proceeds. Cost recovery (a legislative term that is intended to represent the accounting principle of **depreciation,** or **recapture**) represents a partial return of the investment; it allows the owner to recover a portion of the original cost through deductions for the physical loss in value resulting from a property's aging. It is here that expenses categorize as capital improvements as part of an amortization schedule, which depreciates the cost of the improvement according to its useful life. **Sale proceeds** are the difference between a sale price and the costs associated with the sale. The sale proceeds when compared with the original purchase price may represent additional return of investment. An excess between the two is called a gain.

Net operating income (NOI) is a shortened term for the original term, net income before recapture (NIBR), which is rarely used today. The older term more clearly suggests that there is no place for cost recovery in the formula for NOI. Cost recovery does not generally appear in a real estate manager's operating statements. Cost recovery is dealt with below the NOI line in items that are investor decisions, not market-based decisions.

Statement of Changes in Financial Position

As has been illustrated, an accrual-based financial statement can be confusing. It does not directly match cash receipts but is intended to match what *will* be received. Similarly, expenses, whether paid or not, will be reflected on the income statement. The statement of changes helps the reader reconcile the differences between actual receipts and disbursements and those that will occur as a result of activities in the accounting period.

Accounts Receivable Aging

For accrual-basis accounting, a statement will likely be included that schedules out funds due to the property from tenants. The statement may be very detailed, as in the delinquency report, or it may just summarize balances due and the period over which they have remained unpaid. A real estate manager must be alert to informing the accounting department or designated individual to write off rents that are unpaid for an extended period. Some companies establish a policy that any account unpaid over a specified period—perhaps 90 days—is considered a bad debt and deducted from accrued rent revenue. In most real estate management circumstances, especially multi-family properties, eviction proceedings will be well underway for residents or tenants that have reached that level of delinquency.

Accounts Payable Aging

Unpaid invoices are a liability of the property owner, and the amount of money owed to vendors must be properly disclosed in financial statements. The accounts payable aging statement may summarize all unpaid invoices; or it may be a detailed schedule of each invoice not paid, the period that it is past due, and why it was not paid on time. Significant delinquencies in accounts payable should be pointed out to an owner in the cover letter to the financial statements.

In addition to these financial statements, the accounting department usually includes a copy of all relevant reconciled bank statements.

Managerial Reports

While financial statements by their nature are reflections of activity in a prior accounting period, they have the advantage of having gone through verification and a *closing* process before the statement is produced. Managerial reports, usually used for internal purposes, are often real-time reports that have not undergone the scrutiny that a financial statement has. Nonetheless, precise data entry and system-specific controls help promote accuracy, and most companies rely heavily on this type of report to monitor daily operations. Owners with online access to the real estate management company's data may run some or all of these reports on a regular basis. Some of these reports are also included in financial packages to property owners to supplement data on the financial statements.

Rent Roll

While the rent roll is perhaps one of the most popular reports for real estate owners and managers alike, there is little agreement on exactly what it should contain. Most property management software programs have at least one rent roll report that discloses information to varying degrees. In some cases it is a report on unit occupancy; in others it schedules out accounts receivables. The rent roll almost always lists data that is relevant to the specific resident/tenant or unit/suite when vacant (rent, size, lease commencement and expiration, date vacated, etc.).

Delinquency Report

While a rent roll may display balances due, it does not necessarily show the period for which rent has been unpaid. A delinquency report displays the amount due, the detail of what is unpaid, and the number of accounting periods for which a balance has remained unpaid.

Vacancy Report

A vacancy report lists and describes the property's unoccupied space, whether in square feet for commercial space or by unit in the case of multi-family or condominium units. In many cases, it will calculate the accrued loss of rent due to vacancy (economic vacancy) and the number of square feet or units vacant (physical vacancy). Vacancy reports may also include such information as the number of days a particular space has remained vacant or when the apartment will be market ready and re-leased.

Variance Report

Budget variance reports may be needed regularly as part of the reports that a real estate manager prepares for the building's owners. A budget variance report lists budgeted amounts, actual amounts, and budget variances (in dollars and as percentages of the estimated budget amount) for each line item in the operating budget.

At its minimum, it can be software-generated with only figures, but a true variance report also includes a narrative that describes assumptions, amounts, reasons for variances, and plans for correcting them. It communicates to stakeholders that the real estate manager is aware of the variances and will take appropriate action. The details depend somewhat on the policies of the real estate management company and its relationship with the property owner. When discussing budget variances, focus on describing the variances as favorable and unfavorable (see Chapter 5). For example, say a major category such as "repairs and maintenance" has a favorable variance of $1,000, but the subcategory of HVAC repairs has an unfavorable variance of $1,500. Other subcategories would then have favorable variances totaling $2,500 in order for the major category to be favorable. Depending on policy, the real estate manager may need only to comment on the variance in the major category or may need to address every variance for the subcategories as well. It is likely the real estate manager will have to specify how he or she intends to keep variances positive or why a negative outcome will be the ultimate result at the end of a financial period.

In explaining the variances, the real estate manager should give a rationale for any variances that exceed predetermined standards. For example, explanations may be required for any variances that are 10% greater than the budgeted amount. The narrative should also describe any corrective actions taken.

Finally, reports should have a column for approved budget variances. Sometimes budgets allow some midyear adjustments to reflect changes in circumstances, new information, or changing market conditions. Some companies do not revise budgets once the year has begun.

. . . when considering financial reporting:

Questions real estate managers may ask

- What reports does my company generate, both internal and external? What software, if any, is or could be used?

- How and when does my company report variances to the owner?

SHARING OPERATING DATA

Real estate management professionals wanting to compare the operation of properties in their management portfolio with other properties in their markets may want to take advantage of research studies that compile data from many properties in a market and produce a statistical report. One such series of statistical reports is produced and published by IREM. The *IREM Income/Expense Analysis Reports* are published for five property types: conventional apartments, federally assisted apartments, open shopping centers, office buildings, and condominiums/planned unit developments.

The chart of accounts used for each property type is an abbreviated format that includes all sources of income and expense, but they are combined into fewer categories than a real estate manager would use for detailed analysis. IREM includes with its data entry form a manual and worksheet that shows how a typical real estate management firm might reformat data to meet the requirements of the given research.

Real estate managers who understand the organization of charts of accounts and their relationship to owner reporting will find this knowledge most useful. In addition to formatting data for internal use, property owners, and reporting services, there are likely many opportunities to reformat for appraisers and lenders. Real estate managers will also need this knowledge to analyze the financial performance of properties not in their portfolio.

REVIEW QUESTIONS

- What are the differences between financial accounting and managerial accounting?

- What is the difference between internal and external reporting?

- What are common internal financial reports?

- What are common external financial reports?

- Refer back to Exhibits 7.3, 7.4, and 7.5. How would you reformat the information to forecast a pro forma statement of operations for the next calendar year from any one of these statements? What additional information would you need? What data would you eliminate?

Financing Basics

Investment in real estate takes two forms: (1) **equity investment,** where there is a direct or indirect "ownership" interest in property (i.e., property purchaser/owner), and (2) **debt investment,** where funds are loaned to property owners in exchange for a payment of interest (i.e., lender). The equity investor can borrow a major portion of the purchase price of a property. Consequently, financing plays a large role in making decisions about real estate.

In this chapter, much of the focus is on planning and financing for buying or renovating an existing building. Financing of new or existing real estate also is an important concern of real estate managers. Even though few real estate managers make decisions about financing on their own, an understanding of financing leads to better decision making, assessment of financial condition, and knowledge of how a property operates. The knowledge of the basics of real estate financing will allow real estate managers to gather all appropriate documentation, prepare reports, and discuss recommendations for financing that will achieve optimal results for the owner.

A BRIEF HISTORY OF LENDING AND BANKING

Prior to the Great Depression in the 1930s, the U.S. banking system operated largely by accepting deposits from customers and investing those deposits as loans to other customers. Savings and loan institutions lent money secured by mortgages on homes in their community, and commercial banks made loans on larger properties in addition to business loans secured by business assets.

Life insurance companies made loans secured by mortgages on larger properties owned by large investors. When a lending institution did not receive payment, it would foreclose on the security, taking possession of the property. Since the banking system required few reserves, lending institutions could loan most of the funds on deposit to borrowers.

The Lending Process

Consider the fundamental process of lending money from the perspective of any bank. Depositors place funds on deposit in the institution for which they earn interest. This money is a liability of the bank which must be paid back to the depositor either on demand, or as required by the deposit agreement. Some of those deposited funds are set aside as reserves, then the rest are available to be loaned to customers on various terms and conditions, at which point the loaned funds are considered an asset of the bank that can be kept in the bank's portfolio or sold to other investors. Loans that are not sold to a secondary market (see "Government-Sponsored Entities" in this chapter) are considered *portfolio loans.* These loans are paid back to the bank over a period of time with payments going to *interest* representing the financial return on the lender's investment and *principal* usually paid back through an *amortization* process that represents the return on the lender's investment.

In a short-term loan, the principal is recovered in perhaps 90 days, but in a mortgage loan, the lender recovers its investment over as long as 30 years. When a depositor wants to withdraw funds, the bank's cash on hand is reduced. If many depositors withdraw funds at the same time, the bank may need to borrow money to repay the depositor or sell assets to increase its liquidity. If the value of the bank's assets shrinks due to market conditions, as happened during the Great Depression in the 1930s, there may not be enough funds available to accommodate depositors' withdrawals. Absent government regulation and the depositor insurance programs instituted after the Great Depression, a "run" on the bank would take place, and the institution would collapse.

Federal Insurance Corporations

After the rebuilding of the financial system in the 1930s, the players in the lending arena were largely unchanged. However, financial markets were starting to evolve as the country began recovery from the Great Depression. Two important developments took place: The Federal Government began insuring deposits, and it formed the Federal National Mortgage Association.

The government's insuring of deposits took place through the Federal Deposit Insurance Corporation (FDIC) for commercial banks and the Federal Savings and Loan Insurance Corporation (FSLIC) for thrift institutions, such as savings and loans. These entities were created by Congress to maintain stability and public confidence in the nation's banking system. The insured institutions were regulated in terms of liquidity requirements and were also required to pay an interest rate to depositors set artificially low by law.

The creation in 1938 of a secondary market for single family home mortgages through the Federal National Mortgage Association, which came to be known as Fannie Mae, was aimed at increasing liquidity for institutions with portfolios of home loans. Homeowners were defaulting on their home mortgages en masse, and the many foreclosures left lending institutions badly strapped for cash. President Franklin D. Roosevelt signed a bill allocating $1 billion to create Fannie Mae to buy mortgages from banks, freeing up their capital to be loaned to other credit-worthy borrowers.

Government-Sponsored Entities

As the process matured over time, some lending institutions chose to sell some of their loans in the secondary market. The Government National Mortgage Association (Ginnie Mae) was created in 1968 by the Housing and Urban Development Act. Ginnie Mae is a government-owned corporation that guarantees (but does not issue) bonds of the pass-through type as long as the loans backing them are underwritten by the government. Throughout the 1960s, this system remained relatively unchanged. Fannie Mae grew dramatically over that time period, so much so that it was converted from a government agency to a publicly traded corporation. Shortly thereafter, the Federal Home Loan Mortgage Corporation (Freddie Mac), who purchased loans and in turn paid the original lending institution to service collection of loan payments on their behalf, was created as a government agency to prevent Fannie Mae from becoming a monopoly.

Later Freddie Mac was also spun off into a publicly traded entity. These were the first of a series of organizations known as government-sponsored entities (GSE)—ones started by the Federal Government that later became public, but were so large that the investment community sensed an implicit guarantee by the government to prevent their failure. In common business terminology, this type of institution is considered "too big to fail"—the government would not allow failure due to the impact on the national economy.

The ability of banks to borrow money from depositors at low rates eventually was eroded by the creation of alternative investment instruments that paid higher rates but were not government-insured. Also during this period, the GSEs were permitted to package loans and sell them as securities to increase their liquidity, making it possible to purchase more loans from thrifts and banks.

Over the next 40 years, Congress passed a series of laws that completely changed the regulatory landscape of the banking system. These laws included deregulation of interest rates paid to depositors, permitting large-scale mergers and acquisitions and severely blurring lines between banks and thrift institutions.

Commercial Mortgaged-Backed Securities

While the existence of Fannie Mae and the many regulatory changes impacting the residential lending market have had a significant and ongoing impact on single family home mortgages, there was little change in the commercial lending arena. A factor that made mortgages worthy of purchase by Fannie Mae was that a residential mortgage was a relatively uniform document with relatively similar terms, no matter where the loan was made or where the property was located.

This was not true for mortgages on commercial property until the 1990s, when the **commercial mortgage-backed security (CMBS)** became a popular financing vehicle. Early CMBS loans were packaged as the result of a financial crisis in the mid- to late 1980s, when many savings and loan institutions collapsed. The collapse was caused primarily by poorly underwritten loans on office buildings, known as see-through office buildings, which were built as speculative investments inspired largely by favorable tax legislation. Lending institutions financed the construction of millions of square feet of office space for which there were few tenants. Owners defaulted on these loans, many of which were **nonrecourse loans,** meaning the investors' risk was limited to their investment in the property.

Ultimately, the lending institutions collapsed and were taken over by the FSLIC, which was later reorganized as part of the **Financial Institution Reform, Recovery, and Enforcement Act (FIRREA).** Another component of that legislation created the **Resolution Trust Corporation (RTC),** which took ownership of the failed investment real estate properties. The RTC sold many properties with mortgages that it held. Once the buildings began to recover, the RTC sold large packages of its mortgages on the secondary market through Ginnie Mae. Since these initial transactions, billions of dollars of loans have been sold in the secondary market using CMBS loans through investment houses throughout the country.

CMBS loans provided a vehicle for securitizing commercial loan packages similar to the methods used by the GSEs to raise capital. The CMBS market accounts for billions of commercial fixed rate financing. While the lending market for single family homes may influence the availability of funds and interest rates, most transactions involving professional property managers are for larger loans for shopping centers, apartment buildings, and office buildings.

Real Estate Financing Terminology

Throughout the United States, two basic instruments are used in real estate financing. When an owner makes arrangements for a loan, either a mortgage or a deed of trust is the legal instrument used to provide the security. A typical mortgage loan has two parts: the promissory note and the mortgage.

- The first part is the **promissory note,** the legal document that a person executes (signs), in which the person makes the promise to pay back the lender. The promissory note lays out in detail the loan amount (known as the principal), payment terms, interest rate (interest is the charge made by the lender for the use of the money lent, which is the principal), and other conditions of the loan.

- The **mortgage** is the legal document that pledges the real estate as collateral for a loan. **Collateral** is any property pledged for payment of a loan and is said to secure a loan. (Unsecured loans are riskier and have higher interest rates.)

A mortgage is a lien on a property. A lien is a legal requirement that a creditor places against a property to secure the payment of the debt. After selling a property, for example, an owner must pay off the mortgage (and if there are several mortgages, any second, third, or other mortgage, in the order in which they were executed). Taxes and some governmental agency fees have priority over a mortgage. Other liens may be placed against properties, such as the mechanics' liens that are placed against a property by contractors and subcontractors for work that may be in dispute. The priority of liens is determined by the date the lien is recorded.

In some areas, particularly the western United States, a *deed of trust* is used instead of a mortgage. The arrangement is similar to a mortgage, except that a deed of trust introduces a third party, a trustee who holds the title to the property as security. Real estate managers must be familiar with local lending practices.

Legal Theories In the United States, two legal theories govern the property rights of a mortgage lender: title theory and lien theory. Most states follow the lien theory. Both theories are based on the concept of title.

Title Theory In states that follow title theory, legal title right to the mortgaged property actually transfers to the lender or to a third party to hold for the lender by means of a deed of trust. When the loan has been repaid, the property is transferred back to the borrower. This is called title theory because the title of the property actually changes hands.

Lien Theory Under the lien theory, title to the mortgaged property remains with the borrower, and a lien, or claim, upon the property is given to the lender by means of the mortgage. The mortgage is a conditional deed that does not operate to transfer title unless a default has occurred in repayment of the loan.

Virtually every interest in a property can be characterized by a lien:

- **Mortgages and deeds of trust** create one kind of lien on property, a collateral or monetary lien, since the lien is given to secure repayment of the debt.

- **Leases** are another kind of lien, one that creates possession and enjoyment rights because it is a right given to someone to occupy the property for a specified length of time.

- A **mechanic's lien** secures payment for materials or labor used in construction. A person who has not been paid for providing construction labor or material used on the property may petition the court for a monetary lien on the property. Such a lien secures payment for the contractor.

- **Tax liens** are monetary liens by federal, state, or local tax authorities for unpaid taxes.

See Chapter 9 for a further discussion of liens and priority of liens as they relate to lenders' rights.

SOURCES OF FINANCING TODAY

The global financial environment has an impact on investors and managers in commercial real estate. In recent years, the issuance of loans for commercial real estate has decreased, as lenders have sought to limit exposure to the risk of defaulting mortgages. It is imperative that real estate managers keep up with the fast-changing marketplace when it comes to lending trends, the availability of funds, and the cost of borrowing.

Real estate managers are not typically responsible for property financing or refinancing, but they interact regularly with lenders and potential lenders. Some real estate managers do hold additional responsibilities as **asset managers** that may include financing. In either case, real estate managers should be well versed in financing trends, alert to changing conditions, and able to advise property owners as requested.

Debt financing on real estate is available through a number of sources, both private and public (government). Private sector sources range from traditional commercial banks and life insurance companies to the increasingly popular **real estate investment trusts (REITs),** pension funds, and investment banks. To effectively achieve ownership goals and objectives, real estate managers must understand the characteristics of each source of debt financing and the criteria lenders use to evaluate potential borrowers.

Commercial Banks

Commercial banks are the largest financial intermediaries in the United States. They provide:

- Both short-term financing for development and construction and long-term mortgage financing for acquisition.
- Capital improvement loans, equipment loans, and lines of credit to other concerns that invest in real estate.

Federal and state governments heavily regulate commercial banks. Their loan-to-value ratios are monitored, and their real estate is limited to a set percentage of their equity capital.

In the 1990s, commercial bank trust departments began managing sizable pension reserve funds and thus entered the real estate financing marketplace separately from the main bank operations. By law, trust departments are managed independently of the larger commercial banks in which they reside, so it is possible for a real estate project to be funded by a trust department even if the loan department of the same commercial bank turned it down.

Loan issuance by commercial banks was severely contracted by liquidity crisis in the global financial markets. However, according to the Federal Reserve's Senior Loan Officer Opinion Survey on Bank Lending Practices, in April of 2011, 5.5% of respondents said their banks eased standards for commercial real estate lending—the first easing of standards for lending by commercial banks since 2005.

Life Insurance Companies

Life insurance companies are the major lenders in many commercial and industrial properties as well as the oldest and most diversified commercial real estate lending source. Improved commercial, industrial, and multi-family properties constitute the major portion of life insurance company mortgage portfolios. They specialize in placing long-term debt in large amounts. Recently, they have become more common sources of financing for commercial real estate loans.

The amount of money loaned on an individual project is generally influenced by state legislation in the insurance company's state of domicile. In most states, life insurance companies can lend up to 75% of the appraised value of residential property. In other states, commercial loans up to 100% of value are allowed if the income stream is sufficient to amortize the loan and if the tenants have outstanding credit. These loans have maturities similar to those for single family homes, typically 25 to 30 years.

The traditional long-term nature of real estate lending places insurance company lenders in a highly vulnerable position during periods of inflation, when yields on existing mortgage portfolios remain fixed as interest rates are rising. To offset this circumstance, many companies participate in the project's equity through direct ownership, receiving some of the income stream, or both. In direct ownership, the life insurance company may also be the developer, or it may participate in a joint venture with a developer. Participation in the income stream is usually in the form of a percentage of income above a certain point, in addition to payments on the loan. In addition to their own investments, life insurance companies also handle real estate investments for pension funds in the role of an investment manager.

Commercial Mortgage-Backed Securities (CMBS)

Commercial Mortgage-Backed Securities are bonds offered to investors that are collateralized by a pool of commercial mortgage loans from which all of the principal and interest paid on those mortgages flows to investors, according to the CRE Finance Council. CMBS benefit borrowers via access to larger pools of capital than would otherwise be available in traditional lending markets and to lower interest rates.

The CMBS market has been heavily influenced by the global liquidity crisis of recent years. As the market peaked in 2006, the resulting slow-down has since been characterized by losses in value to the real estate that is security for the loans. Many CMBS loans are relatively short-term in nature, which forces property owners to refinance the loans 3 to 5 years after the loans were funded.

The drop in value coupled with an accounting rule known as **mark to market** (an accounting regulation that prevents **workouts** or refinancing under conditions where the value of property has dropped significantly) makes it impossible to refinance these loans. This leaves the CMBS investors in a position of having defaults in payments from real estate owners and property values less than the outstanding loans. These dynamics cause a severe credit crunch for commercial property owners and cool the market for real estate in general.

However, as lenders stop lending to correct their balance sheets and recover equity, the way opens up for increased demand for CMBS. According to an article in the National Real Estate Investor, domestic issuance is expected to rise from $11.6 billion in 2010 to possibly $40 billion in 2011 and $65 billion by 2013.[1]

Federal Government

The Federal Government finances real estate both through direct loans and as guarantor and/or insurer of mortgages held by private insurers. The U.S. Department of Housing and Urban Development (HUD) makes direct loans to public agencies through the Urban Renewal Program and to private developers through the New Communities Act.

In its direct lending activity, HUD provides loans at below-market interest rates and direct rent subsidies to encourage the availability of low-income housing. Past programs have provided this financing to the developers and investors, and some have provided it directly to low-income families. For private developers in new communities, HUD guarantees bonds, debentures, notes, and other financial obligations that it issues to finance land acquisition and development. Congress frequently revises HUD's financing programs.

In addition, the Federal Government provides mortgage insurance through the U.S. Federal Housing Administration (FHA). This agency's only function is to insure loans. It was created in 1934 to encourage improvement in housing standards and conditions, facilitate sound home financing on reasonable terms, and exert a stabilizing influence in the mortgage market. To obtain FHA insurance, lenders, borrowers, and the property must meet specified requirements. Mortgage insurance through the FHA is available for single family, multi-family, cooperative, elderly, and other housing projects. Mortgages for qualified veterans are similarly insured through the U.S. Department of Veterans Affairs.

---

[1] Valley, Matt, " *Why this CRE Market is So Hard to Gauge,* " National Real Estate Investor, February 2011. *http://nreionline.com/finance/why_this_recovery_is_so_hard_to_gauge_698m/*

Real Estate Investment Trusts (REITs)

REITs are companies that own and, in many cases, operate income-producing real estate. They have been a major source of diverse funding. There are several types of real estate investment trusts (REIT). A **mortgage REIT** makes or owns loans and other obligations that are secured by real estate collateral. An **equity REIT** owns or has an equity interest in rental real estate (rather than making loans secured by real estate collateral). A **hybrid REIT** combines the investment strategies of the two.

REITs sell publicly traded shares, similarly to the stock market. To be a REIT, a company must annually distribute at least 90% of its taxable income to shareholders in the form of dividends. REITs do not pay taxes at an entity level, but like limited partnerships and **limited liability companies (LLCs),** they pass returns through to the investor to be taxed at the individual's tax rate. The United States has almost 200 publicly traded REITs, and their assets total almost $400 billion. REITs invest in all property types, but the majority of investments are in retail, office, and multi-family properties.

Congress first created REITs in the 1960s to give any individual the opportunity to invest in large-scale commercial property. Then, as a result of the 1986 Tax Act, real estate prices fell 25%. By 1987, there were widespread foreclosures, and the savings and loan crisis had begun to unfold. By 1988, the government had taken over huge portfolios from the savings and loans through FSLIC. Prices remained stagnant until investors regained confidence that the government would not again impose such severely punitive tax laws. REITs attracted the attention of investment bankers, who realized the REIT structure was a vehicle they could use to make money for themselves. Their solution was to repackage real estate to look more like stocks and bonds. In 1993, these new REITs became a significant force, raising more than $18 billion for real estate acquisition.

Today, many individual investors purchase shares in REITs rather than investing in real estate directly. The focus of this investment is on property income as a source of wealth. REITs have buying power, operating efficiency, and low-cost capital to control the best opportunities. They are corporations with shares that are traded on the stock market, similar to common stock. Share prices in REITs are tied to the perceived future cash flows of the properties involved. Debt leverage in the properties is based on balance sheets as collateral rather than on specific assets.

The value of shares in a REIT is determined by supply, demand, and the trust's **net asset value (NAV).** NAV is a valuation index that reflects the market value of real estate properties held by a REIT. It is usually quoted "per investment unit" where the value is divided by the total number of outstanding investment units. The degree of premium/discount on individual investment unit prices relative to the per-unit NAV serves as the yardstick for assessment. In addition to NAV, **funds from operations (FFO)** and **adjusted funds from operations (AFFO)** are other key statistics used to assess the financial performance of a REIT. FFO is operating profit excluding GAAP-style depreciation and any gains or losses on disposals of properties. AFFO is equivalent to FFO less an allowance for maintenance capital expenditures and leasing costs to reflect the cash a REIT spends to maintain its buildings.

While their number is expected to contract in the future because of consolidations, REITs are predicted to remain a significant and permanent force in real estate financing.

Pension Funds

Pension funds accumulate cash on a tax-exempt basis for future payment to retiring employees. Corporate, labor union, and government employee benefit accounts for future pensions or profit sharing are large sources of pension fund investment capital. The overriding investment objectives of most pension fund managers have been protecting the accumulated capital and maintaining sufficient liquidity to meet future payment requirements.

Before 1974, pension funds were generally composed of stocks and bonds, and to a lesser extent secondary mortgages through Ginnie Mae–backed securities. Since the passage of the Employee Retirement Income Security Act (ERISA) in 1974, pension funds have diversified into real estate investments.

Analysts estimate that pension funds that invest in real estate (not all do) typically allocate between 5% and 7% to the category. Today's most aggressive pension funds are moving above those averages. However, most pensions are governed by disciplined investors who must answer to conservative boards of directors.

Institutions that once focused on the top 20 cities are now looking at secondary markets with healthy economies. In addition, some pensions are increasing their use of leverage. In the past, institutions rarely used leverage for their core holdings—properties designed to provide conservative income streams. In the 1990s, pensions typically paid all cash for such holdings, but now many institutions are borrowing in order to boost returns and stretch equity dollars farther. While many institutions would prefer owning 100% of a project with no debt, they are increasingly taking on partners as a way to win deals.

Not all pension funds are keen on debt, however. Some institutions fear that leverage adds risk. Individual core properties rarely have more than 60% debt, and total portfolios typically have less than 30% leverage. According to the Pension Real Estate Association (PREA), pensions continue to focus on core holdings, keeping 66.5% of assets in that bucket. But in their search for deals, some institutions are looking harder at value-added or opportunistic deals.

Investment Banks

Traditionally, investment banks have been involved in underwriting and distributing initial public offerings and acting as dealmakers for the private placement of debt for corporate mergers and acquisitions. Their business activities in real estate began in the 1970s with brokerage and investment. They created the secondary market for residential mortgage loans where original mortgages (bundled and securitized) are sold.

During the early banking deregulation of the 1980s, commercial banks crossed into the arena of investment banks by beginning to underwrite securities, trade corporate bonds and equities, underwrite and sell mutual funds, and provide full-service investment brokerage and consulting. At the same time, investment banks moved into the commercial bank territories of short-term business loans and the commercial-paper and foreign-exchange-rate markets. Investment banks drew many corporate clients away from the commercial banks.

In the 1990s, when falling property values temporarily dried up financing from life insurance companies, the investment banks stepped in to play a major role in restructuring REITs and making the initial public offerings of their shares. Investment banks created the CMBS secondary market for commercial mortgage loans where original mortgages (bundled and securitized) are sold.

Today, investment banks offer direct commercial mortgage loans. These offerings are typically for hard-to-finance deals, such as properties with past problems, repositioned properties, or properties that have complex financing needs. Investment banks have come to compete directly with REITs, as they do with commercial banks.

Private Sources

Individual investors, acting alone or in limited partnerships, make money available directly for real estate projects in any phase of a property's development: raw land, construction, or improvements. (Often, they are the only source of financing for raw land.) Private sources of financing make up a large share of *mezzanine financing*—financing the gap between traditional loan-to-value ratios and the desires of investors. Typically, the loan amount is small and for a short term. The lending interests of parties in this group are unique and can include any type of funding. Such investors are not a primary source of real estate lending.

Syndicators are a special type of limited partnership that package real estate investments as tax shelters. Their goal is to make ownership of large properties available to numerous small investors who desire an investment with favorable tax treatment. These firms have lost much of their presence due to tax law reform, overbuilding, poor investment decisions, and in some cases, the collection of excessive fees. However, the low-income housing tax syndicators are still a viable market presence and include banks and private firms.

LOAN FUNDING

As described earlier in this chapter, a very traditional approach to lending places the originating lender (bank, thrift institution) in the position of using funds of depositors to make loans to customers. Then the customer repays the loans to the institution so the cycle can continue. However, the fact that loans are paid back over a longer period than a given depositor may intend to keep funds on deposit can create *liquidity* problems for banks that keep too many loans in their portfolios as assets.

In modern lending, the originating lender takes advantage of the loans in its portfolio as assets of the institution, which can be sold to investors by one of several means. Many additional types of loan are now available in which the originator acts simply as an agent for another lender. The end lender agrees in advance to purchase (or fund directly) this type of loan and may have the originating lender remain the "face" for the investor by acting as a **servicing agent.** The servicing agent is responsible for acting on behalf of the end lender in collecting loan payments and taking collection action in case of delinquency.

In general, a lending institution that carefully monitors its loan portfolio, prudently sells loans into the secondary market, and monitors liquidity carefully should be successful in that portion of its business.

In addition to banks and thrift institutions, investment banks, REITS, and other sources mentioned earlier may act as the originating lender in a real estate transaction. Rather than coming from depositors, the funds for the loans come from investors. Later, the originating lender may sell the loans to other investors to maintain liquidity.

Unfortunately, these examples oversimplify modern lending practices. The difference between banks and thrift institutions is murky at best. Originating lenders in a given transaction may also choose to be investors in a CMBS offering secured by other properties. The strong competition for placing loans in the early 2000s caused lenders to underwrite loans on faulty assumptions, including aggressive estimates of value.

The economic conditions of the late 2000s have made it challenging to finance commercial properties. Many investors are unsure of the risk associated with financing real estate and are holding their investment dollars in "safe" alternatives, such as government securities.

While the documentation necessary to **underwrite** a real estate loan—analysis of physical and financial data to make a lending decision—has remained relatively unchanged in the last decade, the scrutiny applied to requests for commercial loans has increased dramatically. In fact, issuance of financing in real estate has declined from 2006 peaks, in part because lenders began to tighten underwriting standards. The requirements have tightened in the following areas:

- More conservative forecasting
- Operational consistency
- Tenant quality
- Cap rate derivation
- Prepayment and extension
- Lease clauses
- Financial reputation
- Predictability
- Mortgage clauses
- Tenant diversity

Specialties in real estate sometimes have differing perspectives, while the economic principles remain unchanged.

TYPES OF LOANS

The various financing sources offer diverse real estate financing options. As mentioned previously, financing for a property may be required for acquisition, major replacements, improvements, renovations, and rehabilitations. Thus, one of a real estate manager's responsibilities may be to compare loan options in order to select the most advantageous loan structure from available financing alternatives. The real estate manager must first understand the various types of loans that can be obtained in the marketplace today.

Interest-Only

An interest-only loan (also referred to as a straight-term, standing, or demand loan) is a type of loan in which the borrower makes only interest payments until the maturity date. Then, the entire principal must be repaid in a single payment. (See Exhibit 8.1.) This type of loan is typically used for construction financing and is the first part of a loan package that would also include a longer-term amortized loan known as a take-out loan, which is permanent financing that is funded at the completion of construction. These funds are used to pay off (take out) the construction lender.

Exhibit 8.1

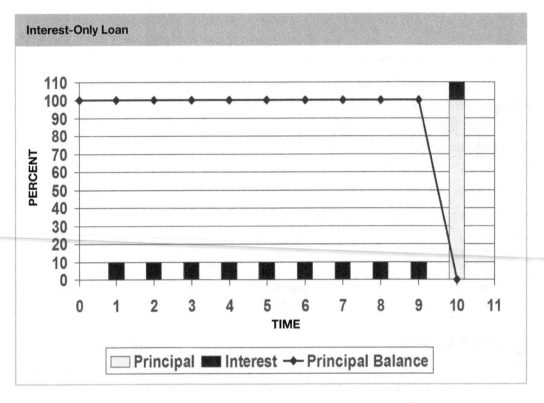

Interest-Only Loan

Fully Amortized

This process of paying off the principal of a loan as part of loan payments is called amortization. A fully amortized loan is characterized by *periodic payments* that include a portion applied to interest and a portion applied to principal. In the early years of the loan, a greater portion of the payment is applied to the interest. As the loan matures, a greater portion of the payment is applied to the principal, and the entire debt obligation is extinguished at the end of the loan term. (See Exhibit 8.2.) Over the course of a fully amortized loan, the borrower builds equity in the property, and the lender gains additional cushioning against loss in the case of default of payment.

There are two types of fully amortized loans: fixed-rate and variable-rate.

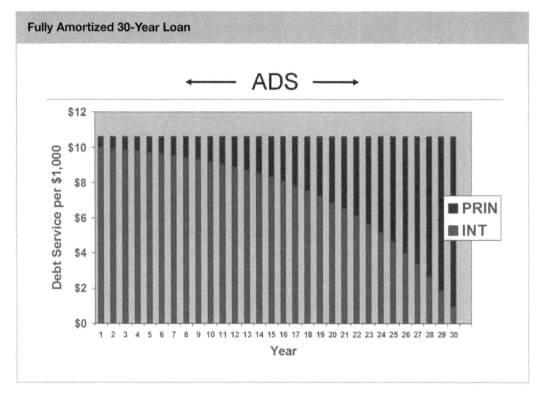

Fixed-Rate

With a fixed-rate, fully amortized loan, the interest rate remains constant over the life of the loan (the entire amortization period). Therefore, the debt service is constant over the life of the loan. [1]

An **amortization schedule** shows the periodic interest and principal components of each individual payment and the amount of the outstanding loan balance after each scheduled payment. An amortization schedule can be generated for monthly, annual, or any other schedule of periodic payments. Amortization schedules can be created using online tools, a financial calculator, or financial analysis spreadsheet tools, such as the *IREM® Financial Analysis Spreadsheet*. (See Exhibits 8.3 and 8.4.)

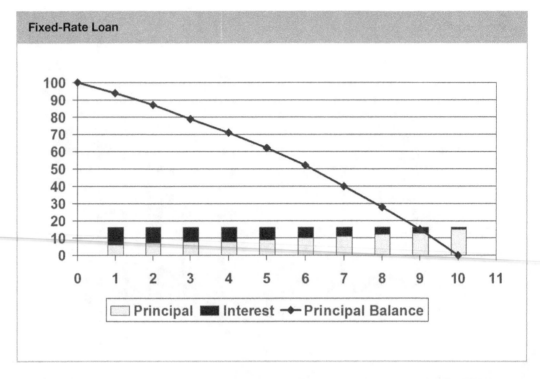

Exhibit 8.3 **Fixed-Rate Loan**

Exhibit 8.4 **Amortization Schedule**

Original Balance			2,320,000
Interest Rate			9.00%
Monthly Payment			($19,272.78)
	Interest	**Principal**	**Balance**
			2,320,000.00
1	($17,400.00)	($1,872.78)	2,318,127.22
2	($17,385.95)	($1,886.83)	2,316,240.39
3	($17,371.80)	($1,900.98)	2,314,339.41
4	($17,357.55)	($1,915.24)	2,312,424.17
5	($17,343.18)	($1,929.60)	2,310,494.57
6	($17,328.71)	($1,944.07)	2,308,550.50

Variable Rate

During periods of volatile interest rates, lenders and borrowers face serious financial risks from long-term fixed-rate loans. A variable-rate loan (also known as an adjustable rate mortgage [ARM]) is an alternative that protects both the lender and the borrower from potential financial shocks due to rapidly changing interest rates.

In a variable-rate structure, the interest rate on the loan is adjusted periodically—usually each year. The amount of the adjustment is tied to an index, typically one of the Treasury Bill rates. Some of the most common indices are the One-year Treasury Constant Maturity Yield, Federal Home Loan Bank (FHLB) 11th District Cost of Funds, Prime Rate, and London Interbank Offered Rate (LIBOR).

The amount of the adjusted interest rate is also capped, commonly by 2% per adjustment period and limited to 5% or 6% over the life of the loan. Payments are recalculated at each adjustment period using the current interest rate and the remaining term from the original loan and using the same method of calculation as the fixed-rate fully amortized loan.

Thus, the first-year loan payment is calculated using the initial-year variable rate (usually below the prevailing fixed rate) and a conventional amortization period such as 30 years. A payment adjustment in the fifth year of an original 30-year loan would be calculated based on the fifth-year adjusted interest rate and 25 years remaining on the loan.

Balloon

A **balloon loan,** or partially amortized loan, refers to a loan where uniform periodic payments include amounts for interest and principal, but the periodic principal payments do not fully amortize the loan because the term of the loan is shorter than the full amortization period. Thus, a substantial single payment, called a balloon payment, is due at the end of the loan term. This balloon payment is typically refinanced at a newly negotiated interest rate or is paid from the proceeds of a sale of the property.

The advantage of a balloon loan to the borrower is that the periodic payments are lower than they would be for a fully amortizing loan because the lender can offer a balloon loan at a lower rate of interest since the loan term is shorter. The advantage to the lender is that the fixed rate of interest is not committed for long periods. The lender will receive the balance of the loan back earlier and will be able to make those funds available for future lending.

Other Loan Types

There are other loan types that are used for various situations in real estate as explained in the following chart.

Loan Type	Description
Interim Financing	Interim financing is a temporary or short-term loan secured by a mortgage and generally paid off from the proceeds of permanent financing. A construction loan, a short-term loan that remains outstanding during the time needed to complete construction, is a common form of interim financing. Construction loans are often replaced by permanent financing—longer-term loans that are usually amortized over 25 to 30 years. Bridge loans may be used for financing between two events; the most common situation being between the construction loan and the completion of permanent financing.
Mezzanine	Most commercial mortgage lenders are limited by regulation, rating agencies, or market constraints to real estate loans with a maximum loan-to-value ratio of 75 to 80%. To reduce the amount of equity required to invest in a real estate project, many borrowers will increase the total property leverage to 85 to 90% through the use of mezzanine debt. Due to first-mortgage lender restrictions on subordinate mortgages, most mezzanine debt is secured by an assignment of the borrower's partnership or membership interests in the entity that owns the real estate rather than the real estate itself.
	Mezzanine lender's returns are derived from a combination of origination fees, exit fees, fixed or variable interest rates (sometimes with accrual features), and participation in property cash flow and/or appreciation, with the structure determined on a deal-by-deal basis depending on the project's characteristics and perceived level of risk. Loan terms typically range from three to five years; although they are sometimes longer. Mezzanine debt is most effectively used in acquisitions, developments, redevelopments, recapitalizations, or refinancing where there is a significant value-creation opportunity.
Rollover	Seen less frequently in recent years, a rollover loan is a long-term loan that sets a fixed interest rate for a certain number of years. At the end of that time, the loan must be rolled over at the prevailing interest rate. (The loan can be paid off to avoid rolling it over, if that is a better business decision.)

Loan Type	Description
Floor-Ceiling	A floor-ceiling loan sets a minimum amount to be loaned (the floor) and a maximum amount (the ceiling). They are also called earn-outs. Floor-ceiling loans are used when buildings are being rented and occupancy is uncertain. The lender commits to the minimum amount, with the maximum amount dependent on the property's progress. If the required occupancy level is not reached, the ceiling amount is not lent. The real estate manager's performance is key to the success of this type of borrowing. Because so much is at stake, owners carefully and frequently monitor property managers to see if they are meeting targets.
Gap	Gap loans are frequently short-term loans used to cover a financial gap such as the amount between the floor and ceiling in a floor-ceiling loan. Typically, interest rates are higher with gap loans.
Secondary Financing	Secondary or junior financing refers to second, third, and other mortgages. The first mortgage has priority after certain governmental rights, such as property taxes—it is the first (or senior) lien against the property and has the first claim. Any other mortgage or financing is junior to it. Secondary financing is a way of using funds for improvements to a property without making changes to the first mortgage, which may have been made at favorable terms. In the discussion of mezzanine debt, we saw one type of the secondary financing structure, for example, when the debt is secured by a membership interest and not the property. The primary mortgage holder may need to approve this type of financing. It is a shorter-term loan that has greater risk and, therefore, usually a higher interest rate.

COSTS OF BORROWING

There are costs involved in getting a loan of any type. Interest represents the primary cost of borrowing money. Some fees (or interest rate charges) are described as basis points (BP), which, as a standard, are 1/100th of one percent of the loan. These costs, which can vary from 4% to 8% of the loan amount, should be included in a real estate manager's budgeting and decision-making.

Depending on the kind and size of the loan, any of the following origination fees may enter into the transaction. Be aware of these miscellaneous costs, and determine whether any others are customary in your region or city.

- Application fees
- Title review
- Survey costs
- Engineering reports
- Closing costs

- Loan (discount) points
- Title insurance
- Property inspections
- Mortgage brokers' fees

- Legal expenses
- Credit report
- Environmental audits
- Appraisal report

Effective Interest Rates

Most loans have additional considerations that cause the stated and actual interest rates on the loan to differ. Because the interest rate is the major determinant of the investor's return, a revised or *effective interest rate* must be calculated to include the effects of these additional factors.

A loan's effective interest rate will vary from the stated interest rate in the following circumstances:

- Lender points and fees paid at the time of loan origination
- Prepayment penalties for repaying a loan before the loan maturity date
- Lender participation in the property's income or equity

In addition to the scenarios listed here, a shortened term is another common reason for a higher effective interest rate. Although we can measure it, we seldom plan for a shortened term. This isn't considered additional interest, but is the amortization of up-front additional interest costs over a shorter period of time.

Note that effective interest rates for loans are calculated differently than effective interest rates for savings. Effective interest rates for loans are calculated by adding prepaid interest and/or penalties to the total interest. Effective interest rates on savings are calculated by compounding interest on interest.

Lender Points and Fees

Lender points paid at the time of loan origination are a common transaction cost in mortgage lending. They represent additional interest on the loan. Each point is equal to an additional 1% interest paid on the total amount of the loan and therefore can represent substantial additional interest. (Loan origination fees may also represent an additional percentage rate of interest on a loan.)

The points and fees are usually included in the total mortgage loan and are collected by the lender by deducting the amount from the loan. Proceeds to the borrower are the amount of the loan minus the points and fees. Some borrowers choose to pay points and fees up front. In larger transactions, it may be desirable to amortize the points and fees over the life of the loan.

Prepayment Penalties

Unlike residential mortgage loans, investment loans might contain penalties for paying off the loan before its maturity date. Although, many commercial lenders allow loans to be paid off early without penalty under certain circumstances. For example, if an owner has a property with a 4% loan, a lender who could reinvest the money into loans at 6% or 7% might allow prepayment even if the loan documents specify that the loan be carried to its full term. Other loans permit prepayment with a built-in penalty. The penalties are described in the **yield maintenance** clause of the loan. Often, the prepayment penalty is specified as a percentage of the remaining balance. See the sidebar for more information about yield maintenance and **defeasance.**

Yield Maintenance and Defeasance

Yield maintenance is a prepayment of the loan with cash, while **defeasance** is a substitution of collateral. As explained by Taylor Liska in the article "Cost Comparison: A Case Study" in CCIM Institute's November/December 2011 issue of *CIRE Magazine,* "Both methods allow the borrower to unencumber the underlying real estate asset, and both compensate for the lender's reinvestment risk following prepayment. However, each method carries unique costs and implications, which can be punitive to a borrower. A considerable advantage of defeasance over yield maintenance is that there is no floor. When the average yield on the substitute collateral is higher than the coupon on the loan, it is cheaper to purchase securities to cover the loan's remaining interest and principal payments than to hold the loan. Conversely, a drawback to defeasance is the complexity of the transaction and the required fees the borrower will incur. The process typically takes 20 to 30 days and can require $50,000 to $100,000 in legal fees."

It is important to understand the difference between the two.

Yield Maintenance and Defeasance *(continued)*

Yield Maintenance

Over a protracted time, lenders may be unsure of how interest rates will move and what affect that may have on their outstanding loan portfolios. To protect against such an event, financial institutions developed a loan requirement called yield maintenance, which guarantees their return, regardless of an early payoff, by making the borrower agree to an additional fee (or penalty) for early prepayment. That is, the borrower guarantees that the lender will receive the full amount of return from the loan as if it had run its full term.

If the rate on the loan being paid off is higher than the market rate of new loans at the time of payoff, the yield maintenance provision can be substantial because it attempts to equalize the amount of return (yield) lost on the money that must be reinvested at a lower rate. If rates on the new loans are higher than the rates on the old loans (and a reasonable demand for new loans exists), then the yield maintenance could well be zero, although a separate minimum prepayment penalty could still be involved.

Defeasance

If an owner wants to decouple a property from its debt obligation, one possible method of releasing the property from the lender's collateral is through a process known as defeasance. A borrower who opts to use defeasance is best described as using "substitute collateral" to satisfy a borrower's loan and then allow the property to be sold or refinanced. The borrower will use the purchase of government-backed securities (e.g., treasury notes and CDs) to substitute the cash flow that the original loan guaranteed. Unlike a yield-maintenance prepayment, defeasance does not prepay the loan, but substitutes a specific set of notes that produce the same income over the same time frame, including any balloon payment that may have been specified in the original loan documents.

Defeasance must be acceptable to the lender and requires a complex series of steps that guarantee the lender's security. There are normally several third party professionals utilized to evaluate, guarantee, purchase, and transfer the securities from one party to the other. Fees can be substantial due to the complexity of the process; therefore, defeasance is not typical in loans that are less than several million dollars. Defeasance is useful especially in markets that see better than expected market appreciation that may prompt an owner to want to sell ahead of the original intention.

CMBS loans often have clauses either prohibiting prepayment prior to the end of a specified "lock-out" period (usually the last 60 to 90 days of the loan term), or imposing very severe penalties for prepayment. The impact of managing properties that have CMBS financing is that sale of the property may not be an option for the owner. For example, a property owner may have four retail centers financed under one CMBS loan that was packaged with several other retail properties. Even if the investor has an opportunity to sell one property at a very high price, if a CMBS loan was used to finance the acquisition, the property may be penalized for repaying the loan before maturity.

Lender Participation

At times, a lender will commit to a short- or long-term loan at a below-market interest rate in exchange for a percentage of the income or equity.

- *Income participation* is an agreement in which a lender receives a percentage, say 15%, of the annual net cash flow at the end of the year. Net cash flow includes all gross income from the property minus operating expenses and the debt service payment associated with the lower interest rate mortgage. In this case, the participation will reduce cash flow in the year it is paid as a result of increasing the annual debt service payment.

- *Equity participation* is an arrangement in which a lender receives a cash sum, such as 20%, of the market value of a property in excess of a specified amount on a specified date. Determination of the market value on the specified date is performed by an agreed appraisal method. The equity payment may or may not be tied to the sale of the property. The borrower may pay the equity participation sum either in cash or in a promissory note.

Examples of lender participation loans include the following:

Type	Description
Convertable Loan	The lender trades a below-market interest rate in return for the option to convert the loan balance at any time during the term into a direct-equity ownership. This type of "partnership" financing is beneficial when an owner wants to cash in on the appreciated value of the property. The proceeds of a convertible loan may be greater than the after-tax proceeds from a sale of the property. Also, the owner retains the ownership rights during the mortgage term.

Type	Description *(Continued)*
Mortgage with Purchase Option	The lender trades a below-market interest rate for an option to purchase the property at a future date.
Joint Venture	This is a partnership arrangement between a property owner and a "money partner" that is an alternative to a permanent loan. Typically, the venture parties anticipate a long-term holding period. The money partner's share of the net operating income (NOI) substitutes for loan interest. Ultimately, the property is refinanced or sold and the money partner shares in the appreciation in the property value.
Interim Joint Venture	This is like the joint venture, except that the money partner is normally an interim lender interested in a short-term investment. This is typical for construction loans.
Shared Appreciation Mortgage (SAM)	The lender trades a below-market interest rate for a share in future equity appreciation.
Sale-Leaseback	The investors actually sell the property and lease it back for a specified number of years at a predetermined rent.

PREPARING A LOAN PACKAGE

Most lenders require the submission of a loan package so they can properly assess the risks and the yields associated with the loan. Lenders may also require other materials such as copies of precommitted leases, title reports, appraisals, and in the case of new construction, evidence of a permanent loan commitment. The elements of a loan package, in fact, are closely related to the elements of a management plan.

Lenders look at the property information as well as the quality of the presentation. The loan package should be thorough and professional; it should present the potential borrower as knowledgeable and experienced. A well-prepared loan package can sometimes make the difference between obtaining a loan and being turned down.

Elements of a Loan Package

A standard loan submission package consists of the following main sections: a cover letter, project overview, appraisal analysis, borrower analysis, rental analysis, and supporting exhibits. The real estate manager needs to be familiar with these elements and may be asked to contribute some of the content, such as the appraisal and rent analyses.

Element	Description
Cover Letter	The cover letter is the first document to be read and can be thought of as the executive summary of the loan package. Therefore, it should emphasize the strong points of the property and summarize the basic loan terms the borrower requests.
Project Overview	The project overview should be a one-page review of the project that describes: • Improvements • Operating costs • Net operating income • Debt service This overview enables the loan committee to get the essential property facts at a glance.
Appraisal Analysis	The appraisal analysis (also called a feasibility analysis) is the substantive information in the loan package about the proposed project. The Appraisal Analysis Checklist that follows describes components of the standard appraisal analysis.
Borrower Analysis	The borrower analysis section should contain an analysis of the loan applicant that describes the type of entity, character and reputation, track record, management capabilities, and financial strength.
Renter Analysis	The rental analysis section describes each occupant of the property, including the tenant's ability to pay rent. Particular emphasis should be placed on lease clauses that might impact rent payments, such as escalation, cancellation rights, subordination, and assignment.

CHECKLIST: APPRAISAL ANALYSIS

☐ *Site Analysis*: should emphasize the adequacy of the site to support the intended use.

☐ *Improvement Analysis:* should focus on the quality and cost-effectiveness of the improvements. Other important aspects include the saleable nature of the real estate and its potential for conversion to another use. Lenders prefer functional, general-purpose properties.

☐ *Regional Analysis:* may be brief, especially if the property is located in an urban area well known to the investment community.

☐ *Neighborhood Analysis:* calls for a detailed knowledge of the immediate surroundings. An assessment should be made of the local market and of any competition or special benefits in close proximity to the property that will help secure the loan.

☐ *Real Estate Tax Analysis:* is an important part of the overall income and expense analysis because real estate taxes typically are the single highest item of annual expense, and they directly affect the cash flow.

☐ *Economic Analysis:* is the most important section of the submission, because it details projected future income. The projected future income is converted into value by using an appropriate methodology, such as capitalization.

☐ *Physical Analysis:* describes the costs associated with a new project's development. This analysis affects the economic analysis.

See Exhibit 8.5 for more detailed information regarding the items representative of those used in a typical loan package.

Cover Letter

Cover Page
- Photo or illustration of property

Title Page
- Name and address of property
- Name of preparer
- Date of preparation

Table of Contents

Project Overview
- Objective
- Description of project

Appraisal Analysis
- *Site analysis*
  - Photo of site
  - Site plan showing boundaries, dimensions, and total area
- *Improvement analysis*
  - Plans and information showing property improvements
- *Regional analysis*
  - Map of region and/or city with boundaries
  - Competition
  - Demographic data of region
  - Economic data of region
- *Neighborhood analysis*
  - Map of neighborhood with boundaries
  - Competition
  - Benefits within proximity of property
- *Real estate tax analysis*
  - Tax-related documents
- *Economic analysis*
  - Relation of net operating income to value
  - Debt service and cash flow projections
  - Return on equity
  - Loan analysis
  - Absorption

- *Physical analysis (for new projects)*
  - Land cost
  - Demolition
  - Construction and contingencies
  - Other development costs
  - Construction and lease-up timetables
  - Architectural and engineering drawings
  - Project supervision
  - Performance bond
  - Construction insurance
  - Real estate taxes during construction
  - Legal and closing costs
  - Operating deficit during lease-up period
  - Permits

Borrower Analysis
- Type and description of entity
- Names of individuals
- Character references
- Historical performance
- Financial data

Rental Analysis
- Tenant profiles
- Rent roll
- Vacancy rates
- Lease clauses pertaining to rent
- Promotion and leasing
- Marketing timetable

Appendices
- Specifications for construction
- Contractors and consultants employed
- Soil test reports
- Lease details
- Regional and neighborhood data
- Financial statements

Exhibits
- Detailed plans and renderings
- Newspaper clippings about project

. . . when considering financing for properties in his or her portfolio:

- Are there ways I can help my property owner choose financing to achieve optimal returns?

- Are there additional sources of financing to explore for the properties I manage?

- How can I improve the loan package information or process for the properties I manage?

· ·

REVIEW QUESTIONS

- List the major sources of real estate financing.

- Define the two documents of a real estate loan.

- What are the types of real estate loans?

- What is amortization? Describe a fully amortized loan.

- How does the note interest rate differ from the effective interest rate? Describe the factors that influence the effective interest rate.

- Explain the relationship between yield maintenance and defeasance.

- What is in included in the Appraisal Analysis section of the loan package?

Loan Analysis

Equity holders and lenders alike invest in real estate because the returns are higher than those from "safe investments," such as government securities. The returns are higher because the risks are higher. Key among those risks is the dynamics of an imperfect and competitive marketplace. For example, when you are borrowing money, there is no certainty about the direction interest rates will go. When you develop a property, future competitive developments may impact a project's success. No one can precisely predict changes in shopping habits of retail center customers or choices of apartment tenants in the face of a dynamic market for home ownership. Office leasing trends change as companies expand or downsize. The results of these various market dynamics may require changing the terms of a loan or paying it off early, or they may prompt the lender to take possession of a troubled property.

Every investment decision is made based on assumptions. Hopefully, the assumptions constitute the best knowledge available to the investor at the time, including a thorough understanding of financial trends and the current and projected future markets for the property type. These details are spelled out in the loan package as well as by real estate managers and by brokers performing investment analyses.

When evaluating a potential loan recipient, lenders examine a number of aspects of the potential borrower and of the property itself and weigh risks associated with financing. This is why the loan package needs to be complete and meet lender criteria.

LENDER CRITERIA

Lenders have criteria that must be met in a number of important areas. These areas can be considered the five "Cs" of credit: character, capacity, conditions, collateral, and capital. The following checklist describes each criterion.

CHECKLIST: THE FIVE "Cs" OF CREDIT

Character

❑ What is the character of the borrowing individual or firm?

❑ Has the borrower ever defaulted on a loan payment or does he or she have an unblemished borrowing history?

❑ Has the borrower hired an experienced, competent real estate manager to manage the property, preferably one with a professional industry credential [e.g., the Institute of Real Estate Management's (IREM) CERTIFIED PROPERTY MANAGER® (CPM®) or Accredited Management Organization® (AMO®), Building Owner and Managers Association International's (BOMA) Real Property Administrator (RPA®), a Certified Commercial Investment Member (CCIM), National Apartment Association's (NAA) Certified Apartment Manager (CAM®), National Association of Residential Property Managers' (NARPM) Residential Management Professional (RMP®) and Master Property Manager (MPM®), among others]?

Capacity

❑ Does the property have the capacity to produce an income stream?

❑ What does the cash flow sheet look like?

Conditions

❑ What are the loan terms?

Collateral

❑ How will the loan be supported?

❑ What is the value of the property?

❑ What is the ability to pay expenses and capital improvements?

Capital

❑ How much does the borrower have at risk?

❑ How much additional capital does the borrower have available to fund unexpected shortfalls or meet other capital needs?

As mentioned earlier, lenders consider two basic factors when pricing loans—***risk*** and ***yield.***

Risk

Measures of risk include:

- Amount of loan as compared to a property's market value, which is generally established by a property appraisal. By law, most institutions are limited to lending only a certain percentage of that value.

- Magnitude and reliability of the property's income stream. Specifically, the risk lies in how well the income stream covers the interest and principal payments on a loan.

- The developer's financial strength and record of completing successfully proposed projects.

Yield

Yield is a function of the ***annual interest rate*** and the term of a loan. As described earlier, the interest rate depends on the current state of the money market and the internal costs of institutional funds. Longer-term loans require a higher yield than shorter-term loans. Both interest rates and the term of the loan influence the risk associated with a loan. *The greater the risk, the greater the required yield.*

LENDER RISK

As discussed previously, equity investment (owning a property directly) and debt investment (lending) are the two forms of real estate investment. One might wonder why wouldn't the investment community simply gravitate to owning a property directly rather than take the position of a lender? And why would an investor not seek to generate money from the investment community to become part owner in a property and pay cash, rather than seek financing? The basic distinction is the way that investors weigh risk in their use of investment capital.

The lender's risk is lower than the owner's risk for two reasons: the lender's return is fixed by contract, and the lender has a preferred position to the owner if there is a drop in value or the loan does not perform as expected. On liquidation, the lender is paid before the owner is paid. Consider the scenarios described in the following example.

Example 9.1

Babylon Associates Office Building

Babylon Associates owns a 40,000-square-foot office building, purchased five years ago for $300,000. The buyers used $100,000 of their own funds to make the purchase and borrowed the remaining $200,000. Today the loan balance is $179,250. The company is putting the property on the market.

- If the market is strong and the property sells for $400,000 (above selling costs), the lender will be paid the mortgage balance and the owners will have positive equity of $220,750.

- If the market is weak and the property loses value and sells for $200,000 above selling costs, the lender will be paid the mortgage balance and the positive equity will be only $20,750.

- If the market is extremely soft and the best offer for the property is $150,000 above selling costs, the entire proceeds of sale would go to the lender; the owners would have to make arrangements with the lender to deal with the shortfall of $29,250. If the owners personally guaranteed the original loan, they might have to pay the difference from their own funds. This is known as a **short sale.** In some cases, the lender may negotiate with the property owner to forgive the deficiency amount and accept the proceeds of the sale as full payment on the loan.

LENDERS' RETURN ON INVESTMENT

Just as owners/equity holders and lenders in a real estate investment each take on risk—though in different ways—so do they each have claims to the net operating income (NOI). The owner is generally the stakeholder who takes the most risk and expects the highest return on investment (ROI). The lender's return is stated in the loan documents and is paid from NOI before any payment to the owner. The rate of return is stated in terms of interest rate; the lender's superior position is further secured by having the right to foreclose on the mortgage in the event of default. The loan may also be structured to include a personal guarantee from the investor. This protects the lender in two ways: If the monthly operations do not produce enough NOI to cover the loan payment, the lender can look to the owner to fund the difference; also, if the lender forecloses on the property due to nonperformance, any loss can be enforced against the owner/guarantor.

CMBS financing differs in that the loans are **nonrecourse,** meaning the property is the sole security for the loan. In fact, CMBS financing typically requires the entity borrowing the money (the property owner) to be a single purpose entity (SPE), meaning the property being mortgaged is its only asset. Usually a limited liability company (LLC) that has the property as its sole asset is created to own a property being considered for CMBS financing.

It may seem counterintuitive to say that the lender faces less risk than the owner in a real estate investment when the lender almost always has more money at stake. An owner may invest 30% of the total funds needed to purchase a property, but the lender is putting up perhaps 70%. Still, having first claim to the NOI and the right to take the property through foreclosure in the event of a default results in a more secure position for the lender.

Some lenders intentionally become part-owners of a property they finance. In a competitive mortgage market, the lender may negotiate a fixed rate of interest for a term of perhaps 30 years. While the mortgage terms probably provided the lender a satisfactory return at the time the mortgage was negotiated, there is no way for the lender to know the future performance of the loan—the owner's ability to repay, possible changes in market interest rates over the holding period, and when, or if, the owner will sell or refinance the property prior to maturity. Since one goal of property ownership is to provide a hedge against inflation, a partial ownership position helps protect against a loss of value in the loan due to inflation.

LOANS AS AN ASSET

In the most pure real estate lending environment, where a bank accepts deposits from savers and reinvests them in mortgages, the mortgage rate will be higher than the rate the bank pays its depositors. This is one of the ways the bank makes money, by having a "spread" between their cost of funds and the earnings they receive on those same funds when loaned back to borrowers. When lenders were more regulated, this calculation posed a rather simple decision for lenders in pricing their loans to borrowers: They made a simple calculation of their cost of funds (interest paid on savings accounts) plus a spread to provide profit and cover overhead. With the increasing complexity of the mortgage environment, loans are active financial assets of the institution. Lenders must price loans to be competitive in the market, but they also want loans to be a performing asset that can be sold to investors. Depositors are no longer the only source of funds to be loaned, so the formula becomes even more complex.

Consider a lender with $25 million of deposits that have been allocated to mortgage loans. Once those loans are made, that $25 million of cash assets is replaced on the balance sheet as a different type of asset: mortgages. The bank then starts collecting payments on those mortgage loans. As a loan amortizes, the lender looks upon the interest portion of that loan as **revenue** to the institution (return on its investment) and the portion of the payment applied to principal as a payment to the institution's **equity** (return of its investment).

If a lender has run out of deposits to use for mortgages and wants to continue making loans, it must find a way to increase its liquidity to have more funds to lend. One way to do this is to sell all or part of its portfolio of mortgages to investors. The price an investor will pay for a group of mortgages depends on the interest rate or yield compared with other investment alternatives. A lender may realize either a **gain** or a **loss** on the sale of mortgages, depending on the prevailing yields expected by investors. Low-yield loans will likely command a lower price than higher-yield loans, given similar risk factors. Lenders must track their portfolios carefully and position them for sale at appropriate times to maximize the liquidity they may realize from the sales. Lenders must always look on their loans as assets that have a market value to other investors.

LENDER TESTS

When establishing their underwriting criteria, lenders often set policies that limit the percentage of value that can be loaned against a particular property. The maximum amount for some lenders is established by law, but lenders can be more restrictive if they choose. Most lenders require that two measures of risk be within their lending guidelines: **Loan-to-Value Ratio (LTV%)** and **Debt Coverage Ratio (DCR).** The borrower must meet the lender's criteria in both of these areas in order to qualify for the loan.

TIPS

LTV and DCR requirements may change with macroeconomic cycles. Some practitioners report that in recessionary times, a 55% loan to value ratio, and a debt coverage ratio projection for five years may be required. However, these numbers are dependent on the type of borrower and the property, and may be higher or lower. Always research current market trends.

Exhibit 9.1 shows the relationship between risk and the two measures.

Exhibit 9.1

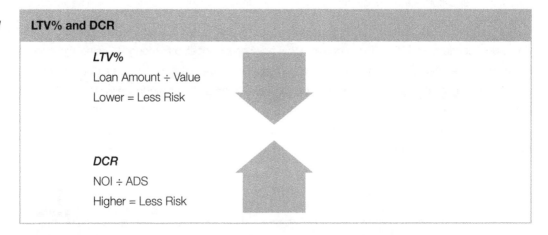

LTV% and DCR

LTV%
Loan Amount ÷ Value
Lower = Less Risk

DCR
NOI ÷ ADS
Higher = Less Risk

Loan-to-Value Ratio (LTV%)

Loan-to-Value Ratio (LTV%) is a lender's test to ensure that the loaned funds are secured by the value of the real estate. It compares the amount of the loan principal to the market value of the property.

$$\text{Loan Amount} \div \text{Value} = \text{LTV\%}$$

The lower the LTV%, the lower the risk to the lender. Most lenders specify a maximum LTV% for the loans they provide. Loan agreements in commercial loans also may require keeping a minimum LTV%. LTV% may be determined based on the bank's policy or the strength of the lender. This ratio attempts to ensure that if market values decline and default or foreclosure is necessary, the property will be worth more than the balance due on the loan.

Calculating LTV%	Example 9.2

Suppose a property's acquisition cost is $2,300,000 and it is financed with a $1,300,000 loan.

A. Calculate the LTV%.

$$\$1,300,000 \div \$2,300,000 = 0.57 = 57\%$$

The LTV% is 57% (low risk).

($1,300,000 ÷ $2,300,000 %= 56.52%)

Now suppose the same property is financed with a $2,000,000 loan.

B. Calculate the new LTV%. Which is riskier for the lender?

$$\$2,000,000 \div \$2,300,000 = 0.87 = 87\%$$

The LTV% is 87%, a higher risk for the lender.

($2,000,000 ÷ $2,300,000 %= 86.96%)

The LTV% normally declines over the life of the loan because principal payments on most mortgages reduce the outstanding loan amount and often value of the property goes up. Therefore, the lender's risk declines in the later years of the loan.

The LTV% formula can be, and often is, used in reverse to determine the maximum amount that can be borrowed. Simply multiply the lender's LTV% criteria by the value of the property. For example, on a $2 million property, an investor may want to find a lender that will loan the most possible money. If three lenders have expressed underwriting criteria of 80% LTV, 75% LTV, and 65% LTV, the maximum amount that could be borrowed from each lender, respectively, would be $1,600,000; $1,500,000; and $1,300,000.

Debt Coverage Ratio (DCR)

The Debt Coverage Ratio (DCR) compares the annual net operating income (NOI) to the annual debt service (ADS) of the loan. This ratio expresses the ability of the property to pay back the loan.

$$NOI \div ADS = DCR$$

NOI reflects income minus operating expenses. ADS includes the loan principal and interest. Thus, NOI should be greater than ADS, resulting in a ratio greater than 1. The closer the DCR is to 1, the riskier the loan. Likewise, the greater the DCR is, the safer the loan is for the lender.

Example 9.3

Calculating DCR

Suppose the NOI for a property is $235,000 and ADS payments total $165,800.

A. Calculate the DCR.

$$\$235,000 \div \$165,800 = 1.42$$

DCR is 1.42, meaning that this property's NOI is 142% of the amount necessary to cover loan payments. Thus, this would be considered a low-risk loan.

Now suppose the same property is financed with $200,000 in ADS payments.

B. Calculate the new DCR. Which is riskier for the lender?

$$\$235,000 \div \$200,000 = 1.18$$

DCR is 1.18, meaning that this property's NOI is only 118% of the amount necessary to cover loan payments. Thus, this would be considered a higher-risk loan.

The DCR formula can be inverted to determine the maximum monthly debt service. This information can then be used to determine the maximum loan amount that can be borrowed when the loan constant is known. Loan constant will be discussed later in this chapter.

Questions real estate managers may ask

. . . when considering lender tests:

- What loan-to-value rates are being required in my market?
- What trends am I seeing in my market with LTV% and DCR ratios?

LENDERS' RIGHTS

As discussed earlier, a mortgage loan is a lien on a property. Lenders have rights with regards to the lien when the property owner is unable to repay the loan or want to release a property from debt obligation.

Priority of Liens

Many different parties can have claims on the same piece of property at the same time. Thus, clarification is required as to who has the right to claim the property in case of a payment default.

When a property is encumbered by competing claims, a determination must be made regarding whose claim should be honored first. Generally, such claims are ranked in the order they are created, with the first having priority over all subsequent claims. That is the reason we refer to competing mortgage claims as a first mortgage, second mortgage, and so on. The mortgage that is created first has priority over all other mortgages, even when the loan amount may be smaller than the amount on a second mortgage, as in the case of a wraparound mortgage.

Thus, the priority of the liens arises from the chronological order of their creation.

1. Property tax (always the first priority)
2. Mortgage
3. Mechanic's lien
4. Lease

Subordination

In some circumstances, a change in the order of priority of liens may be necessary in order to obtain financing. Elevating one lien over another claim that originally had priority is called subordination.

The most typical instance in which subordination arises when a mortgage is taken on an existing property that has current tenants with previously existing leases. Because the leases are in existence before the new mortgage, the leases have chronological priority over the mortgage lien. The mortgage lender typically requests that the leases be subordinated to the mortgage lien. Each tenant is asked to agree in writing to subordinate his or her lease to the mortgage lien. If that is accomplished, the mortgage lien becomes elevated in priority above the leases, and the leases become subordinate to the mortgage lien.

The significance of this procedure arises only if a default occurs in the payment of the mortgage, foreclosure follows, and the mortgage lender takes possession of the property. If the mortgage lender has priority over the leases, the mortgage lender can evict the tenants. If the leases have priority, the mortgage lender must allow the tenants to remain, and the tenants must continue to pay their rent.

Foreclosure of Liens

When a party holds a monetary lien on a property, and the lien has not been paid as agreed, the lien holder has the right to foreclose on the property. Although the exact procedure for foreclosure differs greatly from state to state, the concept is the same.

Once a foreclosure action is instituted, notices are sent out asking every person with an interest in the property to submit his or her claim or lien. The liens are then arranged in order of priority. The property is sold at public auction to the highest bidder. From the proceeds, the liens are paid in order of priority. Once the money has been used up to pay liens, any remaining lien holders are not paid, and their liens are extinguished.

A third or fourth mortgage lien might easily not be paid in the event of a foreclosure sale because the proceeds would not be sufficient. Because a third or fourth lien holder's position is less secure, his or her risk is greater; thus, he or she will demand a higher rate of interest to reflect this greater risk.

LENDER RECOURSE

Measuring risk helps lenders avoid making bad loans. However, even with all the best risk measures in place, lenders must have ways to protect themselves if a loan does not perform as desired or becomes delinquent.

Property Workouts

When a property owner **defaults** on the terms of its mortgage the lender has the right to file a legal action to take ownership of the secured property. This is called a foreclosure action. When a loan becomes delinquent, lending institutions often must adjust their balance sheets, removing these loans from their "good" assets, and must place them into a doubtful account category. This impacts the liquidity of the lender. If they foreclose on the property, the real estate becomes an asset of the lender at its current market value, which is often lower than the original amount of the loan.

Lenders obviously are not always anxious to become property owners and sometimes would rather make arrangements with the property owner to maintain its ownership, and restructure the loan for at least a period of time. An agreement to make temporary arrangements is called a **forbearance** agreement. If the property owner meets the terms, the lender will temporarily withhold any legal action to allow the owner some time to bring the loan current. These loans are not available from all lenders. CMBS lenders are particularly difficult to negotiate with due to the securitized structure of the loans. When workout arrangements cannot be made, the lender is likely to take legal action to gain ownership of the delinquent property.

Foreclosure and Receivership

The first step a lender is likely to take in a foreclosure action is to **accelerate** the loan balance by calling the entire amount due and payable immediately. The amount due will include the delinquent mortgage payments, taxes if delinquent, and severe penalties on top of the late fees. In most states foreclosure actions take several months, and sometimes years, to complete. Bankruptcy on the part of the borrower can complicate matters further. During this period, the lender may have several remedies, including enforcing its security interest in the rents that are being collected. The matter will likely become a complicated legal proceeding.

Also during this time, lenders want to prevent the property owner from committing waste on the property, meaning they want the property kept in a reasonable state of repair and do not want the owner to take any money or property while the action is proceeding. In these circumstances the court will typically appoint a **receiver** to manage the property until the foreclosure is completed. The receiver, often an attorney appointed by the court, may hire a property management company to handle day-to-day operations. Some courts appoint a property management company as a receiver. Either way, opportunities exist for property management companies to take on these responsibilities. While they provide short-term relationships, receiverships can be profitable and place a company in a good position to be chosen to manage a property for the lender or new owner after a foreclosure is completed.

LEVERAGE POSITION

In a traditional lending scenario, the lender receives only the loan balance, no matter how high the sale price goes beyond it. The owner, or equity holder, takes the greatest risk and, therefore, ultimately expects the greatest return. While the lender's return is fixed, the equity holder considers the risks of the marketplace and looks not only at the cash flow from the investment but at the potential of the property to grow in both value and cash returns.

It is important to understand the value of real estate investments in terms of specific owner goals, one of which is generating greater return on investment through **leverage**. Leverage can be thought of as using borrowed funds. Financing allows an investor the opportunity to use borrowed money to acquire investment real estate. This may give the investor an opportunity to diversify his or her portfolio or create an opportunity to increase the rate of return on investment.

Leverage should be analyzed in terms of the impact of borrowing on the equity holder's (owner's) cash flow and return on investment, but the effectiveness of that use of borrowed money should be reevaluated at multiple points across the loan term.

Leverage may be positive or negative. When the rate of return on an investment is increased with the use of debt, the financing offers a *positive leverage* position. Conversely, when the rate of return on an investment is decreased with the use of debt, the investor has a *negative leverage* position. Leverage position is not static—it can change over time from positive to negative or negative to positive.

Financing always creates a risk for the borrower. At the extreme, the risk of borrowing funds for a property investment can result in default and foreclosure.

The leverage position can be determined by comparing three critical measures:

- Free-and-Clear Rate of Return
- Loan Constant (k%)
- Cash-on-Cash Rate of Return ($/$%)

Free-and-Clear Rate of Return

The *free-and-clear rate of return,* also known as ROI or the overall rate, measures the return potential of a property that is free of debt. This ratio compares net operating income (NOI) with the total property value. Note that for purposes of this formula, value is intended to mean the same thing as purchase price.

$$\text{NOI} \div \text{Property Value} = \text{Free-and-Clear Rate of Return}$$

Example 9.4	**Calculating the Free and Clear Rate of Return**

Consider a property in which the NOI is $235,000 and the total property value is $2,300,000.

A. Calculate the free-and-clear rate of return.

$$\$235,000 \div \$2,300,000 = 0.10 \times 100 = 10.22\%$$

($235,000 ÷ $2,300,000 %= 10.22%)

The free-and-clear rate of return for the investor is 10.22%.

Loan Constant (k%)

The *loan constant (k%)* represents the current amount paid for each dollar of borrowed funds. It is the percentage of a loan balance that is required annually to service principal and interest payments on the loan. The term "constant" refers to a constant method of calculation rather than a constant value. Because the loan constant includes both principal and interest payments, it is always higher than the loan's interest rate, except in interest-only loans, where the loan constant equals the interest rate.

Shorter-term debt has a higher constant because more principal is being paid back. Longer-term debt has a lower constant (one closer to the interest rate) because less principal is being paid off. The loan constant represents the amount to be paid for each dollar borrowed.

The equation for the loan constant relates the ADS to the original loan amount:

ADS ÷ Original Loan Amount = k%

Loan constants are used to assess the cost of borrowed funds. When shopping for a loan, the investor usually looks for the loan with the lowest constant since it will produce the lowest annual debt service and, consequently, the highest cash flow. The size of debt service has an important effect on cash flow.

The loan constant varies with interest rates and with the amortization term. For instance, for the same amortization term, the loan constant varies in the same direction as interest rates:

Interest Rate	Amortization Term	Loan Constant
4%	25 Years	6.33%
6%	25 Years	7.73%
8%	25 Years	9.26%

Assuming the same interest rate, the loan constant decreases as the amortization term increases:

Interest Rate	Amortization Term	Loan Constant
4%	20 Years	7.27%
4%	27 Years	6.06%
4%	30 Years	5.73%

A decrease in the loan constant means that the debt service increases. If the interest rate and the amortization period both increase or both decrease, the effects may vary.

Example 9.5	**Calculating the Loan Constant (k%)**

Assume a property has a loan amount of $540,000 in a given year, with an annual debt service of $78,400.

A. Calculate the loan constant (k%).

$$\$78{,}400 \div \$540{,}000 = 0.15 \times 100 = 14.52\%$$
$$(\$78{,}400 \div \$540{,}000 \% = 14.52\%)$$

k% = 14.52%

Example 9.6	**Comparing the Loan Constant**

Here are two instance in which the loan constant (k%) differs only by a single percent. Assume that the loan amount is $1million in each case:

Property 1		Property 2	
NOI	$160,000	NOI	$160,000
ADS (k% = 14%)	$140,000	ADS (k% = 14%)	$150,000
BTCF	$ 20,000	BTCF	$ 10,000

BTCF decreased by half because of the 1% rise in the loan constant.

Note that the interest rate could remain the same, but the constant could change based on the length of time on the loan.

By careful capital budgeting, which determines how much money is needed for improvements, and by shopping for interest rates, a real estate manager can sketch out the kind of financing a project needs. Using different loan constants to determine debt service shows the effect that taking debt will have on cash flow.

Cash-on-Cash Rate of Return ($/$%)

The *cash-on-cash rate of return ($/$%)* measures an investor's rate of return on the capital invested. This ratio compares the equity invested (or current investment) with the before-tax cash flow (BTCF) for one year. It is most commonly used to show year-to-year trends in performance.

$$\text{BTCF} \div \text{Initial Equity} = \text{Cash-on-Cash Rate of Return (\$/\$\%)}$$

The cash-on-cash rate of return measures a one-year return on invested dollars. It is a snapshot of performance, and thus does not consider the effects of time on the investment.

·   **TIPS**

Cash-on-cash rate of return can also be called: equity dividend rate or return on equity (ROE).

Remember that $/$ does not take future cash flows, appreciation, changes in market conditions, and so forth into consideration.

Exhibit 9.2 compares free-and-clear rates of return and cash-on-cash rates of return.

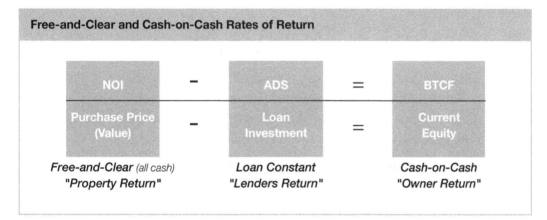

Free-and-Clear and Cash-on-Cash Rates of Return   *Exhibit 9.2*

NOI	−	ADS	=	BTCF
Purchase Price (Value)	−	Loan Investment	=	Current Equity
Free-and-Clear (all cash) "*Property Return*"		*Loan Constant* "*Lenders Return*"		*Cash-on-Cash* "*Owner Return*"

ANALYZING LEVERAGE POSITION

Comparing the free-and-clear rate of return with the loan constant (k%) will indicate whether the leverage position is positive or negative. The result of this positive or negative leverage position will be reflected in the cash-on-cash rate of return ($/$%).

Positive Leverage

When: Free-and-Clear Rate of Return > k%

Then: $/$% > Free-and-Clear Rate of Return

In this case, the cash-on-cash rate of return is greater as a result of placing debt on the property. This circumstance would indicate that the cost of debt on this property is lower than the rate of return the property can produce free and clear of debt. As a result of borrowing this "relatively cheap" money, the investor increases the actual rate of return on the property. (See Exhibit 9.3.)

Exhibit 9.3

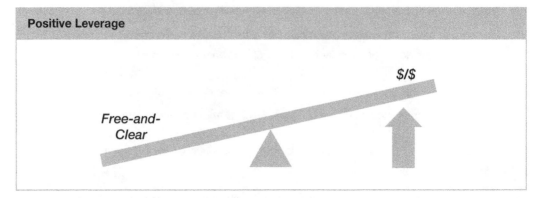

Positive Leverage

Negative Leverage

When: Free-and-Clear Rate of Return < k%

Then: $/$% < Free-and-Clear Rate of Return

In this case, cash-on-cash rate of return is less as a result of placing debt on the property. This circumstance would indicate that the cost of debt on this property is higher than the rate of return the property can produce free and clear of debt. As a result of borrowing this "relatively expensive" money, the investor decreases the actual rate of return on the property.

Even if financing a property puts it in a negative leverage position, an investor still might borrow. Borrowing may be the only way to acquire the investment if there is not enough cash to purchase the property outright. It also allows the investor to invest finite capital in more than one investment. Finally, the rate of return obtained using leverage may still be a favorable one compared to other options in the market. Negative leverage simply tells an investor to be on the lookout for more favorable financing as soon as it may be available. (See Exhibit 9.4.)

Exhibit 9.4

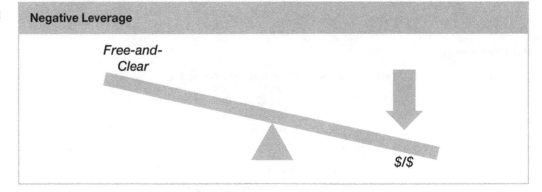

Negative Leverage

Neutral Leverage

When: Free-and-Clear Rate of Return = Loan Constant (k%)

Leverage Loan 1 *Example 9.7*

	Free-and-Clear	Financed with 30-Year, 9.25% Loan
Cost of Property	$750,000	$750,000
− Loan	−　　　0	−　600,000
= Equity	= $750,000	= $150,000
NOI	$ 83,000	$ 83,000
− ADS	−　　　0	−　59,233
= BTCF	= $ 83,000	= $ 23,767

To determine whether the leverage is positive or negative, calculate the free-and-clear rate of return, the loan constant, and cash-on-cash rate of return:

Free-and-Clear Rate of Return = NOI ÷ Value
$83,000 ÷ $750,000 = 11.07%

Loan Constant (k%) = ADS ÷ Loan Amount
$59,233 ÷ $600,000 = 9.87%

Cash-on-Cash Rate of Return ($/$%) = BTCF ÷ Initial Equity
$23,767 ÷ $150,000 = 15.84%

Free-and-Clear Rate of Return (11.07%) > k% (9.87%)
➥ Positive Leverage

Thus, $/$% (15.84%) > Free-and-Clear Rate of Return (11.07%)

Thus, the cash-on-cash rate of return will be higher if the property is financed rather than owned outright. Conversely, negative leverage occurs when the free-and-clear rate of return is lower than the loan constant.

Example 9.8

Leverage Loan 2

	Free-and-Clear	Financed with 25-Year, 11% Loan
Cost of Property	$750,000	$750,000
– Loan	– 0	– 600,000
= Equity	= $750,000	= $150,000
NOI	$83,000	$83,000
– ADS	– 0	– 70,568
= BTCF	= $83,000	= $12,432

To determine whether the leverage is positive or negative, calculate the free-and-clear rate of return, the loan constant, and cash-on-cash rate of return:

Free-and-Clear Rate of Return = NOI ÷ Value

$83,000 ÷ $750,000 = 11.07%

Loan Constant (k%) = ADS ÷ Loan Amount

$70,568 ÷ $600,000 = 11.76%

Cash-on-Cash Rate of Return ($/$%) = BTCF ÷ Initial Equity

$12,432 ÷ $150,000 = 8.29%

Free-and-Clear Rate of Return (11.07%) < k% (11.76%)

➡ *Negative Leverage*

Thus, $/$% (8.29%) < Free-and-Clear Rate of Return (11.07%)

With negative leverage, the greater the amount financed, the lower the cash-on-cash rate of return.

Calculating the Maximum Loan Amount

Once loan terms have been established, an investor may use the debt coverage ratio (DCR) in combination with the loan constant (k%) to determine the maximum loan for which the property may qualify.

$$NOI \div DCR = Maximum\ ADS$$

$$Maximum\ ADS \div k\% = Maximum\ Loan\ Amount$$

$$NOI \div (k\% \times DCR) = Maximum\ Loan\ Amount$$

A greater tolerance for risk (lower DCR) results in a potentially larger loan.

Once the maximum loan amount is calculated, it must be evaluated in light of the LTV% to determine if the property will fully qualify for that amount of borrowed funds. Remember that a borrower must meet both of the lender's underwriting ratios: LTV% and DCR.

BREAK-EVEN ANALYSES

A break-even point is the point at which sales are just sufficient to cover all obligations. For real estate, this is interpreted as an occupancy rate. By performing a break-even analysis, the real estate manager and lender are able to judge how susceptible a property is to declining rental income. The higher the break-even rate (default ratio), the more vulnerable the property is to adverse changes.

Break-even analysis can be applied to residential or commercial property:

- In the case of residential property, the occupancy rate is expressed in terms of the percentage of apartments occupied.

- In the case of commercial property, the occupancy rate is expressed in terms of percentage of square feet occupied. If the break-even occupancy rate is close to or higher than expected occupancy, it is unlikely that the property will generate a profit.

Break-even analysis can be used to determine part of the management fee as an incentive for maintaining high occupancy rates. For example, part of the fee might be a percentage of the amount generated by the property in excess of the break-even point or in excess of the amount required to earn a specified rate of return.

Minimum Break-Even Analysis

The minimum break-even point is sufficient to cover operating costs and debt service only. It is calculated as follows:

$$(Operating\ Expenses + Annual\ Debt\ Service) \div Gross\ Potential\ Income$$
$$= Minimum\ Break\text{-}Even\ Point$$

Example 9.9

Minimum Break Even Analysis

Consider a property with the following financials:

Gross Potential Income	= $685,000
Annual Operating Expenses	= $252,000
Annual Debt Service Payments	= $301,480
Expected Occupancy Rate	= 95%

A. Calculate the minimum break-even point.

($252,000 + $301,480) ÷ $685,000 = $553,480 ÷ $685,000 = 0.81 = 81%

([$252,000 + $301,480] ÷ $685,000 = $553,480 ÷ $685,000 %= 80.80%)

The minimum break-even point for the property is approximately 81% occupancy. Occupancy above this point generates profit. The expected occupancy rate is 95%.

B. Calculate the cash flow for this property if the occupancy is 95%.

(Gross Potential Income × Expected Occupancy Rate) –
Gross Potential Income × Break-Even Rate) = Cash Flow

($685,000 × 95%) – ($685,000 × 81%) = $650,750 – $554,850 = $95,900

Investor's Break-Even Analyses

The *investor's break-even point* covers an additional specified required return on the current investment.

(Operating Expenses + Annual Debt Service + Return on Current Investment)
÷ Gross Potential Income = Investor's Break-Even Point

Example 9.10

Investor's Break-Even Analyses

Consider a property with the following financials:

Gross Potential Income	= $685,000 (100% occupancy)
Annual Operating Expenses	= $252,000
Annual Debt Service Payments	= $301,480
Initial Investment	= $1,000,000
Required Return on Current Investment	= $60,000 (6%)

A. Calculate the investor's break-even point (minimum occupancy rate required in order to earn a rate of return of at least 6%).

($252,000 + $301,480 + $60,000) ÷ $685,000 = $613,480 ÷ $685,000 = 0.90 = 90%

([$252,000 + $301,480 + $60,000] ÷ $685,000 = $613,480 ÷ $685,000 %= 89.56%)

An occupancy rate of approximately 90% is required to earn a 6% return on the current investment.

. . . when considering loan analysis:

- What are the cash-on-cash and free-and-clear rate of returns telling me about the performance of the properties I manage?
- Are the properties I manage in a positive or negative leverage position?
- What are the break-even points of the properties I manage?
- How can I apply the loan analysis concepts to help me recommend leverage strategies to your owners?

REVIEW QUESTIONS

- List the five Cs of credit and, for each, identify one or two things that a lender considers.

- What are the two major ratios used by lenders to evaluate the risk associated with a potential loan?

- List the three variables that must be calculated to determine leverage positions. Explain what each measures and how they are compared to determine leverage position.

- What is the difference between the minimum break-even point and the investor's break-even point?

Time Value of Money

In order to achieve the owner's financial goals and fulfill fiduciary obligations to the client, real estate managers must understand the concept of the **time value of money (TVM).** The basic principle of TVM is this: Dollars in the future are worth less than dollars today. If money is to be received in the future, the recipient is entitled to be compensated for waiting. The amount of compensation will depend on the risk associated with the time it take to get the money.

Money is worth more today than in the future for four basic reasons:

1. Money today can be immediately spent and enjoyed.

2. Money today can be invested and earn interest.

3. Inflation diminishes the buying power of money in the future.

4. Waiting poses the risk of not receiving the money at all—accepting money today eliminates that possibility.

Imagine yourself at a family gathering. A wealthy relative wants to provide inheritances to her loved ones. She offers you $25,000 today, but if you are willing to wait until next year's gathering, she will give you $26,000. Which would you choose? What are the risks and rewards of waiting? Any number of things could occur between now and next year: There may not be a family gathering, the relative may change her mind, she may be anticipating liquidation of an asset that may not materialize, she may die without leaving your inheritance in her will. The logical choice would be to take the $25,000 today. For a premium of only $1,000 to wait a year, the risk isn't worth it.

A quick financial analysis would confirm that decision: If the $25,000 could be invested in a savings vehicle earning 5% interest, it would yield a return of $1,250 at the end of one year, more than the $1,000 the relative is offering. But what if the relative offered $200,000 next year? Or $2 million? Would you be tempted to wait? What factors would you have to consider before deciding?

Inflation is another factor that influences the time value of money. Exhibit 10.1 takes a look at what a $1,000 purchase in 2002 would cost ten years later.

Exhibit 10.1

What's Money Worth in the Future?

| $1,000 (in 2002) | Has the same buying power as | $1,280 (in 2012) |

Source: Bureau of Labor Statistics (data.bls.gov)

So, a purchase you could make for $1,000 in 2002 would cost you $1,280 in 2012 due to inflation.

Note that each year a different rate of inflation is used. The Consumer Price Index (CPI) inflation calculator uses the average CPI for the given calendar year. This data represents changes in prices of all goods and services purchased for consumption by urban households.

For the most part, the demand for goods and services is not related to the market interest rates quoted in the financial pages of newspapers, known as nominal rates. Instead, it is related to real interest rates—that is, nominal interest rates minus the expected rate of inflation. Inflation rates vary over time and can range from close to 10% as in the late 1970s to close to 2% as in the late 1990s.

Two important concepts related to TVM are **future value** and **present value.**

Future Value (FV)	Present Value (PV)
• Refers to how much an investment will be worth after a certain period of time. • Applies to savings accounts and investments. If $1,000 is placed in a savings account paying 4% interest and left there for five years, it will increase in value five years from now. More complicated examples involve real estate investments in buildings over long periods of time and at varying rates of return.	• Is how much a future sum of money is worth now. • Refers to calculating how much money must be set aside at a certain rate of interest for a future use. • Is less familiar because it involves working backwards from a future financial goal to the current value of the funds needed to meet that goal. However, this is exactly what capital budgeting entails—determining how much money to set aside now for a future purchase or major improvement to a property.

Investors in real estate use the concept of time value to find:

- PV of future income
- FV of today's investments
- Rates of return on investments
- Periodic income or payments

Because of major effects of interest rates and inflation, the FV of a mortgage differs greatly from its PV.

COMPOUNDING AND DISCOUNTING

Two fundamental questions are being considered when analyzing an investment under the TVM principle:

1. If an investment is made today, what will it be worth in the future? This is **compounding.**

2. If a payment is to be made in the future, what is it worth today? This is **discounting.**

Present value (PV) or a series of payments (PMT) are compounded over time to determine future value (FV) as shown in Exhibit 10.2. In the case of a savings account with compounding interest, payments of the interest accumulate over time to create a larger future value than the amount originally deposited. The calculations of that future value can be made using multiple tools.

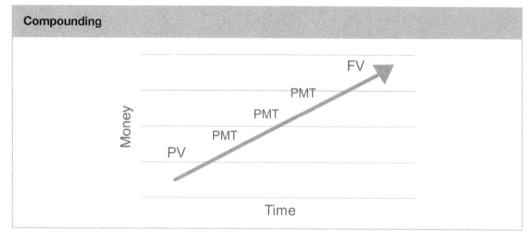

Compounding *Exhibit 10.2*

What if you know a future value but want to determine the present value? Future value (FV) or a series of payments (PMT) are discounted over time to determine present value (PV) as shown in Exhibit 10.3.

Exhibit 10.3

Discounting

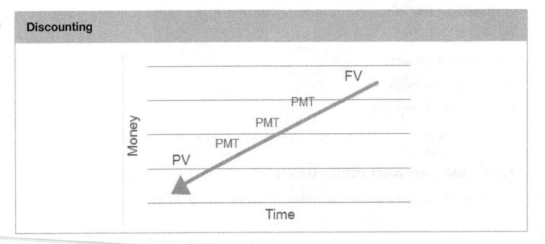

The components of the time value of money calculations may take on different meanings depending on whether money is being compounded or discounted, as shown in the following chart.

	Compounding ➚	Discounting ➘
Number of Periodic Payments (N)	Number of times the payment is made	Number of times the benefit is received
Annual Interest Rate (I/YR)	Interest rate	Discount rate
Present Value (PV)	Current amount or value balance	Current amount or value rate
Periodic Payment (PMT)	Amount of payments made	Amount of benefits received
Future Value (FV)	Future amount or loan balance	Future amount or **terminal value**

All time value of money calculations involve compounding or discounting—that is, moving amounts either forward or backward in time. Questions to consider when analyzing TVM include:

- How long is the investment period?
- When do the dollars go in or come out?
- What information do we already know?
- What is the interest or discount rate?

- How many dollars go in or come out?
- What is the periodic unit (months, years)?
- What is it we are solving for?

TVM Registers

The TVM registers in a financial calculator are used for compound-interest calculations that involve uniform cash flows or payments. These payments must occur at regular intervals. There must be at least one positive and one negative cash flow. Keep in mind that money coming in should be designated by a positive sign, and money flowing out should be designated by a negative sign.

The time value of money has six major components that can be input in different variations, depending on what is being calculated, into a financial calculator or the formula function of a financial spreadsheet:

- *Number of Payments per Year (P/YR):* Number of payments per year (P/YR) is the number of times per year that the cash flow or benefit occurs. This is typically set to one payment per year (annual payments) or 12 payments per year (monthly payments).

- *Number of Periodic Payments (N):* Number of periodic payments (N) is the number of periods or times a cash flow or benefit occurs. In the case of a loan, it is the number of times the loan payment is made.

- *Annual Interest Rate (I/YR):* Annual interest rate (I/YR) represents the rate of return, or the discount rate, on an investment. In the case of a loan, it is the interest rate charged on the loan.

- *Present Value (PV):* Present value (PV) refers to the present value of future benefits. It can be the present value of an investment, or in the case of a loan, the original or current loan balance. Present value is a single, lump-sum amount.

- *Periodic Payment (PMT):* Periodic payment (PMT) is an equal cash flow or benefit that is paid more than once. In the case of a loan, it is the payment on the loan.

- *Future Value (FV):* Future value (FV) refers to the value in the future of a benefit or series of benefits received over time. It can be thought of as a property's *terminal value,* or in the case of a loan, a balloon payment. Future value is a single, lump-sum payment or benefit.

T-BARS AND TIMELINES

The time frames in which money is invested and returned are critical to accurate calculations. The time when a property is valued is **time point zero.** Time point zero can be established any time that an investor, real estate manager, or other analyst looks at future alternatives for an investment. It could take place each year when a budget is prepared, or it could happen when considering refinancing, major capital improvements, or a change in management. The essential point is that investment alternatives are considered to move forward from the current equity position, not from the equity position at an earlier time of ownership.

T-bars and timelines are two common methods used to visualize the flow of cash over periods of time.

T-bars utilize a vertical column to provide a visual representation of the investment questions. Formatting in a vertical manner aligns more clearly with data entered into spreadsheets and financial calculators. Time periods, starting with time point zero, are displayed on the left side of the t-bar and corresponding cash inflows and outflows on the right as shown here:

N	$
0	$ in
1	$ in/(out)
2	$ in/(out)
3	$ in/(out)
5	$ in/(out)

On a t-bar, when an owner pays out money, such as initial investment or negative cash flow, the number is represented as a negative. When funds are received, the number is positive. The term $ in/(out) used in a t-bar can be any type of cash inflow or outflow, including NOI, before-tax cash flow, or proceeds of a sale, depending on the scope of the analysis. Remember that when the investor puts money into the investment—or realizes a negative cash flow—the number is represented as a negative.

Here is an example of how a t-bar can be used:

N	$
0	(PV)
1	PMT
2	PMT
3	PMT . .
.	.
.	.
N	PMT + FV (terminal value)

For example, if a property had an income stream of $10,000 in the first three years and $15,000 in years four and five, and was sold at the end of year five for $600,000, this is what the T-bar would look like:

N	$
0	(PV)
1	10,000
2	10,000
3	10,000
4	15,000
5	15,000 + 600,000 = 615,000

Timelines use a horizontal line to display the same components.

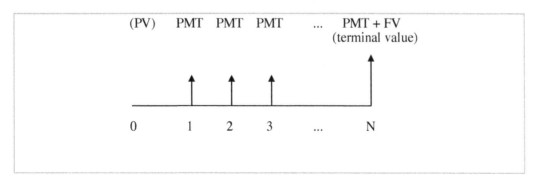

For example:

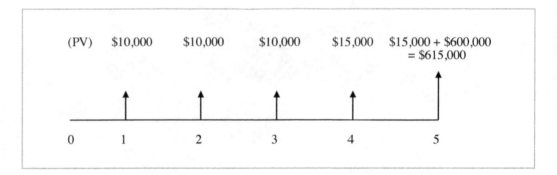

Or:

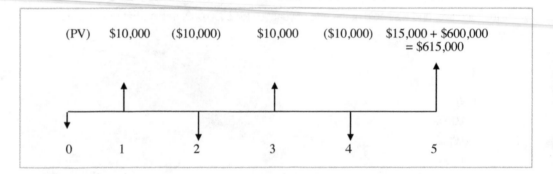

While the holding period and future projections can be represented on horizontal timelines, as has been shown here, the industry standard is to represent the timeline vertically, using the t-bar.

SIX FUNCTIONS OF A DOLLAR

There are six compound interest functions, known as six functions of a dollar, which are used to solve TVM problems.

Function	Description and Use
Future Value of One	*How much will a single amount today be worth at some time in the future?* This function can be useful in calculating investments such as savings accounts and CDs, but it can also be useful for any investment where the cash flows are stable and no funds are withdrawn from the investment until the ultimate sale.
Present Value of One	*How much is a single future amount worth today?* In real estate, this function might be used where an investment is held strictly for its **appreciation** value, such a piece of raw land that is expected to appreciate as its development potential increases.
Present Value of One per Period	*How much is a future series of equal periodic payments worth today?* The present value of one per period, or depositing the same amount in an investment on a regular basis over a given period of time, is sometimes called an **annuity**. Lease payments take on characteristics of an *annuity,* as would a savings account into which a real estate manager deposited a fixed sum every year for a reserve account.
Future Value of One per Period	*How much will a series of equal periodic payments be worth at some time in the future?* This function takes the future value of one and extends it to many payments.
Sinking Fund Factor	*How much must be set aside periodically to accumulate a certain future value?* This function is a most useful tool for real estate managers budgeting for reserve accounts.
Installment to Amortize One	*What is the equal periodic payment necessary to pay off a loan?* Most real estate loans are mortgages that are paid back through a process called amortization, in which periodic payment is calculated so that enough is collected each period to pay both the entire interest and principle balance by the end of the loan.

For each of these functions, there are several options available for solving the TVM. This publication focuses on four common methods:

- Mathematical formula

- Financial tables (3%, 5%, and 10% Annual Compound Interest Tables can be found in the Appendix of this book. The complete set of tables is available in *Ellwood Tables for Real Estate Appraising and Financing* by L. V. Ellwood, 1977, published for American Institute of Real Estate Appraisers by Ballinger Publishing Company.)

- Show more

- Show less

- Spreadsheet functions, such as a Microsoft® Excel spreadsheet

- Financial calculators, handheld and online, are readily available

The first step in solving any TVM problem is to identify the known variables and the variable you are seeking to identify. Keep in mind that the variables are identified as follows:

Interest	= i
Number of Periods	= n
Present Value	= PV
Future Value	= FV
Payment	= PMT

Then, it is often useful to convert the TVM problem to a t-bar to visualize the problem.

Solving for Future Value of One

An analyst can use any of the methods listed previously to solve for FV. Imagine someone depositing $10,000 in a savings account that accumulates interest at 3% for five years. What will be the value of $10,000 investment at the end of the five years?

Known variables:

i = 3% (or 0.03)

n = 5

PV = $10,000

What are you solving for?

The variable you are solving for is the value of the investment after five years, or the FV.

The initial investment and cash flows can be either positive or negative numbers, depending on your perspective. For our purposes—taking the perspective of the investor—when money is placed into a project, it is represented as a negative number. (Think of it as money coming out of the investor's pocket and going into the investment.)

T-bar:

It may be helpful to use a t-bar to visualize the problem.

N	$
0	(PV) ($10,000)
1	0
2	0
3	0
4	0
5	0 +FV

Remember that time point zero is the time the analysis takes place, and all other times on the t-bar are relative to that point in time. In this calculation, funds are deposited at time point zero, and interest is compounded on the investment. Since it is compounded, no cash is received by the investor until the funds are withdrawn at the end of the five years.

Mathematical Formula

There is a mathematical formula to calculate each of the six functions of a dollar. While most people rely on calculators and tools to solve the TVM problems, it is important to understand how the variables are derived. The mathematical formula for FV is:

$$FV = PV\,(1 + i)^n$$

Substituting numbers for the variables in this example creates the following algebraic problem:

$$FV = 10{,}000 \times (1{+}0.3)^5 = 1.03 \times 1.03 \times 1.03 \times 1.03 \times 1.03 \times 10{,}000 = \$11{,}593 \text{ (rounded)}$$

Financial Analysis Tables

There are many tools to help solve the TVM problems so that one does not have to rely on mathematical formulas to derive the unknown variables. Financial analysis tables are one tool that perform some of the math for you already. There is a table to help solve for each of the six functions of a dollar. To solve for our current problem using a financial analysis table, find the 3% annual interest rate table and follow down to the *n* row, in this case 5, and then over to the FV row to find the FV of 1.159 (rounded). Multiply this number by the initial investment (that is, the PV) of $10,000 to get $11,593 (rounded).

Microsoft® Excel and Other Spreadsheets

Problems may also be solved using the formula bar of a spreadsheet. In Microsoft® Excel, for example, select Formula, then select Financial, then select FV, and the Function Argument window is displayed. Enter the known variables in the fields to calculate the FV:

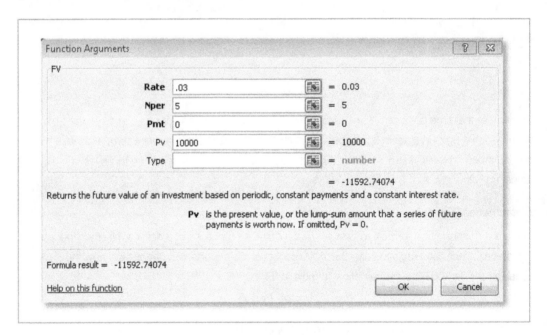

For the FV argument:

- Rate is the interest rate for period expressed as a decimal. In this case, the rate is 3% expressed as a decimal (0.03).

- Nper is the number of compounding periods, which in this case is 5.

- Pmt is the payment made each period. In this case, the cash to be taken out of the investment is 0.

- PV is the present value. In this case, it is the initial investment of $10,000.

With these values entered in the fields, the FV is $11,592.74, which can be rounded to $11,593.

Financial Calculators

Despite the utility and popularity of computers and spreadsheets, many analysts still favor using a financial calculator for quick analysis, especially in situations where it is impractical to use a laptop or desktop computer. As mentioned, there are a number of financial calculators available on the market today, including many online calculators.

For example, to solve our problem using the HP10bll calculator, one would enter the following keystrokes:

Keystrokes	HP10bll Display
1 [SHIFT] [P/YR]	1.00
[SHIFT] [C ALL]	1 P_Yr 0.00
5 [N]	5.00
3 [I/YR]	3.00
10,000 [+/–] [PV]	– 10,000.00
[FV]	11,592.74

Solving for Present Value of One

The example used for finding the future value of one can also be used in reverse to determine the present value of a future payment. Restructuring the previous example, what if an investor knows he or she would receive $11,593 at the end of five years? How much is the investment worth today if the investor's discount rate is 3%? We already know the answer is $10,000, but it is instructive to show how the future value is discounted to identify a present value.

Known variables:

i = 3% (or 0.03)

n = 5

FV = $11,593

What are you solving for?

The variable you are solving for is the value of the initial investment, or PV.

T-bar:

N	$
0	(PV) (0)
1	0
2	0
3	0
4	0
5	0 + 11,593

Mathematical Formula

$$PV = \frac{FV}{(1+i)^n}$$

$$PV = 11{,}593 \times [1 \div (1 + 0.03)^5 = 1 \div (1.03 \times 1.03 \times 1.03 \times 1.03 \times 1.03)]$$

$$= 11{,}593 \times 0.8626 = 10{,}000 \text{ present value}$$

Financial Analysis Table

Just as the tables can be used to solve for future value, they can be used to find present value. By finding the 3% interest rate per year table and following the column down to the number of years (5) and then over to the present value of one column, one can find the present value factor of 0.8626 (rounded). Again, multiplying this by $11,593 results in $10,000 (rounded).

Microsoft® Excel

In Excel, select Formula, Financial, PV, and then enter the known variables in the fields to solve for PV.

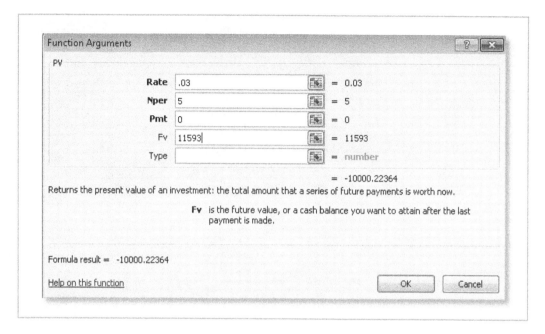

The fields for PV are similar to those in the FV argument; however, since you are solving for PV, you have an FV, or future value, field to complete. After entering all the variables for our example, the answer is $10,000.

Each method described for determining FV and PV can also be used to determine the other functions of a dollar. The following examples show how to solve each function using one or more of the methods available.

Solving for Present Value of One per Period

Consider a property that is leased for annual payments of $10,000 per year for five years. To find the present value of the investment, the sums received must be discounted for the time value of money. A discount rate must be selected based on the risk/return decisions of the investor. For this example, interest will be 10%.

Known variables:

i = 10% (or 0.10)

n = 5

PMT = $10,000

What are you solving for?

What an investor must pay today for the promise of receiving $10,000 each year for five years from the tenant.

T-bar:

N	$
0	(PV)
1	10,000
2	10,000
3	10,000
4	10,000
5	10,000

Mathematical Formula

$$PV = PMT \left[\frac{1 - \frac{1}{(1+i)^n}}{i} \right]$$

Microsoft® Excel

Select Formula, Financial, PV, and enter the known variables of rate, Nper, and Pmt:

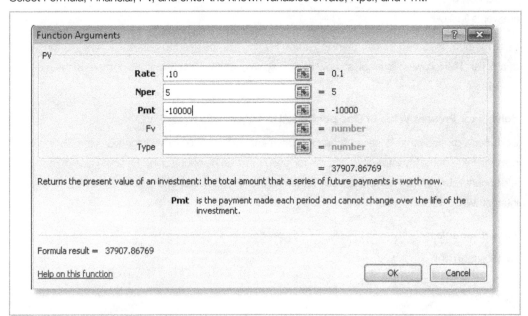

The spreadsheet's financial PV function returns the result of $37,908 (rounded).

Note that the payment is entered as a negative number in this example because it represents money that the tenant would pay—an outgoing cash flow.

About Calculating Annuities

An annuity is a series of constant cash payments made over a continuous period. A car loan or a mortgage is an example of an annuity. When calculating annuities, it's important to be consistent about the units used to specify rate and number of payment periods. If you make monthly payments on a four-year loan at 12% annual interest, use 12% ÷ 12 for rate and 4 × 12 for number of payment periods. In annuity functions:

- Cash you pay out, such as deposit to savings, is represented by a negative number.
- Cash you receive, such as a dividend check, is represented by a positive number.

For example, a $1,000 deposit to the bank would be entered as –$1,000 if you are the depositor and as $1,000 if you are the bank. Spreadsheet formulas and financial calculators solve for one financial argument in terms of the others.

Solving for Future Value of One per Period

Consider the future value of equal payments of $10,000 for five years at 10% interest.

Known variables:

i = 10% (or .10)
n = 5
PMT = $10,000

What are you solving for?

What the future value of these equal payments will be in five years.

Mathematical Formula

The formula is the inverse of the present value of one per period.

$$FV = PMT \left[\frac{(1 + i)^n - 1}{i} \right]$$

Financial Spreadsheet or Calculator

Entering the variables into a financial spreadsheet or calculator, the future value is $61,051 (rounded).

Sinking Fund Factor

Imagine that a condominium association reserve study has indicated that roof replacement, at a future cost of $35,000, will be needed in five years. The association wants to put money away every year so that it has the needed funds five years from now. The association earns 5% interest on its investments.

Known variables:

$i = 5\%$ (or 0.05)

$n = 5$

FV = $35,000

What are you solving for?

How much money must be deposited (PMT) each year to have $35,000 when it is needed in five years.

T-bar:

A t-bar is helpful in visualizing this problem.

N	$
0	(PV) $0
1	PMT
2	PMT
3	PMT
4	PMT
5	$35,000

Mathematical Formula

$$PMT = FV \left[\frac{i}{(1 + i)^n - 1} \right]$$

Financial Spreadsheet or Calculator

Entering the variables into a financial calculator or spreadsheet, the result of the calculation is $6,334 (rounded). Therefore, the association must deposit $6,334 each year in order to have $35,000 five years from now.

Solving for Installment to Amortize One

Consider a loan of $100,000 at 5% interest in which the borrower makes annual payments for five years. As noted in the discussion on leverage, every payment must pay all the interest due on the loan, plus part of the principal. As the loan matures, the amount of interest is reduced, but the payment stays the same, so more of the payment is applied to the principal until the balance is paid off. Calculation of mortgages and loans is addressed thoroughly in other chapters, but for this example, an annual loan payment will be calculated

Known variables:

i = 5% (or 0.05)

n = 5

PV = $100,000

What are you solving for?

What would the annual payment be on this loan?

T-bar:

N	$
0	$100,000 (PV)
1	(PMT)
2	(PMT)
3	(PMT)
4	(PMT)
5	(PMT) + FV = 0

Mathematical Formula

$$PMT = PV \left[\frac{i(1+i)^n}{(1+i)^n - 1} \right]$$

Financial Spreadsheet or Calculator

Entering the variables into a financial spreadsheet or calculator, the resulting annual payment would be $23,097 (rounded). This is what it would look like if entered into a spreadsheet's formula function:

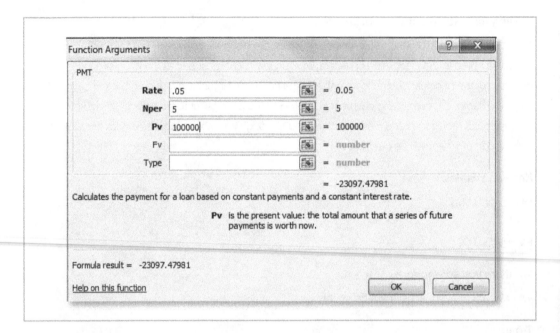

Note that the solution is displayed as a negative since the example takes the property owner/investor perspective.

The concepts underlying the time value of money are very useful both in calculations performed routinely by real estate managers and in showing the power of compounding and discounting. The examples here have isolated certain variables for the purpose of illustration. Some variants that make the concepts even more useful include allowances for cash flows to take place at the beginning or the end of a period and breaking payments down into periodic installments.

MONTHLY INSTALLMENTS AND CASH FLOW TIMING

The TVM calculation methods can be confusing when used with cash flow periods other than annual as well as when funds are received at the beginning of a compounding period rather than the end. However, in actual practice, mortgage payments are made at the end of each period, while rents are paid at the beginning. Both are usually paid monthly rather than annually. Some minor adjustments to the tools explained in this chapter are needed to calculate these elements effectively.

To illustrate the effects of such variables, consider one of the earlier examples: the present value of one per period in which $10,000 was to be deposited into an account annually. Recall the t-bar where:

$i = 10\%$

$n = 5$

PMT = $10,000

N	$
0	(PV)
1	10,000
2	10,000
3	10,000
4	10,000
5	10,000

Using the financial analysis tables, the problem would be solved using the $n = 5$ factor and the 10% interest factor. What changes if payments are made monthly instead of once a year? The payment is then 1/12 of $10,000, or $834 per month, and the payments take place over 60 months. The new t-bar looks like this:

N	$
0	(PV)
1	834
2	834
3	834
.	.
.	.
.	.
60	834

Intuitively, it might appear that all one must do is follow the financial table to $n = 60$ and multiply by that factor, which is 9.967157. The resulting calculation would be $8,312. Given that annual payments returned a value of over $37,000, logic indicates something is wrong with this calculation method.

The problem is that the 10% n factor in the financial table assumes 10% when only one payment is made per year, so the calculation just made would be discounting for 60 years rather than five. The formula must be adjusted to allow for 12 compounding periods per year: 0.10/12, or 0.0083 per month. The adjustment is easy using a financial calculator. The payments per year function must be changed to 12. Entering 60 compounding periods will then provide a solution for five years with monthly (60) payments rather than 60 years of payments. The new result is $39,252—a much more expected solution.

Using the same example for rent payments, valuation of the lease payments would follow the same t-bar, except that the compounding must be adjusted to the beginning of the month. On the financial calculator this is easily done by changing the timing of the compounding periods. The difference is slight, but it is important for an accurate calculation. When using the financial tables, after making adjustments for compounding periods and interest, simply subtract one compounding period to arrive at a solution for payments at the beginning of the period.

CREATING AMORTIZATION SCHEDULES

The financial calculators, spreadsheet, and various other amortization schedule tools can be used to create amortization schedules. Remember, amortization is the process of paying off the principal of a loan as part of loan payments. As discussed in the previous section, principal can be amortized over the term of a loan, repaid at the end of the loan term, or some combination of payment can be used.

An amortization schedule displays the amount of principal paid, the amount of interest paid, and the loan balance after each period of the loan as shown here:

Years (Months)	Principal	Interest	Balance
1 (1–12)	$43,630.46	$117,029.38	$1,276,369.54
2 (13–24)	47,723.31	112,936.53	1,228,646.23
3 (25–36)	52,200.05	108,459.79	1,176,446.18
4 (37–48)	57,096.81	103,563.03	1,119,349.37
5 (49–60)	62,452.88	98,206.96	1,056,896.48

. . . when considering the time value of money concept:

- What role does the diminished value of money over time play in my business dealings?

- Would it be wiser to offer rent concessions at the beginning or at the end of a lease term?

Questions
real estate
managers
may ask

REVIEW QUESTIONS

- What are the basic reasons that money is worth more today than in the future?

- Explain the difference between future value and present value.

- What are the five major components of the time value of money (TVM)?

- Describe the difference between compounding and discounting.

- What are two common methods used to visualize the flow of cash over periods of time?

- List the six compounding and discounting functions (six functions of the dollar) and explain how they are used.

Measuring the Performance of Properties

As mentioned previously, even the simplest forms of investment involve some risk. The ways in which an investor and the current marketplace view risk is a prime factor in determining an investment's potential return and in valuing it as a whole. An investor's risk tolerance will influence the properties that attract her or his attention for investment potential (though real estate investment in general requires a higher level of risk tolerance than many other investment forms). When the time value of money concept is applied to measure investment return, the owner's discount rate and market discount rate are reflective of the risk tolerance of the owner and the market respectively.

Consider two potential investment properties: The first is a retail building leased to a single tenant on a long-term triple-net lease (all expenses are paid by the tenant). The tenant is a national drugstore chain with excellent credit and an excellent track record. The property will provide the owner a 7% return on investment for at least the next 15 years. The second property is a small retail strip center with two strong **anchors** and a mix of smaller neighborhood retailers. It maintains good occupancy and is considered stable. Projections for this property would yield the owner a 25% return the first year, and the potential for future growth could increase the return dramatically.

Assume further that the cash down payment for each of these properties is $200,000. What are the risk factors associated with each potential investment? The drugstore is a relatively safe investment. Risks would relate mostly to the financial strength of the single tenant and its ability to pay rent for the lease term. Liquidation of the property at the end of the lease might be a concern, but that is 15 years away. If the tenant renews the lease, the alternative use for the property is even more years away, but the likelihood of a higher return is probably slim.

The retail strip center also carries risk. Small neighborhood retailers may be stable tenants, but they also may struggle when the economy is weak, increasing the risk of vacancy. The anchor tenants may go bankrupt or have leases that allow them to close a store. Even though they would still have to continue paying rent if an anchor closed, the smaller tenants depend on the traffic generated by the anchors. If an anchor left, the potential for failure among the smaller tenants would increase. This investment obviously has a greater potential for failure, so it is priced to compensate the investor for the additional risk.

Pricing for the risk and the willingness to take the risk will be determined by the investor's risk tolerance. All investors weigh risk on their own terms, which may include the significance of an investment in their portfolio. Some investors will consider the percentage of the worth of their portfolio that goes into an investment. In these retail examples, an investor with a net worth of $20 million might be willing to risk $200,000 for a higher **upside potential** and would purchase the retail strip center. On the other hand, an investor with a net worth of $2 million is more likely to opt for the safer investment, since it will represent a larger portion of the portfolio.

In this example, management is another factor to consider. The triple-net lease requires very little in the way of management, while the retail strip center is very intense from a management perspective. Many investors seek to hold a **balanced portfolio** that consists of a variety of properties and risk levels, the intent being that the "safe" investments will provide returns only as expected and some of the higher-risk ones will be more financially successful, resulting in a higher overall return for the portfolio.

Risk is assessed before a real estate investment is made through forecasting and pro forma analysis. The actual operations of the property and its ultimate performance may or may not meet the forecast expectations. Any number of opportunities can be exploited during the life of an investment, and an equal number of unforeseen circumstances may present themselves. Real estate is never considered a low-risk investment, so while an analysis of just how much risk exists is important, successful operation is critical. Professional management puts the odds in the favor of the investor and helps assure the maximum return possible. It is also the only way the investor can continue to focus on his or her entire portfolio of investments. Real estate investment requires specialized knowledge; hiring a professional real estate manager keeps the investor from getting bogged down in daily operations. Professional real estate managers are also well positioned to take advantage of opportunities for the owner and to guard against unforeseen negative factors.

Before an investor makes a purchase, the real estate manager should reasonably assess the owner's goals in terms of return potential. The ability to analyze investment proposals and assess whether the returns anticipated are reasonably realistic is another benefit of having a professional real estate manager on the team.

The real estate manager evaluates a specific set of factors in assessing the level of risk—the possibility of losing either the principal invested and/or the potential income from an investment—in any given investment proposal. These factors include:

- **Liquidity:** The ability to convert an asset to cash quickly without loss of principal. A savings account, for example, is highly liquid. A valuable painting, by contract, is less liquid because it takes longer to convert to cash at full value. Real estate is considered to have low liquidity because of the time it takes to sell property and the unpredictability of market value at the time of sale.

- **Marketability:** The ability to convert an asset to cash quickly irrespective of price. For example, stocks can be sold any time on an organized exchange at the prevailing market value, which may, however, result in a loss of value at the time of sale.

- **Leverage:** The use of borrowed funds to finance a portion of the purchase price of an investment. The ratio of borrowed funds to total purchase price is known as the loan-to-value ratio. The higher the ratio, the greater the amount of leverage. (Note that this is different from positive or negative leverage.) Real estate transactions can be more highly leveraged (paid for with borrowed funds) than most other types of investments.

- **Management:** The cost of monitoring an investment. There are two types of investment management. Asset management involves monitoring the financial performance of an investment and making changes as needed. Property management, which is exclusive to real estate investment, involves the overall day-to-day operation of the property and the physical maintenance of the buildings. Real estate management companies often have staff members who serve both roles. In a competitive environment, more real estate management companies are offering both services as part of their proposals to owners (to the extent that the line between asset and property management is often blurred).

- **Tax Impact:** The effect of federal income tax laws (governing, for example, capital gains taxes, tax credits, income taxes, and tax deferments) on the income, profits, or losses from an investment.

- **Rate of return (yield):** The percentage return on each dollar invested for each period it is invested. As a measure of investment performance, rates of return are useful for comparing investment alternatives. They can be estimated on either a before-tax or an after-tax basis.

- **Economic factors:** Elements of the economy (including inflation and deflation, prevailing interest rates, and money supply) that affect investment value and are subject to change over the life of an investment. The longer funds are left in an investment, the more difficult these factors may be to predict. They are major factors in analysis of returns and the time value of money.

Additional general concepts already described that impact every investment are the time value of money (TVM), compounding, and discounting.

The risk factors outlined here may be determined by analysis of market forces or they may be specified by the investor. While other disciplines in real estate analysis may take each factor into consideration separately, real estate managers are more likely to analyze risk using a market-derived analysis. Cap rates (see Chapter 12: Property Valuation), for example, are a measure of risk associated with an investment. One way to measure market value by the income approach to value uses the market-derived cap rate and applies it to a stabilized NOI for a property. While the cap rate in theory includes each of the factors above, only a total cap rate found in the market will be used in this publication for analysis.

MEASURING INVESTMENT RETURN

Individual investors may have specific criteria for investment return on their cash equity. Again, each investor may weigh the factors affecting risk separately or may use the returns typical in the market. For an investor who chooses a discount rate based on personal investment needs, the resulting analysis will be an investment value. When equity returns are determined by analysis of typical investment objectives of property buyers, the result will more likely reflect a market value.

Four common calculations are used to measure investment return. The most significant test(s) will vary in each situation based on the individual investor's goals for the asset. For example, if an owner is looking for a short-term gain, cash-on-cash return will take precedence. If the owner is looking for a longer-term income, measures that account for the entire holding period, net present value and *internal rate of return,* will be more important.

Test One: Cash-on-Cash Rate of Return

Cash-on-cash rate of return ($/$%) measures an investor's rate of return on the initial or current investment of equity. This ratio compares the cash invested in a property (equity) with the before-tax cash flow (BTCF) from one year.

$$BTCF \div Current\ Equity = Cash\text{-}on\text{-}Cash\ Rate\ of\ Return\ (\$/\$\%)$$

The cash-on-cash rate of return measures a one-year return on invested dollars. It is a single-year "snapshot" of performance, and thus does not consider the effects of time on the investment. This test is most commonly used to show year-to-year trends in performance.

Test One: Cash-on-Cash Rate of Return

Example 11.1

Year 1 BTCF is $25,000 and the owner's equity is $345,000. What is the cash-on-cash rate of return for Year 1?

$$\$25{,}000 \div \$345{,}000 = 7.25\%$$

Test Two: Value Enhancement

Value enhancement is the expected value at the end of the holding period less the initial value of the investment and the cost of capital improvements. It is a partial measurement of investment return over two periods of time—acquisition and disposition, or the end of the holding period. Though it measures what occurred over a holding period, it does not take into account the effect of time by discounting future value. Also, there may be costs of acquisition and costs of sale that some investors will take into account.

Value at End of Holding Period

– Value at Beginning of Holding Period

– Cost of Capital Improvements
_____

Value Enhancement

Test Two: Value Enhancement

Example 11.2

A property's purchase price was $2,000,000. At the end of the holding period it sold for $3,900,000. During the hold, a $600,000 common area renovation was done. What is the value enhancement?

$$\begin{array}{r}
\$3{,}900{,}000 \\
-\quad 2{,}000{,}000 \\
-\quad\ \ 600{,}000 \\
\hline
\$1{,}300{,}000
\end{array}$$

Test Three: Net Present Value (NPV)

Net Present Value (NPV) is the difference between the cost of an investment and the discounted present value (PV) of all anticipated future fiscal benefits of that investment. Recall that NPV was used previously to calculate present market value.

The PV of an investment is the maximum amount an investor should pay for the investment. It can be used to measure an asking price of a property with an investor's offering price.

NPV is the same analysis, but this time the investment cost is subtracted from the PV of the cash flows. If the difference is greater than zero, a net gain will be realized from the investment and an investor will have exceeded the anticipated rate of return (discount rate). NPV can be used to compare alternative investments and rank them in order of desirability.

NPV is calculated by subtracting the present value of the capital outlay from the present value of the expected returns. NPV is most useful when the required rate of return is already known. A positive NPV means that the PV exceeds cost; in other words, the investment will earn more than the minimum acceptable return. While a negative NPV means that the PV is less than cost, meaning the investment will earn less than the minimum acceptable return. (See Exhibit 11.1.)

Exhibit 11.1   **NPV Impact on PV**

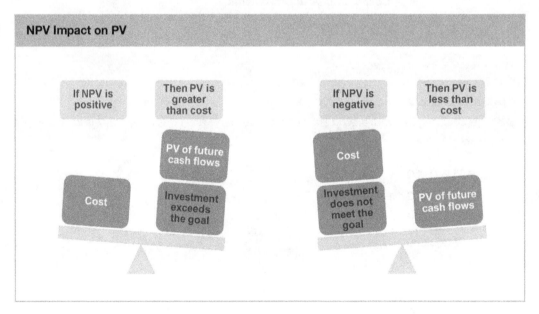

An NPV of zero means that the goal was exactly achieved. (See Exhibit 11.2.)

Test Three: Net Present Value (NPV)

Example 11.3

An investor buys a small building for $100,000 cash and leases it for the following net rent payments over a four-year holding period:

Year 1	$10,000
Year 2	$11,000
Year 3	$12,000
Year 4	$13,000

Net sales proceeds at the end of Year 4 are estimated to be $190,000. Owner's required return is 10%. What is the NPV of this investment?

N	$
0	(100,000)
1	10,000
2	11,000
3	12,000
4	13,000 + 190,000

When you input the above variables into a financial calculator or spreadsheet, NPV = $65,849.33.

Test Four: Internal Rate of Return (IRR)

What if an investor does not have a required rate of return in mind? In such a situation, using the IRR will be effective in evaluating an investment. IRR is defined as the rate of return that equates the present value of the expected future cash flows to the initial capital invested. The IRR is also the rate of return that results in an NPV of zero.

IRR is a calculation that can be applied to even or uneven cash flows. The same basic equation is used for both NPV and IRR, but in each case, a different question is being asked and answered. Like NPV, IRR calculations require a projected sale at the end of the holding period. Even if the owner has no plans to sell the property, this calculation must be included.

Example 11.4

Test Four: Internal Rate of Return (IRR)

Recall from the previous example that NPV was $65,849. The NPV calculation told us that we exceeded the owner's required return of 10%. But what rate of return did the owner achieve? Calculate IRR to find out.

N	$
0	(100,000)
1	10,000
2	11,000
3	12,000
4	13,000 + 190,000

By solving for IRR using these variables, we determine that the owner's actual return is 26.49%.

The Relationship between NPV and IRR

When both NPV and IRR are calculated, comparisons can be made to determine how an investment is performing.

A positive NPV means that IRR is greater than the owner's required rate of return (discount rate). This means that the investment exceeds expectations. A negative NPV means that IRR is less than the owner's required rate. This means that the investment does not meet expectations. (See Exhibit 11.3.) When NPV is zero, IRR will equal the owner's required rate of return.

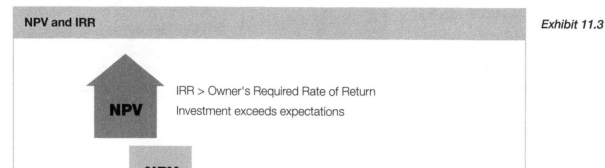

IRR > Owner's Required Rate of Return
Investment exceeds expectations

IRR > Owner's Required Rate of Return
Investment does not meet expectations

Modified Internal Rate of Return (MIRR)

IRR is perhaps the most popular measure of yield or return in analyzing income-producing real estate, yet it has some inherent shortcomings:

- *Multiple Rates of Return.* In most cases, there is only one IRR for a series of cash flows. However, when you have more than one change of sign in a series of cash flows (including the initial investment as one of the cash flows) then the math behind IRR may produce more than one result.

- *Assumed Reinvestment Rate.* IRR is the internal rate of return on capital within an investment. No mention has been made of a rate of return on cash flows withdrawn from the investment. There is an implicit assumption that the cash proceeds from the investment can be reinvested at the calculated IRR, and this may not always be true.

Similarly, if an investment generates negative cash flows, then the investment may potentially need to be funded from sources outside of the investment and funds will have to be borrowed at a rate external to the investment. In those cases, negative cash flows should be discounted at a rate representing the cost of borrowed funds.

Both of these concerns can be accommodated by using a technique known as Modified Internal Rate of Return (MIRR). MIRR discounts all negative cash flows to day one at a "safe rate" representing the cost of borrowed funds. Positive cash flows are compounded forward to the end of the holding period at a "reinvestment rate" that is realistic for market conditions. It is up to the analyst, however, to specify the safe and reinvestment rates.

Despite the many technical problems associated with its use, IRR generally is considered the standard measure of return and is used predominately by the real estate investment community.

Questions
real estate managers may ask

. . . when considering investment return:

- Which test(s) of investment return would be most applicable for the properties I manage given the goals of my owners?

· ·

REVIEW QUESTIONS

- What seven factors does the real estate manager consider in evaluating the level of risk in any given investment proposal? Define each.
- What are the four tests used to measure investment return? Explain what each test measures.
- When NPV is positive, what does this indicate?
- When NPV is negative, what does this indicate?
- When NPV equals zero, what does this indicate?

Property Valuation

In a sense, all of real estate finance is a study of valuation—how much a property is worth. The single most important contribution that a real estate manager makes is to build value for an investor. Consider a few of the ways a real estate manager influences the value of a property through daily work:

- Analyzes the competitive rental market to determine optimum gross potential rent (GPR)

- Negotiates with vendors to find the best combination of quality and price for goods and services

- Pays invoices promptly and takes advantage of discounts

- Enforces leases and collects all fees for late payments

- Monitors the financial markets and recommends refinancing when appropriate

- Maintains a priority list of capital expenses for future owner investment

In addition to affecting actual value, real estate and property managers can directly impact the perception of value. A person who passes by a well-maintained property will notice the **curb appeal** and perceive the property as more desirable and having higher value than one that is run down. A property with high occupancy and many vehicles in its parking structure will create a perception of success compared with one with weeds growing out of cracks in an empty parking lot.

While the perception of value is an important consideration in marketing a property, the investment community evaluates many more criteria. Much of this chapter addresses value from the perspective of the owner/investor in commercial real estate. Real estate managers are not appraisers, who estimate value as their primary profession, but to communicate effectively with various real estate specialists they need to understand some of the considerations appraisers include in their valuation estimates, so that they help owner achieve his or her goals for the property. A firm understanding of valuation is also essential to working with commercial real estate brokers and mortgage professionals.

PRINCIPLES OF LAND ECONOMICS

The theory surrounding valuation of real property is founded in the principles of **land economics,** the study of the geographic, environmental, legal, economic, and social aspects of the primary units of production addressed in macroeconomics—land, labor, capital, and entrepreneurship. In reality, all four units of production are associated with the valuation of real estate, but land provides the location for the income-generating activity.

Land economics, specifically urban land economics, is a major field of study and research at prestigious universities worldwide, including the University of Wisconsin–Madison, the University of California–Berkeley, the University of Pennsylvania's Wharton School of Business, and the London School of Economics.

Economists link value to the interaction of supply and demand. One significant feature of real estate that influences demand is the principle of scarcity, or a limited supply. While scarcity does not create real estate value *per se,* it is the limited supply of land that makes it unique. Real estate exists on the planet only where it is located now. It cannot be moved, whether it is vacant or developed with buildings. Two buildings of equal size and utility on different pieces of land may have considerably different values. Location is not the only factor in a real estate investment decision, but it is a significant one.

Another important principle of valuation is anticipation. Investment real estate (like virtually all investments) is owned, sold, or developed based on the perception of future benefit. A related principle is change. Desire for an item is subject to change based on economic, governmental, or social influences. Because real estate cannot be moved, it is especially subject to changes in its surrounding marketplace.

Unlike some entities, real estate is not traded in an efficient marketplace—one characterized by easy transport of the product, little government regulation, stable prices, and knowledgeable buyers and sellers. As a result, real estate investors and managers alike need a working understanding of real estate investment's fundamentals, including the principles that contribute to value.

Competent management is a foundation for all the economic principles of investment real estate. The responsibilities of real estate managers to their clients include understanding market forces as they fluctuate and providing advice on potential changes that will keep a property competitive and influential in its market.

Nearly all real estate professionals learn the concept of **bundle of rights** early in their education. In theory, ownership of land gives the property owner rights of the surface of the land extended to the center of the earth and into the sky, and the owner can do anything with the land that he or she wishes. In reality, these rights are limited by public and private restrictions. Public restrictions may include state and municipal laws to zone and restrict the land's use **(police power),** to tax the property, and to take control of the property under its power of **eminent domain.** Private restrictions may include **restrictive covenants** to prevent certain uses. For example, a shopping center owner or developer may grant a grocery store the exclusive right to sell certain products in its shopping center, thus restricting other tenants from selling them. Property owners give up additional rights through the ability to mortgage a property for the purpose of financing, pledging the property as security for a debt. Most important for real estate and property managers is whether an owner is giving up the right of possession through leasing to third parties.

When a property is owned subject only to public restrictions, it is said to be under **fee simple ownership**—free and clear of encumbrances. This is the way most people look upon the market value of real estate. When a property appraisal is ordered, the scope of the assignment always indicates the rights to be appraised. Most appraisals appraise fee-simple rights, but there are appraisals of specific interests, such as the value of an easement or right-of-way and value for taking by a public body. (The International Right of Way Association is an organization of appraisers who specialize in understanding unique rights in real estate interests.)

Other interests that may be the subject of an appraisal report include the value of mortgage interest, the value of leasehold interest, and the value of air rights, water rights, mineral rights, development rights, and condominium rights.

THE PURPOSE OF APPRAISALS

One of several procedures of due diligence—the process of verifying details in a real estate transaction—is to support the suggested value of a property with an **appraisal** performed by an independent third party. The appraisal profession has undergone significant regulation, particularly since the 1980s, when many savings and loans collapsed from the inability to manage deregulation, which was afforded them in 1980.

In 1989, the Financial Institutions Reform and Recovery Act (FIRREA) set strict standards for appraisals as part of an overhaul of banking practices. Starting in 1993, all real estate appraisals that were related, in any way, to use of federal funds or to interstate commerce were required to be performed by licensed or certified appraisers holding credentials in the state where the property is located. Whether a license or certification is needed depends on the size and complexity of the property under analysis.

To create consistency nationwide, FIRREA mandated that standards for appraisal reports be established by the Appraisal Foundation, a nonprofit organization affiliated with all major appraisal organizations, including the Appraisal Institute and the National Association of REALTORS. The foundation sets appraisal standards—known as the **Uniform Standards of Appraisal Practice (USPAP)**—through its Appraisal Standards Board and licensing standards through its Appraiser Qualifications Board.

The regulations governing real estate appraisals continue to evolve. Initial FIRREA issues developed as a result of savings and loan failures, most resulting from commercial loans made when S&Ls entered the commercial market following deregulation. The financing and refinancing boom of the late 1990s and early 2000s impacted both commercial and residential transactions, leading to the much-publicized insolvency of Fannie Mae, Freddie Mac, and mortgage insurance reinsurer AIG. Most recently, legislation was passed prohibiting the initiating lender in a single-family home transaction from selecting the person who will conduct the property appraisal. The appraiser is selected by a third party from a list approved by the lender.

Real estate appraisal is a very specialized arena, performed by individuals highly educated in the principles of valuation. More detail on the path of study necessary to become a real estate appraiser is available at the websites of the national appraisal organizations.

Even though real estate managers are not likely to render opinions on value for external reporting, they will use similar techniques in performing any asset management analyses and in estimating value and equity positions to isolate variables for management decision making.

APPRAISAL REPORTS

At one time, a real estate appraisal could take many forms—from a simple letter estimating value to a complex narrative report. Most financing transactions for investment real estate today must meet USPAP standards, which differ based on the type of assignment. Smaller appraisals may be accomplished by a form report—an appraisal submitted on a series of forms approved by the lender—but nearly every commercial and multi-family appraisal is submitted as a **narrative appraisal report.** The narrative report is a thorough discussion of all factors leading to the conclusion of value; it may be hundreds of pages long and include many exhibits.

Whatever the form or lengths of the appraisal report, every real estate valuation should include the following elements:

- Name of the party requesting the report
- Date of the report
- Identification and description of the property
- Purpose of the appraisal, including rights appraised
- Final estimate of value, with calculations
- Certification and signature of the appraiser

According to the Appraisal Institute, a narrative appraisal report uses this basic structure:

- Introduction
- Identification of the appraisal problem and the scope of work
- Presentation of data
- Analysis of data and conclusions
- Addenda

The requirements of an appraisal report are further defined at *www.uspap.org*.

While the discussion of appraisal introduced the way the investment community approaches value in real estate, its relevance to real estate and real estate managers warrants more detail. It is not unusual for real estate managers in the course of their duties to make "asset management" recommendations to property owners. This may include advice about whether the property should be held, sold, traded, or refinanced in order to maximize owner wealth. Anyone assisting an owner in making decisions like these must be well versed in both valuation and finance. When a property is bought, sold, or refinanced, a third-party appraiser is nearly always engaged to verify value. Even before listing a property for sale, real estate brokers likely analyze the property's performance to estimate value. Real estate managers, likewise, must be able to estimate value to protect the **market value** and **investment value** of the property.

VALUATION

One of the goals of managing a property is capital appreciation. Owners want to see the market value of their property increase over time so that it can be sold for more than the purchase price. Therefore, real estate managers should know how to estimate value of a property and apply capitalization techniques to project increases or decreases in equity.

A Word about Capital

The term "capital" comes up often in real estate. *Capital* is money that can be invested and consists of the total assets of a business. Capital is also any form of wealth used, or ready for use, in creating more wealth.

In real estate, capital is often used for making major improvements to a property. Therefore, like any other kind of funds, capital should be budgeted. Previous chapters discussed net operating income (NOI) and before-tax cash flow (BTCF) as important indicators of financial viability. NOI is used to determine whether the property produces enough income to pay debt service and to create a capital budget for major expenses.

Capital is often available for investment because investing money is usually the best way of increasing one's wealth. Investors count on the value of their investment to grow over time. Similarly, property owners buy office buildings, shopping centers, and apartment complexes with the expectation that the value of the property will appreciate over the time that the owners hold the properties.

How Capital Is Used

Starting with the basic definition of capital as money or property available for investment, we can look into several concepts that describe how capital is used. These basic ideas are useful for understanding capital and capitalization.

- *Capital asset:* long-term assets, tangible or intangible, needed to generate income. In real estate, capital assets are often defined as land, buildings, and improvements.

- *Capitalization:* the treatment of future income as part of a firm's capital. In appraisal, it is the process employed in estimating the market value of real property by applying a proper investment rate of return to the annual NOI the property is expected to produce.

- *Equity:* the value of real property in excess of debt. It is the interest or value that an owner has in real estate over and above the mortgage and other financial liens against the property. Sometimes the term *equity investment* is also used. In the banking world, equity may be referred to as *net worth.*

- *Liquidity:* the ability to convert assets into cash. A savings account is liquid. Generally, real estate is not highly liquid (sometimes called ill-liquid), because it rarely can be sold immediately for cash.

- *Working capital:* the amount of money a company has on hand to conduct business over the short term.

Valuation is an estimation, or calculation, of the worth of a property; it is often the result of the process of appraisal. One of the most important tasks of managing real estate as an investment is obtaining an accurate valuation of a property. An accurate valuation is required to assess the risk of financing as well as the return to the investor. Valuation also underlies the manager's ability to assess the benefits of renovations, the decision to sell a property, and local property taxes and insurance. An understanding of valuation facilitates the manager's ability to work with owners.

Highest and Best Use

A real estate manager who analyzes real estate held for investment purposes must determine the property's **highest and best use.** Highest and best use occurs when the property produces the highest value and achieves the fullest economic potential. The Appraisal Institute defines highest and best use as the reasonably probable use of vacant land or an improved property that:

- Is physically possible.
- Is legally permissible.
- Is financially feasible.
- Results in the highest value.

If the value of the vacant land is greater than the value of the property as improved, then the highest and best use becomes the use of the land as though vacant. An appraiser's view of the optimal use for the land may or may not support continued use of the building. A real estate manager, on the other hand, is looking primarily for the highest and best use of the land that utilizes existing improvements.

Some conclusions about highest and best use can be drawn from property and market analyses that detail the condition of the property and its competitive position within the market. The use that maximizes an investment property's value, consistent with the rate of return and associated risk expected by the owner, is its highest and best use.

In many cases, the highest and best use is the current use. However, the highest and best use for the property may not be in line with the owner's current goals. Once a study of the highest and best use has been completed, the real estate manager should discuss with the client any use that is not in line with the stated goals.

Types of Value

In the context of income-producing real estate, real estate has two types of value: market value and investment value. For insurance purposes, there is also a replacement value.

Market Value

Market value is the most likely price the asset would command in the open, competitive market (the price at which a willing seller would sell and a willing buyer would buy).

Increased market value can be due in part to factors over which the real estate manager has little control, such as improved market conditions, short supply, inflation, and changes in tax laws. On the other hand, an effective real estate manager has considerable influence in increasing NOI through cost control, collections, careful budgeting, and rent increases. In addition, innovative management techniques, such as adapting and rehabilitating properties and refinancing, can create higher value.

Implicit in the definition is the consummation of a sale as of a specified date and the passing of the title from seller to buyer under specific conditions:

- Both buyer and seller are typically motivated.
- Both parties are well informed or well advised and acting in what they consider their best interests.
- A reasonable time is allowed for exposure in the open market.
- Payment is made in cash in U.S. dollars or through financial arrangements comparable to cash.
- The price represents the normal consideration for the property sold, unaffected by special or creative financing or sales concessions granted by anyone associated with the sale.

TIPS

Many jurisdictions have a legal definition of market value. Be sure to know yours!

Investment Value

A property may have different values to different investors, for example an adjacent property to a property owned by an investor may be worth more to that investor. Investment value of a property is its worth to a particular investor based on the investor's specific requirements. Investment value changes because it depends on an individual investor's or company's financial strength, skills, and cost of capital. Investment value is calculated for the purposes of making investment decisions, and the financial management of the property may be set to influence investment value in light of these decisions.

Investment Equity

Both the value of the debt and the value of the equity must be considered when making investment decisions. Investors often will want to see the value of the equity, investment equity, when considering the best use of the property.

The equity of the property can be derived by subtracting the outstanding loan balance and anticipated costs of sale, if sold, from the current market value.

Replacement Value

A third type of value to be aware of is replacement value. Replacement value reflects the cost to replace or restore a building to its pre-existing condition and appearance. It is a common method of determining insurance coverage. In appraisal, replacement value equals the cost at current prices to replace an existing building with one of equal utility.

VALUATION APPROACHES

Since at least the 1950s, formal appraisal reports have estimated market value by analyzing a property from three different approaches: the **cost approach,** the **comparable sales approach** (or **market data approach),** and the **income capitalization approach.** The three approaches, which rarely yield the same result, are used to assure that no important detail is overlooked. The final estimate of value is not an average, but rather is the result of the appraiser's best judgment in light of the results of the three approaches.

Cost Approach

The cost approach is a method of appraisal in which a property's value does not exceed the market value of the land plus the value of the existing building on it. It often sets the upper limit of value on a property. The economic principle of substitution dictates that no one would pay more for a property than they would pay to buy a similar parcel of land and construct a building of the same utility. This approach to value generally yields the highest estimate of the three valuation approaches.

Consider a 20-year-old strip shopping center. Assume there is a vacant parcel of land of the exact same size as the property under consideration. If you were to buy that land and build a strip shopping center on it, the cost would equal the price of the land plus all of the costs of development and construction. (For this purpose, tenants and their leases are not a consideration.) Of course, an investor would not pay more for a 20-year-old building than for a newly constructed building, which raises the question of what purpose it serves to value the 20-year-old structure. The appraiser, after calculating the cost of development, must consider the condition of the 20-year-old property and deduct for the condition of the older structure. The appraiser estimates its **effective age** by deducting for such factors as **obsolescence** and **physical depreciation.** A building in excellent condition will have fewer deductions than one in poor condition.

Under the cost approach, the value of any improvements is estimated based on the cost to reproduce them minus accrued depreciation. Current construction prices for the existing building may be referred to as a reproduction cost or a replacement cost:

- **Reproduction cost** is the cost at today's prices to construct an exact duplicate of an existing building using the same type and quality of materials and construction standards and embodying all of the characteristics, negative and positive, of the subject building. Because the same materials may no longer be available—or, if available, may be extremely costly—and building codes and newer construction techniques may supersede those that applied originally. Reproduction cost is generally only applicable to newer buildings.

- **Replacement cost** is the cost at today's prices to replace an existing building with one of equivalent utility using current materials and construction standards. Replacement cost is the basis for the cost approach to appraisal.

The cost approach to appraisal is:

- Most commonly used for new or recently constructed buildings.

- Most appropriate for non-income-producing, special purpose properties such as churches and schools.

- Conducted as outlined in the following checklist.

CHECKLIST: COST APPROACH

☐ The appraiser obtains the cost to reproduce the existing building as a new structure. Costs may include: labor, materials, equipment, subcontractor fees, financing charges, selling costs, insurance costs, permits, licenses, survey and architectural fees, builder's profit and overhead, and legal fees. Cost information service companies publish cost data for these items in different geographic markets across the country. This data can be used as a starting point or checkpoint for obtaining accurate data.

☐ The appraiser adjusts the costs for the depreciation of the existing building. The following types of depreciation are considered:

Physical depreciation is the aging or deterioration of the property; these defects may be curable through property maintenance.

Functional obsolescence is the condition of obsolete design or use of the property that detracts from its marketability; these defects may be curable or incurable.

Economic obsolescence refers to elements that make the property less desirable that arise from economic sources outside of the property, such as the deterioration of the surrounding region. Even when the surrounding environment is good, the market for a particular type of use may have shifted away from the property's geographic area.

☐ The appraiser estimates the value of the land by using sales information on comparable undeveloped parcels of land.

☐ The land value and depreciated replacement cost are added together to arrive at a cost estimate.

Cost Approach *Example 12.1*

In a simplified example of appraisal using the cost approach, consider a 5,000-square-foot single-story storefront building located in the central business district of a small city. Buildings of this nature are typical for the area and are often occupied by businesses for office or retail purposes. The building is 25 years old and in reasonably good condition, with modern upgraded mechanical systems.

Cost-estimating software would be used to determine the replacement cost of the structure new: $503,676 in this case. The appraiser would then make deductions from the replacement cost for physical depreciation, economic obsolescence, and functional obsolescence on the subject property. These total $400,000, leaving a net structure cost of $103,676.

Having also estimated the value of the vacant land (at $215,000), the appraiser adds that figure to the depreciated value of the building, yielding a final value of $338,676.

Replacement Cost	$503,676
– Depreciation	$400,000
= Depriciated Costs	$103,676
+ Land Value	$215,000
= Value	$338,676

Comparable Sales Approach

Using the comparable sales approach (also called the market data approach), an appraiser estimates a subject property's market value by comparing it to similar properties that have sold in the area. Since no two properties are exactly alike, the appraiser studies the differences in the comparable properties and makes adjustments to bring their cost more in line with the subject property. The give-and-take result is a figure that shows what each comparable property would have sold for if it had the same qualities as the subject property. The figures are then analyzed to estimate a market value of the subject property.

The comparable sales approach is conducted as described in the following checklist.

CHECKLIST: COMPARABLE SALES APPROACH

☐ The appraiser obtains recent sales information on comparable properties. An appraiser's report typically shows side-by-side comparisons of three comparables. Multiple listing services (MLS), local appraisers, and county courthouse records are the most dependable sources for this information.

☐ The appraiser identifies and lists the key features of the subject property and the comparable properties that may require adjustments. Examples of key physical features include: location, size of property, type of construction, quality of construction, interior and exterior condition, and amenities such as proximity to restaurants, transportation, or health clubs. Financing terms, market conditions, date of sale, and conditions of the sale are other key features that are examined for adjustments. This information can be obtained from the buyer, seller, broker, or lender.

☐ The appraiser makes adjustments to the comparable sales prices to bring their cost more in line with the subject property. These adjustments are based on the differences in the features identified in the previous step and may be adjusted up or down depending on how the sold property compares to the subject property.

☐ The appraiser averages the adjusted sales prices of the comparable properties to arrive at a figure for the subject property. The weighting reflects the appraiser's judgment of the degree of resemblance between each of the comparable properties and the subject property.

The comparable sales approach is best used when there is an active market for a given property type in which the appraiser can find any number of comparable sales.

Consider the same 5,000-square-foot storefront building of office and retail space described in the example. The property is in a downtown area and relies on foot traffic and downtown parking ramps. It has no parking of its own. Several comparable freestanding buildings have sold recently.

- Sale 1, a 7,000-square-foot building two blocks away, is structurally identical and has similar mechanical systems to the subject property. This comparable sold for $372,000 two months ago.

- Sale 2 has 5,500 square feet and is identical in terms of construction, but it has a lot with 20 parking stalls behind the building. It is located on the outer edge of the downtown area, with virtually no foot traffic or parking ramps. Comparable 2 sold for $295,000 last month.

- Sale 3 is a 10,000-square-foot building, also downtown, with no parking and similar condition and building systems. This property sold 18 months ago for $515,000.

In comparing these three properties, the appraiser notes the following details:

- Sale 1: Sold for $53.14 per square foot. No adjustments are needed for location or condition.

- Sale 2: Sold for $53.63 per square foot. Adjustments are needed for location and parking.

- Sale 3: Sold for $51.50 per square foot. The larger size may require an adjustment for building efficiency. Because it sold 18 months ago, an adjustment may also be needed for time.

Note that the appraiser would consider other things as well, such as lease terms, tenants, vacancies, and so on. However, details have been simplified here for purposes of this example.

The value range for the appraised property is thus established as $51.50 to $53.63 per square foot, but the appraiser must render a single opinion of value. The appraiser uses her or his best judgment to determine the value of the differences, creating a comparison matrix (similar to a comparison grid used for establishing market rents) that might look like Exhibit 12.1.

The appraiser might further adjust or, if appropriate, average the adjusted sales or perform a weighted average giving more weight to the most comparable sale. Using the simple averaging method, the indicated value would be $53.29 per square foot, or $266,450:

$$266,450 = \left[\frac{\$53.14 + \$53.23 + \$53.50}{3} \right] \times 5,000$$

Exhibit 12.1

Feature	Subject	Sale 1	Sale 2	Sale 3
Property Comparisons and Adjustments				
Location	Downtown	Downtown	Fringe + 0.35	Downtown
Parking	None	None	– 0.55	Downtown
Time				+ 1.50
Total adjustment (per sq. ft.)	0	0	– 0.20	+ 1.50
Indicated value of subject	TBD	$53.14	$53.63	$51.50
			– 0.40	+ 3.00
			$53.23	$53.50

Income Capitalization Approach

The income capitalization approach (also called the economic analysis approach) is the preferred appraisal method for income-producing properties. Its premise is that the future benefit of owning a property is based on its net operating income and the risk factors for that class of property as determined by the marketplace. If the marketplace of investors accepts a certain risk factor in considering one property's income stream, they probably would accept a similar risk factor for a similar property.

This method estimates the value of a property by applying a proper capitalization rate to the annual net operating income (NOI) the property is expected to produce, using the formula:

$$\text{Income (I)} \div \text{Rate (R)} = \text{Value (V)}$$

It may help to think of the IRV formula in the form of a house, as in Exhibit 12.2.

Exhibit 12.2   **IRV**

Note that in the "house" image the I is "over" R to derive V.

That is:

Net Operating Income (I) ÷ Capitalization Rate (R) = Value (V)

- I is stabilized net operating income (NOI).
- R is the capitalization rate found in the marketplace for the subject property type.
- V is the market value of the subject property.

Two key elements in the formula are the stabilized NOI (I) and the capitalization rate (R).

Stabilized NOI (I)

Stabilized NOI (I) is the true earning potential of the property. It reflects income achieved at full market occupancies and expenses incurred at full building operations, including full real estate tax assessments. It is NOI projected out into the future so as not to underestimate NOI because of a new building lease-up or repositioning mode. An accurately projected NOI is a critical component in determining value.

Buyers and sellers will look at NOI from different perspectives. Sellers will want to focus on projecting future NOI. Buyers, on the other hand, will want to focus on actual results, or past NOI. This is where negotiation over price takes place in the competitive marketplace. Appraisers attempt to establish the most probable NOI by focusing their attention on a stabilized NOI projection.

In practice, NOI projections produced by appraisers can be for as long as 15 years. In selling situations, a real estate manager is likely to project income for 5 years. Following are the steps involved in projecting stabilized NOI for one year:

1. Effective gross income is calculated. This is done by examining market rent levels and vacancy rates in the area and determining gross potential income and typical vacancy losses. Effective gross income is then derived from the gross potential income plus other miscellaneous income minus estimated vacancy and collection losses.

2. A forecast of operating expenses is performed. This requires an analysis and documentation of continuous operating requirements. Next year's expenses are forecast from these requirements. Unusual capital expenditures, such as a new roof, are not included in these estimates.

3. NOI is obtained by subtracting the forecasted operating expenses from the forecasted effective gross income.

Real estate managers rely upon the income capitalization approach for projections and planning because it is the method in which they have the most information, such as NOI estimates and the ability to derive capitalization rates.

Capitalization Rate (R)

The **capitalization rate** (R), or cap rate, is a single rate that converts a single year's income into value. It is the rate of return to estimate the property's value. Cap rates are a measurement of risk used by real estate managers and their clients to make a variety of investment decisions because they provide a method of relating a property's income to its value. In the stock market, a similar analysis can be done through a price-to-earnings ratio. In the bond market, a yield rate is used. In real estate, the capitalization rate is used.

The value calculated from a capitalization rate can be thought of as a price paid for a given income stream. Therefore, the capitalization rate can be used to compare different properties when making real estate investment decisions. The capitalization rate also makes choosing between real estate investments and stock or bond investments possible.

As you would expect, the capitalization rate varies between properties and property types. Variables that influence the capitalization rate include:

• Demand for a particular type of property

• Quality of the property

• Future potential benefits

For example, a prime shopping center with a strong operating history and excellent future potential may sell at a 7% capitalization rate while a small strip center may sell at a 9.5% capitalization rate.

Information inherent in the derivation of capitalization rates includes:

• Investment returns

• Expectations of market value appreciation or depreciation

• Financing information

• Inflation expectations

• Operating expenses

Because of the variety of the information involved in the capitalization rate, several methods exist for deriving it. Each method emphasizes physical, financial, and market concerns to different degrees.

Using IRV to Calculate the Cap Rate

In general, one can find the cap rate by using the IRV equation. Since IRV is an equation, the three elements can be flipped to derive each other. If R is known, that rate may be applied to I to determine an estimated V. If R is unknown, recent sales of properties where the NOI (I) and sale price (V) are known can be substituted into the formula to estimate the market cap rate (R). Therefore, you can use the same formula to find the capitalization rate when you know NOI and value:

$$NOI\ (I) \div Value\ (V) = Capitalization\ Rate\ (R)$$

This formula is one of the central tools for understanding the relationship of income to value of the asset.

Capitalization Rates and Value

Since capitalization rates reflect the nature of risk taken with a real estate investment, there is an inverse relationship between capitalization rates and value. The lower the capitalization rate, the higher the value of the property. The higher the capitalization rate, the lower the value as shown in Exhibit 12.3.

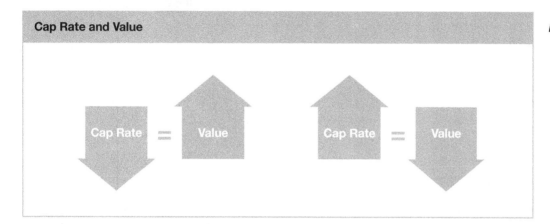

Cap Rate and Value   *Exhibit 12.3*

TIPS

Because the capitalization rate is used to estimate value, extreme care must be used to select the appropriate rate. Minor differences in the rate used can create large variations in the resulting value. For example, for a property with a projected NOI of $750,000, an 8% capitalization rate would produce a value [750,000 (I) ÷ 0.80 (R)] of $9,375,000. A capitalization rate of 8.5% would determine a value of $8,823,529. The difference in value is more than half a million dollars from a one-half of one percentage point difference in the capitalization rate.

This raises a rather significant ethical issue when estimating any cap rates. Small differences in cap rates have a much greater impact on value than small differences in NOI.

Going-In and Going-Out Cap Rates

Sometimes cap rates must be forecast. For example, a real estate manager or investor with the goal of selling a property at a future date may want to project proceeds of sale in several years. No one can predict with certainty what investors will consider the appropriate risk rate in the future, so it must be forecast. Therefore, it is important to understand that, in any test for value over time (e.g., at acquisition and at sale in the future), the real estate manager is required to make assumptions about the cap rate at the start point of the test (i.e., the **going-in cap rate),** and at the terminal point of the test (i.e., the **going-out cap rate).**

A capitalization rate is influenced by market conditions. Desired risk and yield, for example, are influenced by the larger economic cycles of demand and swings in the costs of financing. Generally, the going-out cap rate is higher than the going-in rate to reflect the potential risk associated with the passage of time. However, going-out cap rates can be lower than the going-in rates. Following are a few factors that could lead to this:

- Investors may desire the property's investment class more in the future than they do today.

- The economic climate could be better, affecting all property classes.

- The property could be repositioned.

Because markets change, cap rates will fluctuate, in some markets widely, over time. Cap rates indicate value as a snapshot in time. Therefore, while we can determine the market's appetite for a certain investment today, the further we project in the future the less certain our forecast can be. The going-in cap rate is a result of today's market. Will the going-out rate 5 years later be the same as today? While no one can predict the future, your research should justify the assumptions you make with a regard to going-out cap rate when performing analyses for an investor.

Philosophies vary on estimating going-out cap rates. For example, some investors plan to make their properties less risky than when they bought them. Perhaps an owner will purchase a rundown property at a 9% cap rate but plan to put considerable money into remodeling. The newly renovated property will better meet market standards, and the investor can project that, when it is stabilized and operating successfully, it will be a less risky investment—and will therefore project a lower going-out cap rate. Other investors prefer a more conservative approach, in which they always increase the cap rate by, say, one-half to three-quarters of a percent higher than the going-in cap rate. Their premise is that the economy is unpredictable and it is safer to err on the side of a weaker market. Real estate managers usually prefer this approach. If their projections work at the higher cap rate (lower value), then they surely will work if the market improves and cap rates decrease (higher value).

Income Capitalization Approach

Example 12.3

Continuing with the example of the small retail and office storefront, consider the following additional information on the comparable sales:

Subject property: Leased to a credit union. Next year's expected NOI is $29,000.

- Sale 1: Leased to an accounting firm. NOI is $36,395.

- Sale 2: Divided into two leased spaces, both occupied by attorneys. NOI is $29,500.

- Sale 3: Leased to a real estate office. NOI is $60,000.

Dividing NOI by the sale price yields the cap rate for each property:

- Sale 1: $36,395 ÷ $372,000 = 9.78%

- Sale 2: $29,500 ÷ $295,000 = 10%

- Sale 3: $60,000 ÷ $515,000 = 11.65%

The appraiser must then make a judgment of the most appropriate cap rate for the subject property. In this case it might be best to consider only the two cap rates that apply to recent sales and eliminate the older sale altogether. Or the cap rates could be averaged, or a weighted average could be used. The appraiser's experience guides the decision.

For this example, average the cap rates of sale 1 and sale 2 to yield an indicated cap rate of 9.89% ([9.78 + 10] ÷ 2). Substituting variables for the subject property into the IRV formula indicates a value of $293,225 ($29,000 ÷ 0.0989).

Final Value Estimate

After completing calculations for each of the three approaches to value, the appraiser presents a final estimate of value. This figure is often referred to as the **appraised value** of a property, but it is really the appraiser's estimate of market value as of the date of the appraisal report.

The property example used for illustration here yielded these estimates for the three approaches:

- Cost approach: $338,676

- Comparable sales approach: $265,950

- Income capitalization approach: $293,225

For the final estimate for this property, the appraiser might rely solely on the income capitalization approach or might choose the income capitalization approach as the main determinant but modify it slightly in light of the much lower value indicated by the comparable sales approach. The cost approach would be considered a way to provide a check on the other two methods, with the awareness that with an older building, more error is likely in estimating depreciation. Using his or her best judgment, the appraiser renders a final value estimate and must justify the decision thoroughly in the narrative report.

Since NOI for the year after the start of the analysis is a key variable in the valuation formula, errors in forecasting must be minimized. The examples here were used to simplify the concept of determining a cap rate, but budgeting accurately and extracting precise data from the market are essential to the effectiveness of the IRV (income capitalization) formula. Remember that the formula only works when NOI is considered stable and there is sufficient data to determine or estimate cap rates. The formula for a cap rate takes into account the ultimate sale of the property at the end of a typical holding period. So where the variables have been properly determined, this approach to value is easy to calculate.

The income capitalization approach to value can also be used to estimate value where NOI is not stable through *discounted cash flow analysis,* which will be discussed in a later chapter. Essentially, where the IRV formula incorporates into the cap rate the stability of income and ultimate sale of the property, discounted cash flow analysis evaluates each income stream, including the estimated income resulting from sale of the property, then discounts each income stream back to present value. This approach works when NOI is unstable or expected to become unstable due to operational changes or improvements to the property.

DERIVING THE CAPITALIZATION RATE

Common methods for deriving the capitalization rate include the comparable sale analysis, extrapolation of surveys, and mortgage equity analysis. A comparison of data generated from multiple methods of deriving the capitalization rate will yield the best results.

Capitalization Rate Components

The capitalization rate is the sum of many different measures. One way to formulate this is to compute, and then add together, several figures that measure return on investment, including the following.

CHECKLIST: CAPITALIZATION RATE COMPONENTS

☐ *Safe rate:* a rate of return on low-risk investments such as treasury notes, bank and insurance company CDs, or high quality bonds

☐ *Risk rate:* an additional premium added for taking on risk above that of a low-risk investment reflecting the strength, length, and durability of the anticipated *net income* stream

☐ *Fee or entrepreneurial rate:* the base profit rate that will compensate you for investing in this opportunity in addition to the safe rate choice

☐ *Non-liquidity rate:* the rate that will compensate for anticipated marketing costs and time required to convert the investment into cash

☐ *Recapture rate:* the rate that will return your invested capital over the investment's anticipated holding period; a sinking fund rate for the return of invested capital

Here is an example of how these five figures can be summed to determine a capitalization rate:

Safe Rate	3.5%
+ Risk Rate	1.5%
+ Fee	1.0%
+ Non-Liquidity Rate	1.0%
+ Recapture Rate	1.5%
Built-up Cap Rate	8.5%

Note that these quantitative components relate back to the theoretical factors discussed in Chapter 11 (i.e., liquidity, marketability, leverage, management, tax impact, rate of return, and economic factors) that real estate managers evaluate when assessing risk of an investment proposal.

Comparable Sales Analysis

The comparable sales analysis for cap rates is similar to the comparable sales approach for property valuation in general. It involves analyzing sales and net operating income (NOI) figures of similar properties to compile a list of cap rates in the marketplace. This method inherently considers physical, financial, and market risks.

Although comparable sales analysis is often used because of its convenience, there may be circumstances in which it cannot be utilized, such as a lack of recent comparable sales data or if sales of similar properties took place under different market conditions. Other distortions in the data can occur from, among other factors, operating differences, variations in financing terms, and differences in land-to-building utilization.

With comparable sales, when the NOI and sale price are known, the relationship is very clear using the income capitalization formula. Some caution must be exercised to ensure a reasonable level of comparability; adjustments may be in order if the sale did not take place in the recent past or is not "at arm's length." Further, variances in calculation methods may cause inconsistency in NOI between properties.

An example of this would be such line items as "reserve for replacements." Many property owners make an allowance for capital improvements in their operating statements. Technically, the overall cap rate used in these problems includes allowances both for capital improvement and for the ultimate sale of the property. The analyst should be careful that the reported NOI is calculated consistently.

CHECKLIST: COMPARABLE SALES ANALYSIS

☐ For each comparable, divide the NOI by the sales price to derive the capitalization rate.

☐ Compile a list of capitalization rates.

☐ Summarize the collected capitalization rates using an arithmetic mean, weighted mean, median, or mode as described in the subsequent sections.

Arithmetic Mean

The arithmetic mean is the average of all of the capitalization rates collected. If the capitalization rates are close in value, the average will be representative of the capitalization rate you are seeking.

Arithmetic Mean Cap Rate	Example 12.4

Consider the following rates that were collected in the marketplace:

Comparable	Capitalization Rate (%)
A	9.86
B	10.11
C	9.72
D	9.99
E	9.72

A. Calculate the arithmetic mean (average) capitalization rate.

$$9.86 + 10.11 + 9.72 + 9.99 + 9.72 = 49.40 \div 5 = 9.88$$

The average capitalization rate = 9.88%.

Weighted Mean

Often, the comparable properties for which sales data are available possess important differences that affect value. The weighted mean calculation can reflect those differences in order to obtain a capitalization rate that is representative of the subject property.

When a weight is assigned to comparables, those that are most similar to the subject property receive the highest weight, while those that are the most dissimilar receive the lowest weight. The weighted mean is calculated by multiplying each comparable capitalization rate by its weighting factor, then adding the results.

Example 12.5

Weighted Mean Cap Rate

Using the cap rates from the preceding example, assume that comparables A and D are the most similar to the subject property, comparable B is closely similar, and comparables C and E are the least similar:

Comparable	Capitalization Rate (%)	Weight
A	9.86	30%
B	10.11	20%
C	9.72	10%
D	9.99	30%
E	9.72	10%
	Sum of weights =	100%

A. Calculate the weighted mean capitalization rate.

Weighted Capitalization Rates

9.86	×	30%	=	2.96
10.11	×	20%	=	2.02
9.72	×	10%	=	0.97
9.99	×	30%	=	3.00
9.72	×	10%	=	0.97

$$2.96 + 2.02 + 0.97 + 3.00 + 0.97 = 9.92$$

The weighted mean capitalization rate = 9.92%.

Median and Mode

Sometimes an average does not reflect a representative capitalization rate. When the sample size is large, median and mode can be used to summarize the comparable capitalization rates.

The *median* is the middle value among the series of figures in which half of the data lie above it and half the data lay below it. The *mode* is the most frequently occurring figure in the data set.

Consider the same capitalization rates. Reordering the data to view the greatest to the least capitalization rate would produce the following:

Comparable	Capitalization Rate (%)
B	10.11
D	9.99
A	9.86
C	9.72
E	9.72

A. Calculate the median capitalization rate.

The median capitalization rate is the value in the middle of the data, in this case 9.86% (comparable A).

B. Calculate the mode capitalization rate.

The mode is the most frequently occurring capitalization rate, in this case 9.72%.

Extrapolation from Surveys

Extrapolation is a method of estimating capitalization rates from survey information found in a variety of sources. The data collected may be current acceptable capitalization rates or capitalization rates on recent property sales.

Published capitalization rates reflect information derived from institutional investors who are most likely purchasing "best in class" properties in large markets. It is important to keep in mind that these rates may not be applicable to smaller properties in secondary markets, or to anything other than a Class A property.

Capitalization rate information is available from a variety of sources:

- **Pension funds:** generally have articulated investment criteria indicating a minimum acceptable capitalization rate. Pension funds tend to purchase only prime property, but the capitalization rate can be adjusted to the subject property based on perceived risk.

- **Real Estate Investment Trusts (REITs):** must file information with the U.S. Securities and Exchange Commission (SEC). These public disclosures provide useful data on acquisitions and can be obtained directly from the REITs or from the SEC.

- *American Council of Life Insurance (ACLI):* produces a quarterly report of capitalization rates and other useful data.

- *Professional associations:* such as the International Association of Assessing Officers (IAAO), the National Association of Real Estate Investment Trusts (NAREIT), and the Appraisal Institute publish capitalization rates.

- *Brokers, assessors, and appraisers:* have exposure to data on similar properties (e.g., value, offers made) that reveals the level of market interest and buyers' expectations of value.

- *Institutional and foreign investors:* view real estate as part of a larger portfolio that includes stock and bond investments. Consequently, expected rates of return on investment instruments such as U.S. Treasury Bills, long-term government bonds, corporate bonds, and stocks can be used to derive a competitive cap rate for a property.

Mortgage Equity Analysis

Mortgage equity analysis is typically used to confirm capitalization rates found in the marketplace, or in the absence of any market data. Mortgage equity analysis is more complex. Most people who buy real estate do so at least in part because of the benefits they derive from leverage. It is logical to consider nearly every real estate investment to have two components: the investment of the buyer, represented by the cash down payment; and the investment of the lender, represented by a note and mortgage.

When a property is purchased, a negotiation takes place between buyer and lender in which down payment, interest rate, escalations, and other factors are considered. The condition of the capital markets at the time of purchase will influence the negotiating positions of both parties. The end result, the purchase price, is satisfied by paying the seller a combination of borrowed funds and equity funds.

Mortgage equity analysis involves estimating value based on both the lender (mortgage) and investor (equity) returns. The returns of these two stakeholders are calculated as follows:

- *Lender:* The total funds needed to service the debt payment, both principal and interest, are represented in percentage terms by the loan constant.

- *Buyer:* The funds needed to satisfy a typical equity holder in terms of return on cash invested plus ultimate return from sale of the property is the equity dividend rate.

The capitalization rate for the mortgage component is the loan constant (k%). The capitalization rate for the equity component is cash-on-cash rate of return ($/$%). These two rates are weighted and summed to calculate the overall capitalization rate. The weights used are the available new loan loan-to-value (LTV%) ratio, applied to the debt component, and the (1 − LTV%) ratio applied to the equity component.

$$(\text{k\%} \times \text{LTV\%}) + [\text{\$/\$\%} \times (1 - \text{LTV\%})]$$

Consider a loan market where loans are typically available for up to 80% of value (LTV%) at 11.75% for 30 years. The loan constant is 12.11%. Further assume that investors are seeking a 7% cash-on-cash rate of return.

Calculate the capitalization rate using mortgage equity analysis.

$$k\% \times LTV\% = 12.11\% \times 80\% = 0.10 \times 100 = 9.69 \text{ (weighted mortgage rate)}$$

Or

$$12.11 \times 80\% = 9.69$$

$$\$/\$\% \times (1 - LTV\%) = 7\% \times 20\% = 0.01 \times 100 = 1.40 \text{ (weighted equity rate)}$$

Or

$$7 \times 20\% = 1.40$$

$$9.69 + 1.40 = 11.09$$

The capitalization rate = 11.09% (rounded to 11.1).

This analysis makes several assumptions:

- Fixed-rate financing is available and will be used at conventional rates under conventional terms.

- A relatively consistent loan-to-value ratio exists in the marketplace.

- Interest rates are relatively stable.

- There is relatively low variability among lenders.

Much of the foregoing analysis relies on clearly understanding the financial positions of the two major stakeholders in a real estate investment—first, the lender, and second, the owner, who holds the equity position. The motivation for any financial investment is for each party to realize both a return *on* the invested capital and a return *of* the invested capital. The lender receives a return in the form of the payment on the mortgage. Remember the discussion of leverage: the loan constant provides for both an interest payment to the bank (return on investment) and a principal payment to the lender (return of the investment). The equity holder receives a return on the investment through periodic cash flows and a return of the investment through sale of the property, and to some extent through tax benefits created by cost recovery.

It is important to remember that the lender in a transaction is also an investor in real estate. The lender assesses risk a bit differently than the equity holder, but both parties must consider the impact of the risk factors of investment, namely, liquidity, marketability, leverage, management, tax impact, and return on investment.

EQUITY CAPITALIZATION AND INVESTMENT VALUE

As mentioned, income capitalization focuses on estimating a property's market value—its likely sale price based on NOI. A technique for estimating a specific investor's value is called equity capitalization. Equity capitalization is based on cash flow, rather than NOI, and it measures the value of the equity. From the owner's point of view, BTCF takes into account the property's financing (debt service) and is a measurement of cash-on-cash rate of return.

Equity capitalization does not use the capitalization rate. Instead, it incorporates the cash-on-cash rate, which was discussed earlier in this course.

Cash-on-Cash Rate of Return ($/$%) = BTCF ÷ Initial Equity

Rearranging the equation to fit the IRV formula gives:

I (BTCF) ÷ R (Cash-on-Cash Rate of Return) = V (Equity Value)

The cash-on-cash rate of return is the desired rate of return to the investor on the invested capital (either initially or over time).

When a property is bought using a loan, its total value can be thought of as having two components: equity and debt. One way to buy a property for $1 million (total price) is to pay for it with $800,000 in borrowed money (debt) and $200,000 in cash (equity). Capitalizing before-tax cash flow using the cash-on-cash rate reveals only the value of the equity. To find the total investment value of the property, add the loan amount to the value of the equity:

Equity Value + Loan Amount = Investment Value

Investment Value

Example 12.8

An investor borrows $1,200,000 for a property. The desired cash-on-cash rate of return is 8%. The NOI is $78,000 and debt service is $56,000, which gives a before-tax cash flow of $22,000.

How much will the investor pay in cash for the property?

$$I \text{ (BTCF)} \div R \text{ (Cash-on-Cash Rate of Return)} = V \text{ (Equity Value)}$$

$$V \text{ (Equity Value)} = 22{,}000 \div 0.08 = \$275{,}000$$

Investment Value = Equity Value + Loan Amount

$$= 275{,}000 + 1{,}200{,}000$$

$$= \$1{,}475{,}000$$

The investor will pay $1,475,000 to get $22,000 in before-tax cash flow.

Change in Investment Value

Example 12.9

Consider an example where a real estate manager is evaluating spending $20,000 to insulate drafty corridors in a building. The cash flow increase is $3,000. Suppose that the building's owner asks for a minimum rate of return of 10%.

Calculate the change in investment value.

While equity and debt are both part of investment value, the insulation will be bought with cash. Only the equity portion of investment value, then, will change. The debt portion is unaffected and can be ignored.

The following calculation shows the change in equity:

$$I \text{ (BTCF)} \div R \text{ (Cash-on-Cash Rate of Return)} = V \text{ (Equity Value)}$$

$$V \text{ (Equity Value)} = \$3{,}000 \div 0.10 = \$30{,}000$$

The increase in the investment value is $30,000. The insulation costs less than $30,000, which means that the cost of insulation fits the owner's investment goals; the money can be spent for the insulation.

These are just a few of the tools that can be used to analyze a real estate investment. Here's a capitalization recap:

Type	Rate Used	Income Capitalized	Results
Income Capitalization	Capitalization Rate	NOI	Market Value
Equity Capitalization	Cash-on-Cash Rate of Return	BTCF	Equity Value + Loan Amount Investment Value

ETHICAL VALUATION

A real estate manager will face many opportunities to analyze forecasts of income, expense, and value estimates that come from third parties, including owners, brokers, appraisers, and bankers. The real estate manager will also make forecasts that are transmitted to third parties for various reasons. Perhaps a client is preparing to sell a property and needs to provide operating statistics to a broker. Or a client may be considering purchase of a property, and the real estate manager must analyze a pro forma statement prepared by a broker or seller.

As has been shown, values can be manipulated rather easily by only a small difference in cap rate forecast. NOI can be manipulated by moving expenses to or from the balance sheet to the operating statement or by misforecasting revenue. The real estate manager must not participate in manipulation of values in any manner. For example, say a property owner suggests "tweaking" the operating statement to show a higher NOI for a prospective buyer or lender. The professional of integrity will provide an honest operating history and best estimates of future revenue and expenses.

Real estate managers also ought to remain alert to manipulation of value by others. For example, if a client receives a pro forma statement for a property under consideration, the real estate manager may be asked to analyze the statement and render an opinion. The real estate manager's knowledge of current cap rates and the ability to see the trending methods used by third parties may assist the client's decision making.

The role of a real estate manager is to provide honest historical information and forecasts into the future that are honest and justifiable. Not only is it unethical to manipulate data, but it can come back to haunt the manipulator in other ways. There are many stories of real estate managers who tinkered with data to help a client sell a property only to be hired to manage the same property for the new owner. The real estate manager's abilities will be called into question if she or he can't operate the property for the new owner according to the projections provided prior to the sale. The story needs to be the same for everyone when it comes to reporting historical data, and projections need to be based on clear owner goals.

Real Estate Manager's Impact on NOI and Value

The real estate manager plays a key role in ensuring the quality and stability of a property's net operating income. A market-based budget and solid performance under that budget are the operational activities that maximize NOI (net operating income), an essential component of the income capitalization approach to value. So what is meant by a market-based budget? A good budget begins with a thorough analysis of the marketplace in which the property is located. While rents may have some relevance to cost, the rent charged at a property is a function of other rents being offered locally. As part of her or his core functions, the real estate manager should regularly "shop" a property's competition to ensure that the property is offering its vacant space at current market levels. Gross potential income (GPI) as defined by IREM, is potential income the property could make if all space was leased at 100% occupancy at market rents. Note that some real estate managers use the term *gross potential rent (GPR)* interchangeably with GPI.

Even in the best-managed properties, not all occupied space is likely to be leased at full market rent. In a commercial building, for example, long-term leases govern income even as market rents shift. If market rents increase, the real estate manager should act quickly to reflect those increases in proposals to new tenants. Existing tenants remain at their contract rents until the lease expires, which the pro forma statement reflects in the "loss to lease" category.

Similarly, if market rents drop, the pro forma might reflect a "gain to lease" on occupied space. Adjustments may be appropriate under these circumstances, because any tenants who know they are paying more than market rent may try to modify or terminate their leases in favor of space priced at current rates.

In multi-family properties, where leases are typically shorter than in commercial space, knowing the trends in market rents is even more important because rents can be adjusted more quickly for occupied space. With the use of a revenue management system, rates can be adjusted potentially every day, or even several times a day. This has presented challenges in valuation because GPI, as traditionally defined, is difficult to assess. When valuing a property in a revenue management model, some appraisers assess income using a hotel model for occupied units (averaging the rents) and the traditional model for vacant units.

Real Estate Manager's Impact on NOI and Value *(continued)*

Appraisers are trained to analyze potential market rents in much the same way that real estate managers are trained. They likely will engage in a thorough investigation of competitive rent rates, though not all practitioners present GPI in the same way. Some appraisers and many real estate managers use *"gross possible income"* as the top line of the pro forma statement. This method reports occupied space at contract rent (the rent reported on the lease) and vacant space at the current market rent, less a market-derived vacancy rate. Most appraisers use the GPI approach rather than taking into account undervalued leases.

Problem	Impact on GPI	Result	Value Impact at 9% Cap Rate
GPI is $10 lower than competitive rents	$5,000 less per month ($60,000 per year)	At 95% occupancy, EGI will be reduced by $54,000 per year	$600,000 of lost value due to missed opportunity
GPI is $10 higher than competitive rents	$5,000 more per month ($60,000 per year)	EGI could be reduced by $54,000 due to higher vacancy	$600,000 of lost value due to higher vacancy

A real estate manager who does not offer vacant units at rents consistent with the competition could cost the property owner considerable revenue. In an upward market, if rents are too low the property is likely to experience a misleading high occupancy. In a downward market, if rents are too high the property may experience unneeded vacancy loss. Consider a 500-unit apartment community. Assume that operating expenses stay the same regardless of GPI. Note that whether rents are higher or lower than the competition, GPI, EGI, and value are all negatively affected. (Remember that GPI is gross potential income and EGI is effective gross income.)

Another popular appraisal approach reflects occupied space at contract rent and vacant space at whatever rate is currently being offered at the property (whether market rate or a promotional rate). Whatever method is used, the real estate manager's choice of rents being offered will be brought into question if they do conflict with what the appraiser finds elsewhere. The ultimate goal should be to reflect an EGI consistent with competing properties. A real estate manager who does consistent market research will also save the appraiser time by justifying the rates at which rent is offered. This is not to say that all units must be offered at the top rent in the market at all times. Real estate managers may have reasons—such as temporary high vacancy or slow absorption—to offer incentives to potential renters in order to fill space more quickly.

Another way real estate managers can impact value is through carefully budgeting expenses. A stable NOI requires that operating expenses be consistent with the expenses of similar buildings. Particular care must be exercised in allocating capital expenditures. A capital expenditure reported as an operating expense will inappropriately reduce NOI, and an operating expense reported as a capital expenditure will inappropriately increase NOI.

Another way a manager can impact NOI is by reducing expenses through means such as lowering energy use, instituting sustainable practices, renegotiating contracts with vendors, and so on.

Sometimes real estate managers will be pressured by a broker or an owner to capitalize an expense (perhaps some repairs), which will inappropriately increase NOI. On the other hand, reporting a capital item (such as a roof replacement) as an operating expense will both reduce and destabilize NOI. Both will impact value. The real estate manager must be able to explain the reasoning behind each allocation and the risks associated with incorrect reporting. The table here outlines the impacts to a property when expenses are reported inaccurately.

Real Estate Manager's Impact on NOI and Value *(continued)*

Problem	Result	Impact on GPI	Value Impact at 9% Cap Rate
An operating expense is reported as a capital expenditure	Increases NOI but will be inconsistent with market operating expenses and taxation rules	May reduce the stability of NOI but also falsely increases NOI	Using income capitalization, value would be increased appropriately
A capital expenditure is reported as an operating expense	Decreases NOI and likely will make operating expenses inconsistent with the market	May reduce the stability of NOI and inappropriately decreases NOI	Using income capitalization, value would be decreased inappropriately

The due diligence process before closing a property sale should include a careful analysis of expenses and capital improvements to ensure proper allocations. During analysis, real estate managers should also look at ways to reduce expenses.

Another important way real estate managers influence value is through effective long-term planning. As part of ongoing communication with the owner, the real estate manager must clearly assess and reassess owner goals. Keep in mind that both increasing income and reducing expenses will raise the bottom line—NOI—which will then raise the value of the property when using income capitalization.

. . when considering the time value of money concept:

- How is market value defined in my state?

- What capitalization techniques do I use to project the market value and investment value of the properties I manage?

- What investment measures might I use to derive a capitalization rate?

- What strategies do I have in place to manage factors, including depreciation and obsolescence, which are considered as part of the cost approach to appraisal?

- How does recent sales data for comparable properties compare to the perceived value of your property?

REVIEW QUESTIONS

- List some reasons why a real estate manager may want to estimate the value of a client's (or potential client's) real estate?

- Define "highest and best use."

- Describe the difference between market value and investment value.

- List the key features of each of the following valuation approaches:

    –Cost approach

    –Comparable sales approach

    –Income capitalization approach

- What is IRV, and how does income capitalization estimate market value?

- Explain what a capitalization rate is, and describe the difference between the going-in and going-out cap rate.

- What is the relationship between cap rate and property value?

- List the five capitalization rate risk factors.

- List several methods that can be used to derive the capitalization rate?

- What is equity capitalization and how does it relate to investment value?

- How does the real estate manager impact NOI and value?

Discounted Cash Flow

As described in the previous chapter, capitalization is an appraisal method used in real estate valuation. Keep in mind that direct capitalization estimates the value of a property by applying an estimated capitalization rate to a single year of income [annual net operating income (NOI) the property is expected to produce], using the IRV formula [I/R = V]. However, the property income can vary from year to year. A property may experience unstable NOI for a variety of reasons, including the loss of a large tenant, remodeling, ineffective management, or a management change. For example, an office building that has major leases expiring in two years could have a significant decrease in income in the future. (See Understanding Stability of Income sidebar.) Discounted cash flow analysis uses multiple years of income to provide a more accurate measure of value.

Understanding Stability of Income

The terms stable and unstable with regard to income can be misleading. Stability refers not to reliability of an income stream, but rather to income that remains essentially the same for each succeeding period. For example, a five-year lease calling for the tenant to pay rent of $5,000 every month for the entire period would be considered a stable income stream. By contrast, a lease in which the landlord provides a concession of 6 months free rent followed by rents of $5,000 per month the first year and specified higher rents in each successive year would likely be considered an unstable income stream for the purpose of DCF analysis.

Also, the value of a property to a specific individual investor differs from that property's value in the general market. Capitalization of NOI is a technique that estimates market value, or most probable selling price. That market value is comprised of the theoretical behaviors of all potential buyers, and it becomes an average of those behaviors. Because of individual financial circumstances, income tax situations, and the like, specific investors may find particular properties more or less desirable than others in the market. One may not like the type of property, its location, its age, its rent roll, and so on.

A **discount rate** is the investor's required rate of return. An investor must consider many factors to determine the appropriate required rate of return, taking into account **opportunity cost** (earnings that could have been made had the money been available for immediate investment), inflation, and certainty of payment (risk). (See Exhibit 13.1.)

Exhibit 13.1   **Investor Discount Rates**

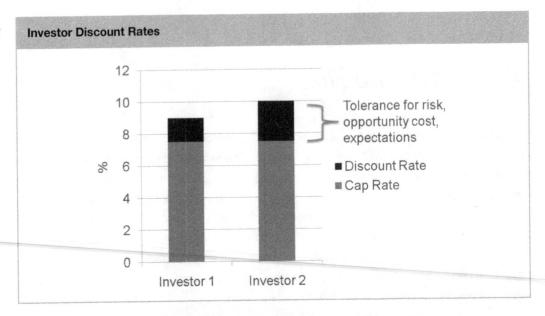

In summary, capitalization uses *single-year* NOI, while discounted cash flow (DCF) uses *multiple-year* cash flows. DCF analysis is the process used to discount future cash flows to arrive at present value. When the cash flows are stable the calculations are relatively simple. When the income stream is not stable, the property can still be valued, but the methodology must be modified. Unstable cash flow must be calculated individually to their present values. Using DCF for property valuation requires discounting income streams (including the sale proceeds of the holding period) by a market-derived discount rather than a cap rate.

COMPONENTS OF DCF ANALYSIS

Discounted cash flow (DCF) analysis uses the concept of the time value of money to determine how much a series of payments over several months or years into the future would be worth in present dollars. Therefore, it is a sound method used to calculate the real value of long-term leases. The mathematical formula for DCF is:

$$DCF = \frac{CF_1}{(1+r)^1} + \frac{CF_2}{(1+r)^2} + \dots + \frac{CF_n}{(1+r)^n}$$

$$FV = DCF(1+i)^n$$

$$DPV = \frac{FV}{(1+i)^n} = FV(1-d)^n$$

Where:

- *DPV* is the discounted present value of the future cash flow *(FV),* or *FV* adjusted for the delay in receipt.

- *FV* is the nominal value of a cash flow amount in a future period.

- *i* is the interest rate, which reflects the cost of tying up capital and may also allow for the risk that the payment may not be received in full.

- *d* is the discount rate, which is $i/(1+i)$, i.e., the interest rate expressed as a deduction at the beginning of the year instead of an addition at the end of the year.

- *n* is the time in years before the future cash flow occurs.

Suppose you were offered a piece of land that you forecast could be sold for $100,000 five years from now. Would you pay $100,000 for that land today? No, because you would receive no compensation for the time that your money would be tied up. In addition, you would not be compensated for the risk that you would encounter with this investment. Consequently, you would purchase the land at an amount less than $100,000 (a discount). The amount of the discount would be determined by the rate of return that you would require to entice you to invest. You could use discounted cash flow analysis to determine what you should pay today for cash flow you would receive in the future.

Components of DCF analysis follow. (Note that abbreviations in parentheses are the most common way the components are identified on financial calculators and in formula functions of spreadsheets.)

- **Number of Payments per Year (P/YR):** Number of payments per year (P/YR) is the number of times per year a cash flow or benefit occurs. This is typically set to one payment per year (annual payments) or 12 payments per year (monthly payments).

- **Number of Periodic Payments (N):** Number of periodic payments (N) is the number of periods or times a cash flow or benefit occurs.

- **Annual Interest Rate (I/YR):** Annual interest rate (I/YR) represents the rate of return or discount rate.

- **Cash Flow (CFJ):** Cash flow is the even or uneven cash flow or benefit that is paid or received.

- **Number of Consecutive Cash Flows (NJ):** Number of consecutive cash flows is the number of periods or times the same cash flow or benefit occurs consecutively.

- **Net Present Value (NPV):** Net present value (NPV) is the difference between the cost of an investment and the discounted present value (PV) of all anticipated future fiscal benefits of that investment.

When solving for PV using uneven cash flows on some financial calculators, you must use the NPV key. This is because, when initial cash flow equals 0, the NPV function becomes the PV function.

MARKET AND INVESTMENT VALUE

Market value and investment value can be calculated by using the discounted cash flow technique. In both cases, future income is discounted at a particular rate to determine present value.

Regarding market value:

• Market value is estimated by forecasting annual Net Operating Income (NOI) and the future sales proceeds over a reasonable holding period. The final annual cash flow includes the sales proceeds. These cash flows are discounted to PV using a market discount rate.

• Under this technique, market value is equal to the PV of all future cash flows (NOIs) and sales proceeds.

Regarding investment value:

• Investment value requires you to determine the PV of the equity position. This is done by forecasting the annual before-tax cash flow (BTCF) and the future net sales proceeds. Cash flows are discounted to PV using the investor's required return rate. The PV of the BTCF for each year is the value of the equity position in the property. Then the amount of the mortgage is added to current value of the equity to determine the investment value of the property.

• Under this technique, investment value is equal to the sum of the PV of the equity position and the value of the mortgage position.

	Market Value	Investment Value
Income Stream Used	Net Operating Income (NOI)	Before-Tax Cash Flow (BTCF)
Loan Balance Added	No	Yes
Discount Rate Used	Market Discount Rate	Investor's Required Rate of Return

CALCULATING MARKET VALUE

Calculating market value is a four-step process.

Step 1: Forecast Net Operating Income (NOI)

First, forecast NOIs that are likely to accrue to the owner for a typical holding period. While appraisers may use longer periods, real estate managers commonly use five-year holding periods. Projecting over periods longer than five years is much more difficult; consequently, figures are not as reliable.

All assumptions used to project NOIs should be explained and should have a sound economic basis of support. Income does not need to be stable.

Step 2: Estimate Sales Proceeds

Next, estimate the terminal value, or what the property will sell for at the end of the holding period. This is accomplished by using capitalization to divide the *following year's* NOI by a capitalization rate (often referred to as the going-out cap rate, a measure of the market's perception of risk at the end of the holding period).

Remember, we use the IRV formula [I/R = V] to do this.

Next year's NOI is used because we are selling next year's benefits. Subtract the cost of sale (typically brokerage fees) from this terminal value to arrive at *sales proceeds*.

Terminal Value – Cost of Sale = Sales Proceeds

For example, for a five-year holding period, the terminal value is estimated by dividing the projected NOI for the sixth year by the going-out capitalization rate expected at that time. Sales costs are then subtracted to arrive at sales proceeds.

Sales proceeds are added to the NOI of the last year of the holding period.

Step 3: Select a Discount Rate

When estimating market value, the discount rate can be viewed as the market-driven return from the property. It includes the annual return from rental income *plus* any return from price appreciation. (Remember, a capitalization rate is simply a one-year return from rental income only.)

When selecting an appropriate discount rate for calculating market value, real estate managers should look to the broader investment markets and determine typical rates of return. A look at equity dividend rates from comparable risk investment alternatives might be one source of finding an appropriate discount rate.

When market value is sought, the discount rate must be found from market data. Market discount rates may be obtained from the following sources:

- Active market investors, experienced property managers, lenders, and appraisers

- Source books and published surveys

- Trade articles and websites

To ensure accuracy, the source used should be corroborated by the results of at least one other source. When using these sources to obtain a discount rate, compare investments of similar quality and risk. Keep in mind that large institutional investors tend to buy only top quality, lower risk properties.

Step 4: Sum Discounted NOIs

Next, all of the discounted NOIs plus the sales proceeds are summed to arrive at the present value of the property.

Example 13.1

Calculating Market Value Using DCF

A new office building is opening this year. Due to a weak market, the owner is offering tenants periods of free rent as an incentive to move in. Therefore, NOI will not reach a normal level for several years. The owner intends to sell the building after four years and the building should be fully leased at that time.

According to budget projections, annual NOI forecasts are as follows:

- Year 1 $18,000

- Year 2 $61,300

- Year 3 $85,800

- Year 4 $107,200

- Year 5 $111,500

The market-driven rate of return on investments of this type is 10%. The going-out capitalization rate for similar four-year-old buildings is 8.5%. Cost of sale is 3%.

Calculating Market Value Using DCF *(continued)*

What is the present market value of the property?

1. Forecast NOIs:

NOIs for the holding period (Years 1–4) have been provided.

2. Estimate sales proceeds:

First, determine terminal value by capitalizing the next–year's NOI.

$$\$111,500 \div 8.5\% = \$1,311,764.71$$

Next, subtract cost of sale to arrive at sales proceeds.

$$\$1,311,764.71 - \$39,353 = \$1,272,411.71$$

This figure is added to the Year 4 NOI.

3. Select a discount rate:

Assume a discount rate of 10%.

4. Sum the discounted NOIs:

Use a financial calculator or spreadsheet to determine that the present market value is $1,073,781. This means that if the investor pays this amount today for the property and receives these benefits, the 10% return will be realized.

CALCULATING INVESTMENT VALUE

Unlike when calculating market value, investment value is found by using a required rate of return that pertains to a particular investment and investor, instead of the market in general.

Calculating investment value is a five-step process.

Step 1: Forecast Cash Flows

Forecast NOIs, then subtract annual debt service (ADS) to arrive at cash flows that are likely to accrue to the property owner for a typical holding period. Remember:

$$NOI - ADS = BTCF$$

ADS will be unique to each investor and particular investment. Along with the unique investor's required rate of return, the real estate manager is able to calculate a true investment value that is unique to this investor and particular property. All assumptions used to project cash flows should be explained and should have a sound economic basis of support.

Step 2: Estimate Net Sales Proceeds

First, estimate a terminal value, or what the property will sell for at the end of the holding period. Like with market value, this is accomplished by using capitalization to divide the next year's NOI by a capitalization rate (i.e., the going-out cap rate).

Remember, we use the IRV formula to do this.

$$\text{Income} \div \text{Rate} = \text{Value}$$

Once you have estimated a terminal value, subtract the cost of sale *and the remaining loan balance* to arrive at net sales proceeds.

$$\text{Terminal Value} - \text{Cost of Sale} - \text{Loan Balance} = \text{Net Sales Proceeds}$$

For example, for a five-year holding period, estimate the terminal value by dividing the projected NOI for the sixth year by the capitalization rate expected at that time. Subtract sales costs and the remaining loan balance to arrive at net sales proceeds.

Add net sales proceeds to the cash flow of the last year of the holding period.

Step 3: Input the Investor's Required Rate of Return

When selecting a required rate of return for calculating investment value, real estate managers should ask the client what is appropriate for them to attract their money to the risk associated with the particular investment.

Step 4: Sum Discounted Cash Flows

Sum all of the discounted before-tax cash flows plus the net sales proceeds to arrive at the present value of the *equity* portion of the investment value.

Step 5: Add Original Loan Balance

After the cash flows have been discounted to the present time and summed together, add the original loan balance to the present value of the equity to arrive at the total investment value.

$$\text{Present Value of Equity} + \text{Original Loan Balance} = \text{Investment Value}$$

The present value of the loan will always be the initial loan amount when estimating investment value for a property yet to be built. When evaluating an existing property, the present value of the loan will be the loan balance at the beginning of the analysis period, not the outstanding balance at the end of the holding period.

An investor has purchased a commercial property that has an $850,000 mortgage and is expected to have the following cash flows:

- Year 1   ($55,000)
- Year 2   ($6,000)
- Year 3 $16,000

Year 4 NOI is projected to be $100,000. The going-out capitalization rate for similar properties is 9% and the cost of sale is expected to be 5%. The loan balance at the end of Year 3 will be $834,000. This investor normally requires a 10.5% rate of return on similar properties.

What is the investment value?

1. Forecast cash flows:

Cash flows for the holding period (Years 1–3) have been provided.

2. Estimate net sales proceeds:

First, determine terminal value by capitalizing the next year's (Year 4) NOI.

Terminal value ($100,000/9%)		$1,111,111
Cost of sale (5%)	−	55,555
Remaining loan balance	−	834,000
Net sales proceeds		221,556

3. Input the required rate of return:

The investor's required return is 10.5%.

4. Sum the discounted cash flows:

The present value of equity is $121,380.

5. Add the original loan balance:

121,380 + 850,000 = $971,380

The total present investment value of this property to this particular investor is $971,380.

TIPS

One can look at this problem in a different way. Essentially, what the discounted cash flow calculation is doing is taking each year's income and discounting it back to today's value, then adding it all up. So Year 1 cash flow is discounted back one year at 10.5%. Year 2 cash flow is discounted back two years at 10.5%. Year 3 cash flow is discounted back three years at 10.5%.

All of the discounted cash flows are summed to give us present value of equity. Finally, the loan balance is added to arrive at total investment value.

Remember, real estate managers often favor discounted cash flow analysis over capitalization for valuation because it accounts for multiple-year cash flows and may provide a more realistic estimate of property value.

Questions real estate managers may ask

... when considering the value of the properties he or she manages:

- What is the investment value of one of the property's I manage to my particular owners and how does it compare to market value?

- How does this compare to the *fair market value*?

- How can I apply the TVM and DCF concepts to make the best decisions for the properties I manage?

REVIEW QUESTIONS

- When is discounted cash flow analysis used, and what are its components?

- How does the market discount rate compare to the market capitalization rate?

- What are the steps used to estimate sales proceeds when determining market value?

- What are some sources of determining market discount rates?

- What are the two major differences between calculating market value and calculating investment value?

Financial Analysis and Making Recommendations

Real estate managers use measures of return to make the best financial decisions regarding the property in order to meet ownership goals. To that end, real estate managers must analyze a property's financial performance by conducting cash flow projections over the holding period and evaluating possible courses of action for a property. Performing cash flow analyses allows the real estate manager to more accurately forecast the value and performance of real estate. This type of analysis examines figures such as purchase price, equity, loan variables, income and expenses, and required rates of return to determine the overall financial health of the asset.

In this chapter, we will use many of the concepts presented in this book to conduct a before-tax cash flow analysis in order to examine possible courses of action for a property and make a sound recommendation about the future of the asset to ownership. Note that in the subsequent examples, a copyrighted spreadsheet tool (the *IREM® Financial Analysis Spreadsheet*) is used to complete the financial analysis. However, any financial analysis tool from spreadsheet software to financial calculators could be used to perform these.

BEFORE TAX CASH FLOW ANALYSIS

To apply what has been discussed thus far, let's conduct a before-tax cash flow (BTCF) analysis.

BTCF Analysis	*Example 14.1*

The Mayfair property was purchased by your client for $6,000,000 with a $1,500,000 down payment and a 30-year $4,500,000 mortgage with a 7% interest rate (assume monthly payments). No points or fees were charged.

Gross potential income (GPI) is expected to be $775,000 in Year 1. Operating expenses are expected to be $300,000 in Year 1. Both are expected to increase by 2% each year. The property is expected to sell at the end of Year 5 at an 8% going-out capitalization rate. Assume a cost of sale to be 5%. The owner's required return is 10%.

Using this information, perform a cash flow analysis for the Mayfair property, rounding all figures to the nearest dollar.

A. What is initial equity?

B. What are principal and interest payments for each year and the loan balance at the end of
   Year 5?

C. What are before-tax cash flows over the holding period?

D. What are the net sales proceeds?

E. What does the T-bar look like?

F. Calculate the four tests of investment return.

The following sections provide answers to these six questions.

A. What is initial equity?

INITIAL ANALYSIS	
	Initial Value
Purchase Price	$6,000,000
+ Acquisition Expenses	$0
+ Points, Fees	$0
= Original Basis	$6,000,000
- Loan Amount	$4,500,000
= Initial Equity	$1,500,000
MIDSTREAM ANALYSIS (if applicable)	
Current Market Value	$0
- Cost of Sale	$0
- Current Loan Balance	$0
= Cash-Out Potential	$0
+ Capital Improvements	$0
- New Loans	$0
+ New Points, Fees	$0
= Current Equity	$1,500,000

B. What are principal and interest payments for each year and the loan balance at the end of Year 5?

	Principal Pmt	Interest Pmt	Balance
Year 1	45,711	313,552	4,454,289
Year 2	49,016	310,247	4,405,273
Year 3	52,559	306,704	4,352,713
Year 4	56,359	302,905	4,296,355
Year 5	60,433	298,830	4,235,922

C. What are before-tax cash flows over the holding period?

	Year 1	Year 2	Year 3	Year 4	Year 5
NOI	$475,000	$484,500	$494,190	$504,074	$514,155
- Loan Principal	$45,711	$49,016	$52,559	$56,359	$60,433
- Loan Interest	$313,552	$310,247	$306,704	$302,905	$298,830
- Capital Expenditures	$0	$0	$0	$0	$0
= BTCF	$115,737	$125,237	$134,927	$144,810	$154,892

D. What are the net sales proceeds?

					PROCEEDS OF SALE ANAL
					Terminal Value
Sale Price	$6,000,000	-	-	-	$6,555,480
- Cost of Sale	$300,000	-	-	-	$327,774
- Loan Balance	$4,454,289	$4,405,273	$4,352,713	$4,296,355	$4,235,922
= Net Sale Proceeds	$1,245,711	-	-	-	$1,991,784

E. What does the T-bar look like?

5 Year T-BAR			
N	$		
Current Equity	(1,500,000)		
BTCF Year 1	115,737		
BTCF Year 2	125,237		
BTCF Year 3	134,927		
BTCF Year 4	144,810	Year 5 BTCF	Sales Proceeds
BTCF Year 5 + NSP	2,146,676	154,892	1,991,784

F. Calculate the four tests of investment return.

FOUR TESTS OF INVESTMENT RETURN: Year 5			
Year 1 $/$%	Value Enh.	NPV	IRR
7.72%	$555,480	$241,913	13.82%

Cash on Cash

Year 1 BTCF ÷ Initial Equity = $115,737 ÷ $1,500,000 = 0.077158 x 100 = 7.72%

Value Enhancement

Value at End of Holding Period	$ 6,555,480
–Value at Beginning of Holding Period	– 6,000,000
–Cost of Capital Improvements	– 0
Value Enhancement	$555,480

NPV and IRR

After inputting the above variables from the T-bar into a financial calculator or spreadsheet:

- NPV = $241,913

- IRR = 13.82%

MIDSTREAM ANALYSIS

The previous example was conducted at the beginning of an initial investment. A *midstream analysis* is performed when an investor wants to examine equity and investment return from a point in time other than the original purchase date. Situations that necessitate a midstream analysis may include:

- Change in management

- Infusion of capital

- Refinancing

- Testing alternative courses of action

A midstream analysis can tell the real estate manager and owner:

- The owner's cash-out potential, or the income he or she would have received had the property been sold at that time.

- The owner's current equity in the property after capital improvements are made. These figures can then help in assessing investment return at the midstream point.

Cash-Out Potential

Midstream analysis is used to determine cash-out potential as follows. Cash-out potential can also be referred to as opportunity cost—the cost for the opportunity to receive future cash benefits.

> Current Market Value
> − Cost of Sale
> − Current Loan Balance
> ——————————————
> = Cash-Out Potential

Current Equity

If a midstream analysis is conducted due to the infusion of new capital, the equation is continued as follows:

> Cash-Out Potential
> + Capital Improvements
> − New Loans
> + New Points and Fees
> ——————————————
> = Current Equity

For example:

Current Market Value	$ 2,000,000
– Cost of Sale	– 60,000
– Current Loan Balance	– 1,000,000
= Cash-Out Potential	= 940,0000
+ Capital Improvements	+ 200,000
– New Loans	– 150,000
+ New Points and Fees	+ 0
= Current Equity	= $990,000

Importance of Understanding Current Equity

A more detailed analysis of income property requires understanding that all investment returns are based on the current (time point zero) equity, not the equity from the past. Once current equity is determined, the real estate manager is in a position to consider potential alternatives for long-term growth and to weigh them against both market expectations and individual investor goals.

It is very important that a real estate manager who is evaluating alternatives for a property keep current equity as the focus for the analysis. Understandably, investors tend to focus on their successes with an investment from the time of purchase, but the real estate manager, when looking toward the future, must focus on current value and current equity in order to set realistic expectations. When values grow or drop, the new equity position is the focus of the analysis and is always used as time point zero of the t-bar analysis.

Keep in mind that current equity represents the money the investor would receive if the property was sold today. Based on the current equity, decisions can then be made as to how to invest available capital. One alternative is to keep the money in the property and forecast alternatives for growth. Another is to use the money in an alternative investment. Midstream analysis examines these alternatives—reinvesting money elsewhere or keeping it in the property—and focuses on focuses on the current equity and value rather than the past.

PERFORMING A MIDSTREAM ANALYSIS

It's time to apply midstream analysis to an example property.

A Complete Midstream Analysis

Example 14.2

Consider a commercial property that was purchased in Year 1 for $2,300,000 with a $1,725,000 loan at 9% interest for 30 years. You begin managing the building at the beginning of this year, Year 4. Your client requires an 8% return on real estate investments. Your research has established that a typical capitalization rate for this property type is 9.5% at this time. Assume selling costs of 7% of the sales price.

The owner has agreed to invest $300,000 into the electrical and HVAC systems, which are in need of an overhaul.

According to budget forecasts, annual GPI is projected to be $602,500 and escalate by 3% yearly. Operating expenses are projected to be $300,000 and escalate by 3% yearly as well. Your client plans to sell the property at the end of Year 7 when the going-out capitalization rate is predicted to be 11% and cost of sale is still estimated at 7%.

Before proceeding with this example, we will enter the relevant variables in the *IREM® Financial Analysis Spreadsheet*.

Purchase price, loan terms, analysis begin month, required return, capitalization rates, and cost of sale are all entered in the Owner Goals tab as shown in Exhibit 14.1.

Owner's Goals and Objectives

Exhibit 14.1

Owner Goals and Objectives
Enter data in the yellow highlighted cells only.

Site:	For:

ANALYSIS VARIABLES	
Loan Amount ($)	$1,725,000
Loan Interest Rate (%)	9.00%
Loan Pre-paid points (%) (EFI%)	
Loan Amortization Period (years)	30
Loan Balloon (years) (EFI%)	
Loan Penalty (%) (EFI%)	
Analysis Begin Month	Loan 2 Begin	37
Owner's Required Return (%)	8.00%
Going-IN Capitalization Rate (%)	9.50%
Cost of Sale (%)	7.00%

INITIAL ANALYSIS	
	Initial Value
Purchase Price	$2,300,000
+ Acquisition Expenses	
+ Points, Fees	
= Original Basis	$2,300,000
- Loan Amount	$1,725,000
= Initial Equity	$575,000

Gross potential income (GPI), operating expenses, and annual escalation amounts are entered in the Pro Forma Statement tab as shown in Exhibit 14.2. Note that several columns have been hidden for display purposes. Also, total operating expenses were placed in the first row (Heat) and will carry down to the bottom of the statement to calculate Net Operating Income (NOI).

Exhibit 14.2	Pro Forma Statement

Pro Forma Statement
Enter data in the yellow

Site:	For:		By:			
		Annual Increase				
Income		Increase	Year 1	Year 2	Year 3	Year 4
Gross Potential Income (GPI)		3.00%	$602,500	$620,575	$639,192	$658,368
- Loss to Lease		0.00%	$0	$0	$0	$0
- Vacancy and Collection Loss		0.00%	$0	$0	$0	$0
= Net Rent Revenue			$602,500	$620,575	$639,192	$658,368
+ Miscellaneous Income		0.00%	$0	$0	$0	$0
+ Property Tax Reimbursement		0.00%	$0	$0	$0	$0
+ Utility Reimbursement		0.00%	$0	$0	$0	$0
+ CAM Reimbursement		0.00%	$0	$0	$0	$0
+ Other Reimbursement		0.00%	$0	$0	$0	$0
= Effective Gross Income (EGI)			$602,500	$620,575	$639,192	$658,368
Operating Expenses						
Utilities						
Heat		3.00%	$300,000	$309,000	$318,270	$327,818
Electric		0.00%	$0	$0	$0	$0
Water and Sewer		0.00%	$0	$0	$0	$0
Total Utilities			$300,000	$309,000	$318,270	$327,818

Now that we've entered the variables, let's conduct our midstream analysis.

What is the cash-out potential?

Cash-out potential, or the amount that would be achieved if the owner were to sell the property today, is $1,275,092. Current market value was first found by capitalizing this year's NOI. Then the cost of sale and the current loan balance were deducted.

INITIAL ANALYSIS	
	Initial Value
Purchase Price	$2,300,000
+ Acquisition Expenses	
+ Points, Fees	
= Original Basis	$2,300,000
- Loan Amount	$1,725,000
= Initial Equity	$575,000
MIDSTREAM ANALYSIS (if applicable)	
Current Market Value	$3,184,211
- Cost of Sale	$222,895
- Current Loan Balance	$1,686,224
= Cash-Out Potential	$1,275,092

Analysis begins year 4
(Rounded Up)

What is the current equity?

Current ownership equity in the property is $1,575,092. This was found by entering the $300,000 capital improvement figure which was added to cash-out potential.

INITIAL ANALYSIS	
	Initial Value
Purchase Price	$2,300,000
+ Acquisition Expenses	
+ Points, Fees	
= Original Basis	$2,300,000
- Loan Amount	$1,725,000
= Initial Equity	$575,000
MIDSTREAM ANALYSIS (if applicable)	
Current Market Value	$3,184,211
- Cost of Sale	$222,895
- Current Loan Balance	$1,686,224
= Cash-Out Potential	$1,275,092
+ Capital Improvements	$300,000
- New Loans (Mid Stream)	$0
+ New Points, Fees	
= Current Equity	$1,575,092

Analysis begins year 4
(Rounded Up)

What is the midstream net present value? What assumptions can you make from this number regarding the internal rate of return?

Midstream NPV, assuming a holding period of four years, is ($153,326). Because NPV is negative, we can assume that IRR has not met ownership goals.

	$/$%	Value Enh.	NPV	IRR
		TESTS OF INVESTMENT RETURN		
Year 2	9.21%	($566,736)	($416,693)	-8.14%
Year 3	9.80%	($479,211)	($282,163)	0.45%
Year 4	10.41%	($389,061)	($153,326)	4.87%

What is the midstream internal rate of return?

Midstream IRR is 4.87%. As predicted by the negative NPV, this is less than the required goal of 8%.

	$/$%	Value Enh.	NPV	IRR
		TESTS OF INVESTMENT RETURN		
Year 2	9.21%	($566,736)	($416,693)	-8.14%
Year 3	9.80%	($479,211)	($282,163)	0.45%
Year 4	10.41%	($389,061)	($153,326)	4.87%

What is your overall assessment of the performance of this property?

The property does not meet the financial performance goals of ownership. Alternative courses of action should be considered for the property.

ANALYZING PROPERTY ALTERNATIVES

Changing the investment performance of a property requires the exploration and possible selection of alternative courses of action for that property. A real estate manager should analyze the property in its "as-is" condition first to establish a baseline of performance. He or she may then test several other alternatives as illustrated in Exhibit 14.3.

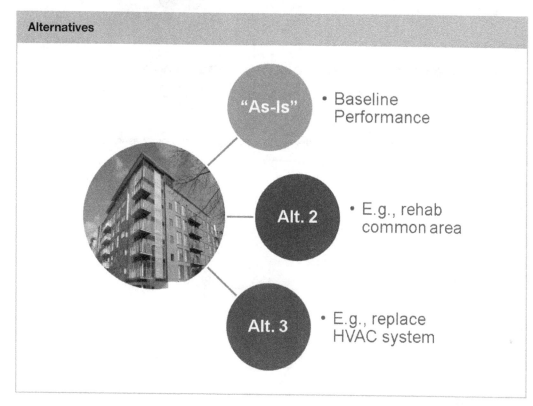

Alternatives   *Exhibit 14.3*

- "As-Is" • Baseline Performance
- Alt. 2 • E.g., rehab common area
- Alt. 3 • E.g., replace HVAC system

The owner's goals and objectives as well as results from the manager's previous property and market analyses will help identify possible alternatives to test. Each option could have an impact on the property's income, expenses, future value, and investment return. Conclusions about the alternatives chosen are drawn from thorough financial evaluation of each.

For the property in its "as is" state, as well as for any possible courses of action, develop the following:

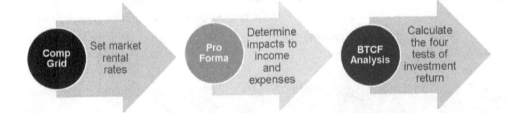

EXAMPLE: MIDSTREAM ANALYSIS OF ALTERNATIVES

InvestGroup, the investors in the City Tower project, require a 14% rate of return as well as at least $3,000,000 in value enhancement.

They are considering some alternatives for an investment property they purchased five years ago. They would like the real estate manager to perform an analysis of the next five years, assuming a sale at the end of Year 5. Note that this analysis begins in month 61 as analysis years and ownership years are not the same. For example, Year 1 of the analysis is actually Year 6 of ownership.

The property was purchased based on the following information:

- Purchase price: $6,000,000

- Initial loan amount: $5,100,000

- Interest rate: 9.5%

- Loan term: 30 years

- Current (going-in) market cap rate: 8%

- Going-out capitalization rate: 10.5%

- Cost of sale: 3.5%

As-Is (Alternative One)

Note that an *as-is analysis* is done because it provides a baseline for comparison.

Figures from the Pro Forma Statement include:

- Gross potential income (GPI): $2,000,000 (Based on lease escalations, GPI is expected to increase 5% per year starting next year.)

- Operating expenses: $850,000 (Based on the efficiently run property, expenses are expected to increase by only 2% per year starting next year.)

A. What is midstream current equity?

INITIAL ANALYSIS	
	Initial Value
Purchase Price	$6,000,000
+ Acquisition Expenses	$0
+ Points, Fees	$0
= Original Basis	$6,000,000
- Loan Amount	$5,100,000
= Initial Equity	$900,000
MIDSTREAM ANALYSIS (if applicable)	
Current Market Value	$14,375,000
- Cost of Sale	$503,125
- Current Loan Balance	$4,908,290
= Cash-Out Potential	$8,963,585
+ Capital Improvements	$0
- New Loans	$0
+ New Points, Fees	$0
= Current Equity	$8,963,585

B. What are the before-tax cash flows for the next five years?

	Year 1	Year 2	Year 3	Year 4	Year 5
NOI	$1,150,000	$1,233,000	$1,320,660	$1,413,223	$1,510,945
- Loan Principal	$50,475	$55,485	$60,992	$67,045	$73,699
- Loan Interest	$464,127	$459,118	$453,611	$447,558	$440,904
- Capital Expenditures	$0	$0	$0	$0	$0
= BTCF	$635,397	$718,397	$806,057	$898,620	$996,342

C. What are the net sales proceeds at the end of the holding period?

					Terminal Value
Sale Price	$14,375,000	-	-	-	$15,372,328
- Cost of Sale	$503,125	-	-	-	$538,031
- Loan Balance	$4,857,814	$4,802,329	$4,741,338	$4,674,292	$4,600,593
= Net Sale Proceeds	$9,014,061	-	-	-	$10,233,703

D. What does the T-bar look like?

5 Year T-BAR				
N	$			
Current Equity	(8,963,585)			
BTCF Year 1	635,397			
BTCF Year 2	718,397			
BTCF Year 3	806,057			
BTCF Year 4	898,620		Year 5 BTCF	Sales Proceeds
BTCF Year 5 + NSP	11,230,046		996,342	10,233,703

E. Perform the four tests.

FOUR TESTS OF INVESTMENT RETURN: Year 5			
Year 1 $/$%	Value Enh.	NPV	IRR
7.09%	$997,328	($944,781)	11.11%

Note that the real estate manager is looking at Year 1 $/$% even though this is a 5-year analysis.

Alternative Two

After discussions with the owners, the real estate manager decides to test the feasibility of an alternative course of action, which is to perform a moderate renovation of common areas at a cost of $200,000 as well as a moderate upgrade of the common exterior and landscape area at a cost of $100,000, for total capital improvements of $300,000.

Based on a survey of comparable properties and an analysis of the supply, demand, and absorption statistics, the real estate manager concludes that the combination of these projects will increase the GPI by 7% per year total starting next year. Expense escalations are projected to remain the same (2% annual increase). Note that operating expenses did not change in this case.

A. What is midstream current equity?

INITIAL ANALYSIS	
	Initial Value
Purchase Price	$6,000,000
+ Acquisition Expenses	$0
+ Points, Fees	$0
= Original Basis	$6,000,000
- Loan Amount	$5,100,000
= Initial Equity	$900,000
MIDSTREAM ANALYSIS (if applicable)	
Current Market Value	$14,375,000
- Cost of Sale	$503,125
- Current Loan Balance	$4,908,290
= Cash-Out Potential	$8,963,585
+ Capital Improvements	$300,000
- New Loans	$0
+ New Points, Fees	$0
= Current Equity	$9,263,585

B. What are the before-tax cash flows for the next five years?

	Year 1	Year 2	Year 3	Year 4	Year 5
NOI	$1,150,000	$1,273,000	$1,405,460	$1,548,059	$1,701,525
- Loan Principal	$50,475	$55,485	$60,992	$67,045	$73,699
- Loan Interest	$464,127	$459,118	$453,611	$447,558	$440,904
- Capital Expenditures	$0	$0	$0	$0	$0
= BTCF	$635,397	$758,397	$890,857	$1,033,456	$1,186,922

C. What are the net sales proceeds at the end of the holding period?

					PROCEEDS OF SALE ANAL
					Terminal Value
Sale Price	$14,375,000	-	-	-	$17,777,474
- Cost of Sale	$503,125	-	-	-	$622,212
- Loan Balance	$4,857,814	$4,802,329	$4,741,338	$4,674,292	$4,600,593
= Net Sale Proceeds	$9,014,061	-	-	-	$12,554,669

D. What does the T-bar look like?

5 Year T-BAR			
N	$		
Current Equity	(9,263,585)		
BTCF Year 1	635,397		
BTCF Year 2	758,397		
BTCF Year 3	890,857		
BTCF Year 4	1,033,456	Year 5 BTCF	Sales Proceeds
BTCF Year 5 + NSP	13,741,591	1,186,922	12,554,669

E. Perform the four tests.

FOUR TESTS OF INVESTMENT RETURN: Year 5			
Year 1 $/$%	Value Enh.	NPV	IRR
6.86%	$3,102,474	$227,487	14.63%

Alternative Three

After discussions with the owners, the real estate manager decides to test the feasibility of another alternative course, which is to perform an upgrade to the energy consuming equipment at a cost of $200,000.

Because of the installation of the energy saving equipment, the real estate manager expects that the operating expenses will only increase by 1% annually instead of the 2% originally projected. Income is still projected to increase by the original 5% per year.

A. What is the midstream current equity?

INITIAL ANALYSIS	
	Initial Value
Purchase Price	$6,000,000
+ Acquisition Expenses	$0
+ Points, Fees	$0
= Original Basis	$6,000,000
- Loan Amount	$5,100,000
= Initial Equity	$900,000
MIDSTREAM ANALYSIS (if applicable)	
Current Market Value	$14,375,000
- Cost of Sale	$503,125
- Current Loan Balance	$4,908,290
= Cash-Out Potential	$8,963,585
+ Capital Improvements	$200,000
- New Loans	$0
+ New Points, Fees	$0
= Current Equity	$9,163,585

B. What are the before-tax cash flows for the next five years?

	Year 1	Year 2	Year 3	Year 4	Year 5
NOI	$1,150,000	$1,241,500	$1,337,915	$1,439,494	$1,546,499
- Loan Principal	$50,475	$55,485	$60,992	$67,045	$73,699
- Loan Interest	$464,127	$459,118	$453,611	$447,558	$440,904
- Capital Expenditures	$0	$0	$0	$0	$0
= BTCF	$635,397	$726,897	$823,312	$924,891	$1,031,896

C. What are the net sales proceeds at the end of the holding period?

					PROCEEDS OF SALE ANALY
					Terminal Value
Sale Price	$14,375,000	-	-	-	$15,801,948
- Cost of Sale	$503,125	-	-	-	$553,068
- Loan Balance	$4,857,814	$4,802,329	$4,741,338	$4,674,292	$4,600,593
= Net Sale Proceeds	$9,014,061	-	-	-	$10,648,287

D. What does the T-bar look like?

5 Year T-BAR			Year 5 BTCF	Sales Proceeds
N	$			
Current Equity	(9,163,585)			
BTCF Year 1	635,397			
BTCF Year 2	726,897			
BTCF Year 3	823,312			
BTCF Year 4	924,891			
BTCF Year 5 + NSP	11,680,183		1,031,896	10,648,287

E. Perform the four tests.

FOUR TESTS OF INVESTMENT RETURN: Year 5			
Year 1 $/$%	Value Enh.	NPV	IRR
6.93%	$1,226,948	($877,252)	11.39%

Questions real estate managers may ask

. . . when considering making recommendations:

- What do the before-tax cash flow analyses of my properties tell me?
- When might I conduct a midstream analysis? How might my knowledge of this type of analysis highlight my value to a client?
- Knowing my owners' goals for your properties and based on my analyses, are there improvements that might help achieve the owners' desired return?

RECOMMENDING A COURSE OF ACTION

After the "as is" and alternative analyses are conducted, it is time to compare the results of each scenario and make the best recommendation, based on the specific goals of ownership.

The following matrix can be used to present the results of these financial tests:

Test	Alternative 1 (As Is)	Alternative 2	Alternative 3
$/$%			
Value Enhancement			
NPV			
IRR			

The goal of the tests is to provide a means of comparison for each alternative. Some of the tests may not be applicable in certain situations. More than likely, all tests will not point to the same alternative. When this occurs, the real estate manager must determine which analytical method or methods are preferable given the circumstances. Ownership goals should always be the driving factor for any decisions made.

TIPS

Not all tests may point to the same alternative—determine which test(s) are preferable given ownership goals. Explain why adoption and implementation of the alternative you recommend is preferable given your analyses.

CHECKLIST: WHAT TO INCLUDE

- ❏ Operating plan for property
- ❏ Implementation timeframe
- ❏ Any perceived risks and exposures
- ❏ Any financing recommendations
- ❏ Marketing and leasing plan to achieve results

EXAMPLE: MAKING A RECOMMENDATION

Let's take the example from the midstream analysis of alternatives for the InvestGroup's City Tower project to the next step: making a recommendation.

The real estate manager begins by placing the financial test results in the matrix to compare the three alternatives. Recall that ownership stated desired goals of a 14% return as well as a minimum of $3,000,000 in value enhancement

Test	Alternative 1 (As Is)	Alternative 2	Alternative 3
$/$%	7.09%	6.86%	6.93%
Value Enhancement	$997,328	$3,102,474	$1,226,948
NPV	($944,781)	$227,487	($877,252)
IRR	11.11%	14.63%	11.39%

Based on the analyses, which alternative should the real estate manager recommend? The real estate manager should recommend Alternative 2 because the clients require a 14% return as well as at least $3,000,000 in value enhancement. Alternative 2 is the only scenario that meets both of these goals.

However, not all the tests point to the same alternative. Alternative 1 has the greatest $/$%, but single-year return was not a goal of the owners. Alternative 2 has the greatest value enhancement, NPV, and IRR, meeting all of the ownership goals.

This example shows how important it is to make recommendations to ownership based on their specific goals for the property.

REVIEW QUESTIONS

- How is before-tax cash flow calculated?

- When is a midstream analysis is performed?

- What is cash-out potential?

- What is current equity?

- What calculations differentiate a midstream analysis from a purchase (initial) analysis?

- Why would a real estate manager analyze property alternatives?

- Which alternative provides a baseline for a property's performance?

- What are the four financial tests, and what is the best way to organize and summarize data from the four financial tests for each alternative?

- What is the most important thing to keep in mind when determining which scenario to present to ownership?

- What other information should be shared with the owner when making a recommendation?

Lease Analysis

Many of the concepts discussed thus far can also be applied to analysis of leases. For example, discounted cash flow analysis is a key tool to determine the financial impact lease terms and concessions have on property income. The real value of leases drives cash flow, which in turn drives property value.

Keep in mind the following definitions:

- **Base Rent:** Quoted contract dollar amount of periodic rent
- **Present Value of Rent:** Base rent net of concessions over the term of the lease discounted at a given rate
- **Effective Rent:** Present value of base rent amortized over the lease term at the given discount rate into equal payments and further converted into a rental rate per square foot

LEASE CONCESSIONS AND EFFECTIVE RENT
(Short-Term and Long-Term Leases)

Many residential leases are for terms of one year or less, while commercial leases may run five to 25 years. Certainly, though there are short-term commercial leases, especially **sublet space,** which is space vacated before a lease expires. Rent concessions are benefits used to encourage a tenant to enter into a lease. Concessions and terms are negotiated as landlords and tenants perceive their position of strength in the lease market. Concessions have a financial impact on the effective rent.

In residential property management, effective rent is the rent per month reduced by the monthly value of any leasing concessions computed on a per month bases for that unit. It is also the cumulative rental amount collected over the full term of a lease. In commercial properties, effective rent is the amount of rent a commercial tenant actually pays after base rent is adjusted for concessions, pass-through charges, and tenant improvements. Thus, effective rent differs from the quoted base rent set forth in the lease.

The short-term nature of residential leases is one factor that makes calculating effective residential rent simple. There is no need to incorporate the time value of money. Another simplifying factor is the similarity of residential leases. Rent concessions, which are benefits used to encourage a tenant to enter into a lease, usually take the form of free rent, typically for one or more weeks. Though concessions are generally discouraged as a residential leasing strategy, marketplace competition sometimes warrants their use. A particular slow leasing period may be energized by a manager who advertises a concession to attract new tenants. Revenue management programs that design leasing strategies, including rent price and concessions may change often, even daily in some situations.

Commercial leases, on the other hand, typically are more difficult to analyze because lease terms are longer and lease negotiation usually includes multiple factors. In a residential setting, the landlord creates the lease document, and it is generally the same for every tenant. A residential tenant does not have the negotiating power of a large commercial tenant. In commercial real estate, the lease document may be different for every tenant, especially among large users of space that are represented by brokers (or tenant representatives and national tenants). The negotiating points to be considered may include free rent, tenant improvements, buyouts of existing leases, reimbursements of tenant costs, the amount of space to be occupied, and so on.

Short-Term Leases

Effective rent on short-term leases can be calculated by averaging the rent net of the rent concessions. For example, if a property charges $800 per month, per unit, and one month of free rent is offered, total rental income would be $800 x 11 months = $8,800. The total rental income is then divided by the term, and the payment is averaged. So, $8,800 ÷ 12 months = $733.34 effective rent accounted for monthly. Note that $733.34 is effective rent used for analysis purposes only; the tenant or resident will actually get the entire concession in a single month and the stated rent, in this example $800, is paid each of the other months of the lease term (e.g., the tenant or resident doesn't pay the first month's rent but then pays the full $800 per month each month after that).

Long-Term Leases

Concessions associated with long-term leases must account for the passage of time by discounting concessions when they occur. Merely averaging the cash flows (as is done for short-term leases) will not result in effective rent. Rather, to determine effective rent, the sums of all cash flows associated with the lease are discounted to present value. This present value is then amortized into equal payments over the lease term and further converted into a rent rate per square foot per year.

To achieve this, discounted cash flow analysis is used:

1. Enter the lease payments net of concessions. These are the cash flows or benefits received each period.

2. Enter the discount rate, or the rate at which you are discounting these cash flows back to today's value. This is the required rate of return on the money associated with the concession.

3. Solve for the present value of the cash flows using the NPV button.

4. Calculate the payments over the term of the lease. Then calculate the annual rental rate per square foot.

When calculating effective rent for a long-term commercial lease, the final step of calculating on a per-square-foot basis is particularly important for two reasons:

- First, the property owner may have established goals (and property budgets) that assume a specific minimum rent per square foot.

- Second, rental spaces in most commercial buildings are flexible, and a prospective tenant may be interested in space that is already leased to someone else.

Making effective use of space and maximizing rent per square foot are important leasing considerations.

Effective Rent on a Long-Term Lease　　　　　　　　　　　　　　　*Example 15.1*

Suppose you are considering a 10-year gross lease on 1,200 square feet of space that calls for annual rent payments of $20.00 per square foot and free rent for the first 24 months. The owner's required return is 10%. What is the effective rent per square foot per year?

(1,200 sq. ft. x $20/sq. ft. = $24,000 ÷ 12 months = $2,000 rent/month)

N	$
0	(PV)
1	0
2	0
•	•
•	•
24	0
25	2,000
•	•
120	2,000

Enter the variables into a financial spreadsheet or calculator to get an effective rent of $14.27 per square foot per year.

. . . when considering lease analysis:

• How does time impact the present value of my long-term leases?

Consider the rental rate comparisons here. Which would be the most accurate reflection of the effective rent being received?

No Concession	Concession Averaged	Concession Discounted
$20/sq. ft.	$16.00/sq. ft. ($20 x 8 years of rent payments ÷ 10-year term)	$14.27/sq. ft.

Example 15.2 | **Another Look at Effective Rent on a Long-Term Lease**

What if the free rent were given at the end of the term? Calculate the new effective rent per square foot per year and compare the two.

N	$
0	(PV)
1	2,000
•	•
•	•
96	2,000
97	0
•	•
•	•
120	0

Enter the variables into a financial spreadsheet or calculator to get an effective rent of $17.42 per square foot per year.

Note that the timing of the free rent greatly impacts the net effective rent per square foot. Providing the free rent at the end of the term benefits the owner. This is because money today is worth more than money in the future.

Free Rent at Beginning of Term	Free Rent at End of Term
$14.27/sq. ft.	$17.42/sq. ft.

Example 15.3

Actual vs. Effective Rent

Another way a real estate manager might present potential deals to an owner is to plot effective rent versus actual rent. See the simplified example here.

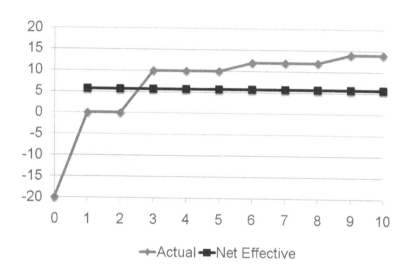

In this case, both lines represent the same net present value. However, based on the owner's goals, he or she may prefer a more consistent annual rent or may prefer a higher effective rent in later years.

Solving for PV of base rent is only part of the process. Variables such as the amount and timing of concessions, discount rate, square footage, and lease duration all affect PV.

Exhibit 15.4	Differing Lease Terms

Let's look at another example—this time using differing lease terms. Consider the three deals below:

- **Deal 1:** 10,000 square feet at $10/sq. ft. for 7 years
- **Deal 2:** 10,000 square feet at $7/sq. ft. for 10 years
- **Deal 3:** 8,000 square feet at $10/sq. ft. for 10 years

When the PV calculation is applied to each deal, the resulting income can be compared.

Deal	SF	Rental Rate	Years	Total Rent	PV@ 10%
1	10,000	$10/SF	7	$700,000	$486,841.88
2	10,000	$7/SF	10	$700,000	$430,119.70
3	8,000	$10/SF	10	$800,000	$491,565.37

Which lease deal would you take? Deal 2 is clearly not attractive, but how might you choose between Deal 1 and Deal 3? When presented to the owner in this manner, the owner may be theoretically willing to take either deal. Perhaps more leased square footage is important to this owner. Perhaps a longer lease is more important. Ownership goals always drive the best decision-making for the property.

CHECKLIST: USES OF EFFECTIVE RENT

☐ To analyze the impact of changing base rent and concession amounts and timing

☐ To consider "what if" alternative deals

☐ To compare actual deals to budgeted income

☐ To examine the impact of deals on property value—you may drop your overall property value even if you are enhancing cash flow in a given year

LEASE BUYOUTS

The buyout of an existing lease by a landlord or a tenant may occur to achieve numerous outcomes. A landlord may want to buy out a tenant's occupancy if the tenant is paying below-market rent or if the space is needed to meet operational or leasing needs. In situations where potential future credit issues impact rent collectability or the landlord is dealing with a problem tenant but eviction isn't desirable, a lease buyout also may be considered.

The tenant may want to buy out the landlord's rights if the tenant needs less space, is experiencing financial difficulties, or wants to release themselves from current lease obligations.

Determining the appropriate payment when buying out a tenant's current lease may be difficult to calculate because the lease may not expire for many months or years. The real estate manager can use the time value of money concept to gain an objective estimate of the appropriate value of a lease buyout by using a desired discount rate.

When market rents exceed contract rents, a **leasehold advantage** for the tenant can occur in the form of below-market rent enjoyment. When this occurs, the cash flow specifically associated with the leasehold advantage is estimated from the market. The leasehold advantage is then discounted to determine its present value.

Note that if the owner or manager is negotiating the buyout of the lease or leasehold advantage, he or she will want a higher discount rate, thus creating a lower PV.

Blend and Extend

When market conditions are unstable, it may result in the tenant paying a rental rate that is greater than the current market warrants. If there is a significant term left on the lease, it is not uncommon for the tenant to want a rent reduction and the landlord to want an extended term. The real estate manager may consider "blend and extend," where the rental rate and term are renegotiated so that the rent is reduced (usually the resulting reduced rent is still above market) and the term extended by adding years to the end of the remaining term (usually five years).

Example 15.5

Buying Out a Leasehold Advantage

Your tenant has nine years remaining on a lease at $6,000 per year. The space is worth $10,500 per year today. The adjacent tenant wants to expand into the space. You want to make the arrangement, but first you must buy out the leasehold advantage. The current market rate of return is 11%.

What is the maximum amount that should be paid to buy out this leasehold advantage?

Market Rent	=	$875 per month
Contract Rent	=	$520 per month
Leasehold Advantage	=	$375 per month

Therefore, in buying out the tenant's lease, the landlord must focus on the net benefit received from the new lease (the leasehold advantage)—in this case, $4,500 per year or $375 per month.

N	$
0	(PV)
1	375
2	375
3	375
•	•
•	•
108	375

Enter the variables into a financial spreadsheet or calculator and the present value of the future payments associated with the leasehold advantage is $25,639.52. This is the maximum amount that should be paid to buy out the existing tenant's lease.

You are interested in buying out a prospective new tenant's current lease and are negotiating a buyout price with the tenant's previous landlord. The lease expires in 16 months (too short to make subleasing viable), and $5,500 of rent is due each month. Similar investments yield 10%. In this case, we are only buying out the lease. Leasehold advantage is not being considered.

What is the maximum amount that should be paid to buy out the potential tenant's current lease?

N	$
0	(PV)
1	5,500
2	5,500
3	5,500
•	•
•	•
16	5,500

Enter the variables into a financial spreadsheet or calculator and the present value of these future payments is $82,066.40, so this is the maximum amount that should be paid to buy out the lease. If the previous landlord demands a higher price, a 10% return on the lease buyout will not be realized.

COMPARING LEASE PROPOSALS

Discounted cash flow calculations allow you to discount future income benefits to a present value, even if they are uneven in nature. Therefore, discounted cash flow calculations can be used to compare two leases that do not have uniform variables.

Example 15.7

Lease A vs. Lease B

A tenant needs to expand into new space requiring $5,000 of tenant improvements (TI). Two lease options are on the table for the 2,000 square foot space, each having different variables. Under Lease A, monthly rent is fixed and the tenant has to pay for the tenant improvements. Under Lease B, monthly rent escalates each year, but the landlord will pay for the tenant improvements.

Terms	Lease A	Lease B
Monthly Rent	$3,750	$2,900 with $400 increase/year
TI	$5,000 TI paid by **tenant**	$5,000 TI paid by **owner**
Sq. Ft.	2,000 sq. ft.	2,000 sq. ft.
Term	5-year term	5-year term
Discount Rate	9%	9%

What is the effective rent per square foot per year of these two lease proposals? Which provides the higher income stream for the owner?

Lease A			Lease B	
N	$		N	$
0	0		0	(5,000)
1	3,750		1–12	2,900
•	•		13–24	3,300
•	•		25–36	3,700
•	•		37–48	4,100
•	•			
60	3,750		49–60	4,500

Enter the variables into a financial spreadsheet or calculator and the effective rent per square foot per year for each lease is:

- Lease A is $22.50.
- Lease B is $21.15.

From the owner's perspective, Lease A has the higher effective rent per square foot per year and is therefore the best choice.

As these various examples have shown, the real estate manager must analyze all economic factors affecting a lease including concessions, buyouts, and alternative leases to understand the true impact on the property's financials.

- -

REVIEW QUESTIONS

- Define effective rent, and explain how it differs from contract rent.

- Why is present value of a lease calculated ?

- How is short-term effective rent calculated?

- How is long-term effective rent calculated?

- When would a real estate manager use effective rent?

- What is a lease buyout, and when might it be used?

After-Tax Cash Flow

Prior to 1986, one of the prime motivators of owning investment real estate was income tax savings due to favorable federal tax legislation. The Tax Reform Act of 1986 and subsequent legislation dramatically changed the tax benefits of real estate ownership, through a complete redefinition of rules associated with investment income. The income tax laws are frequently a topic of political discussion, and modifications are often on the horizon. While it is not the responsibility of a real estate manager to be an expert in tax law, every real estate manager should understand how tax laws impact the cash flow of the investment properties they manage.

This section is intended to provide an overview of federal income tax rules, and their impact on cash flow. Tax laws are highly complex, and the property owner must obtain all tax advice from a tax accountant or tax attorney. In many jurisdictions, giving any form of tax or legal advice is unlawful if you are not licensed to practice accounting or law. A professional real estate manager must avoid giving any legal or tax advice for which he or she is not professionally trained. However, real estate managers should keep themselves up to date on the basic concepts of income taxation so that they may participate in meaningful discussions with property owners and tax professionals on the best steps to take to attain owner goals for a property.

A real estate manager's clients are subject to two forms of federal tax on their real estate investments:

1. Annual income tax on rental income

2. Capital gains tax as a result of a sale of the property

INCOME TAX

As has been discussed previously, before-tax cash flow (BTCF) from real estate is the amount of cash available to the owner after disbursements for operating expenses and mortgage payments have been subtracted from effective gross income.

On the other hand, **taxable income** is the effective gross income less IRS allowable deductions. Income tax liability is calculated on taxable income, not cash flow. The tax liability is deducted from before-tax cash flow to determine after-tax cash flow (ATCF).

Taxable Income = EGI – IRS Allowable Deductions

Income Deductions

The tax code specifies allowable deductions from income to determine taxable income. These deductions include the following:

Factor	Description
Operating Expenses	• Tax laws provide for deductions for all expenses related to the production of income. These deductions include normal operating expenses.
	• Capital Improvements may be treated as an allowed expense deduction and require the expertise of an accountant to make that determination. A common mistake that owners and property managers make is to improperly classify an expensive repair as a capital improvement because of the large dollar amount. Even "big ticket" items such as an exterior paint can be expensed rather than depreciated over several years if it restores a property to a sound state. A capital improvement would be an expenditure that increases property value, extends its life expectancy, or supports a business expansion.
	• The difference in treating a repair as an expense or a capital item has a significant impact on an owner's tax obligation. A most notable case is FedEx vs. United States, in which FedEx challenged the purchase of engines as an expense and not a capital improvement. The courts agreed that the airplane was the unit of property and the purchase of an engine was a maintenance expense. This case revolutionized how IRC section 195 is interpreted and real estate owners treat large expenses. There have been many more court cases to follow in support of the FedEx ruling.
Mortgage Interest	• While the total mortgage payment (Annual Debt Service includes both principal and interest) represents a direct reduction in cash flow, only the interest portion of the annual debt service may be deducted to calculate taxable income.
	• The amount borrowed is not treated as income when received, so principal payments are not treated as expenses and the principal portion reduces the liability on the balance sheet.

Factor	Description
Cost Recovery	• The deduction for cost recovery (also called depreciation) relies on the premise that real estate is a wasting asset. That means the asset loses value with age and use. Therefore, under federal tax law, the owner may take a deduction from taxable income for the tangible property used up (through exhaustion, wear and tear, and normal obsolescence) in a trade or business or for the production of income.
	• Cost recovery reduces the net taxable income of the property.
	• Cost recovery deductions do not represent cash payments and therefore have no impact on cash flow. They are a "paper" expense only that is recognized on the taxpayer's income tax form.
	• Cost recovery deductions are most often calculated using percentage tables provided in IRS Publication 946, How to Depreciate Property.

How to Depreciate Property (IRS Publication 946)

Cost recovery deductions are most often calculated using percentage tables provided in IRS Publication 946, *How to Depreciate Property.*

- *Table A-6: Residential Rental Property:* Table A-6 is for Residential Rental Property using Mid-Month Convention and Straight Line depreciation—27.5 Years and lists the percentages for years 1 through 29 by month placed in service.
- *Table A-7: Nonresidential Real Property:* Table A-7 is for Nonresidential Real Property, using the Mid-Month Convention and Straight Line depreciation—31.5 years and lists the percentages for years 1 through 33 by month placed in service.
- *Table A-7A: Nonresidential Real Property:* Table A-7a is for Nonresidential Real Property, using the Mid-Month Convention and Straight Line depreciation—39 years and lists the percentages for years 1, 2–39, and 40 by month placed in service.

The mid-month convention is used for real property. This means that only half of a month's depreciation is allowed in the months of acquisition and disposition, regardless of when during the month the property acquisition or disposition occurred.

Visit the IRS Web site at *www.irs.gov* for more information and to download IRS Publication 946, *How to Depreciate Property.*

Cost Segregation

Until recently, it was common to use the straight-line method (27.5 or 39 years) to calculate annual depreciation. Recent tax court rulings have acknowledged property owners' ability to exercise accelerated depreciation using a method known as cost segregation. Using this method, the investor is allowed to take a higher amount of cost recovery in the early years of the investment by categorizing major building components into shorter life categories. For example, the HVAC system may be given a 7-year life span, the roofing a 15-year life span, etc. In so doing, the investor can take advantage of higher deductions in early years and use the savings for other investments. The total allowable cost recovery does not change, so if the investor holds the property long enough, the later years will see a smaller cost recovery allowances. In order to take advantage of this method, the owner must hire a professional analyst (usually an appraiser) to survey the building and make a reasonable determination of what the life span of each component is and categorize each item into 5-, 7-, and 15-year life spans. The Cost Segregation Study can cost several thousand dollars, so not all properties may benefit. However, the study can go back to when the property was purchased or 1986, whichever occurred later, so the accumulated tax savings could be substantial.

Example 16.1	Cost Segregation

As shown in the following example, it may be advantageous for an owner to consider the cost of the study. A commercial building that costs $7,000,000 and has a land value of 20% would have a depreciable basis of $5,600,000 or $143,590 per year of allowable cost recovery. The table below displays cost recovery if the same building had itemized and totaled its components into the shorter life span categories:

Item Cost Recovery Allowed

Item		Cost Recovery Allowed
5-year items	$400,000	$80,000
7-year items	$150,000	$21,429
15-year items	$150,000	$10,000
39-year items	$4,900,000	$125,641
Annual Total Years 1 to 5		$237,070

As shown, for the first five years of the investment, the owner would be able to claim a deduction of $237,070 annually instead of $143,590, which would amount to $467,400 over the five years. As with most items related to ownership accounting, it is important to make sure your client gets professional advice from his or her accountant as to how cost segregation will fit specific needs.

Legal Issue: *Congress has anticipated a review of depreciation since 2000, but other tax policy debates have intervened. If no new legislation is passed, the leasehold improvement depreciable life of nonresidential property will continue to be up to 39 years.*

A 39-year depreciable life for tenant improvements is unrealistic in the eyes of investors. A realistic cost recovery period, such as 10 to 15 years, is a reasonable incentive to keep office, commercial, and retail space modern, efficient, and competitive between urban and suburban space. In addition, such a change would more closely mirror corresponding lease terms for these properties.

Before-Tax Cash Flow versus Taxable Income

The differences between calculating BTCF and taxable income in the following example result from amortization of principal in the BTCF column and allowance for cost recovery in the taxable income column.

	Before-Tax Cash Flow	**After-Tax Cash Flow**
Effective Gross Income	$61,000	$61,000
Expenses	30,000	30,000
Net Operating Income	31,000	31,000
ADS–Principal	466	*Not Deducted*
ADS–Interest	27,971	27,971
Cost Recovery	*Not Deducted*	7,273
Taxable Income	$2,563	($4,244)

Passive Income

A potential tax advantage exists whenever the operating income of a real estate investment is legitimately reduced through the application of the tax code. Today, potential tax advantages exist because of the mortgage interest deduction and the cost recovery deduction.

To reduce the role of tax shelters, the Tax Reform Act of 1986 created three categories of income-producing activities: active, portfolio, passive as shown in Exhibit 16.1. By dividing income into three categories, Congress reduced much of the appeal of tax shelters. Now, only a limited amount of loss generated by passive activities can reduce taxable income generated by nonpassive activities.

| Exhibit 16.1 | Income-Producing Activities |

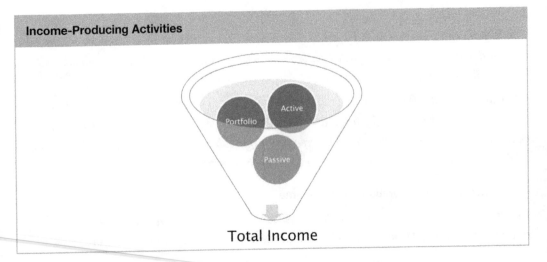

Total Income

Total income is comprised of:

- **Active:** income and losses from salaries, wages, tips, commissions, and other trade or business activities in which a taxpayer materially participates

- **Portfolio:** income and losses from interest, dividends, and royalties

- **Passive:** there are three categories of passive income:

  - Investments in which the taxpayer does not materially participate. Material participation means involvement in the operations of an activity throughout the year on a regular, continuous, and substantial basis.

  - Limited business interest includes interest in investments in which the taxpayer's liability is limited, for example, a limited partnership. Partners receive a K-1, which reports their portion of the property's income and cost recovery.

  - Most rental activity is specifically included in the passive income category, whether the taxpayer materially participates or not. Rental activity produces income that consists of payments for the use of tangible property rather than the performance of services.

All income and losses from activities within a category are aggregated within that category. Generally, net losses from passive activities can only offset net income from other passive activities. Any resulting net passive income is fully taxable in the year generated. The passive income is added to the taxable income from other income categories. Any resulting net passive loss is generally suspended until it can be used to offset net passive income generated in a future tax year or until the owner disposes of the property. Net losses from passive activities are allocated each year to those passive activities experiencing losses. Suspended passive losses may be carried forward indefinitely.

The suspended losses attributed to a property that have not been used against other income in previous years can be used to reduce taxable gains when the entire interest is sold to an unrelated third party in a taxable transaction. Offsetting ordinary income with the losses is better than using them to reduce capital gains on the property's sale because ordinary income is taxed at a higher rate than capital gains. Because income and losses from all passive activities are aggregated, the law provides a method for allocating excess losses to a particular property. Generally, the portion of the suspended loss attributable to a specific property depends on the ratio of the loss from the property to the total loss from all passive activities. Suspended losses are deductible against income at the time of sale in a specific order—first, any gain recognized on the transaction; second, net income or gain for the tax year from all passive activities; third, active or portfolio income when interest in the activity is sold. If the taxpayer has already used the losses attributable to a property to offset income from other passive activities, he or she cannot use them again at disposition.

Exemptions and Exceptions

A limited exemption to the passive loss rules is available for taxpayers who invest in rental real estate. If three conditions are met, the taxpayer can use up to $25,000 in losses from real estate activities to offset nonpassive income:

1. The taxpayer must have an adjusted gross income (AGI) of less than $150,000. For every AGI dollar over $100,000, the $25,000 allowance is reduced by 50 cents. Therefore, the $25,000 exception is totally eliminated when AGI reaches $150,000.

2. The taxpayer must actively participate in the investment. Here, active participation is not the same as material participation. *Active participation* is far less restrictive and is only used when applying this limited exception. A taxpayer actively participates in an investment if he or she participates in making management decisions or in arranging to have others provide services (such as repairs) in a significant sense. The relevant management decisions include approving new tenants, rental terms, capital and repair expenditures, and other similar decisions.

3. The taxpayer must own at least a 10% interest in the investment—but not as a limited partner.

The taxpayer can only offset active income under this exception if net passive losses exist. Passive losses in excess of the $25,000 exception are suspended and carried forward subject to the same restrictions as other passive losses. If, due to insufficient active income, a taxpayer cannot use any of the passive losses under this exception, the unused loss becomes an active loss that can be carried back or forward as any ordinary loss can.

Real estate professionals can also write off the full amount of their net losses from real estate rentals against any category of income. The taxpayer must satisfy three conditions to qualify for this exception:

1. The taxpayer must materially participate in the real estate business. His or her activity must be regular, continuous, and substantial and not as a limited partner.

2. More than half the personal services the taxpayer performs for any business (as defined below) must be for his or her real property.

3. The taxpayer must perform more than 750 hours of service during the year in real property trades or businesses. Real property trades or businesses include real property development, redevelopment, construction, reconstruction, acquisition, conversion, rental, operation, management, leasing, or brokerage. Each rental real estate operation is generally treated as a separate activity to test the taxpayer's level of participation. However, the taxpayer may elect to treat all interests in rental real estate as one activity.

If a taxpayer meets the previously stated conditions, the excepted passive losses may be used against all other income, whether it can be used in that tax year or not. (Whether a taxpayer qualifies for the exception is determined each year.) The taxpayer cannot make use of the deductions available under the exceptions unless net passive losses are available from real estate. For example, if an investor has two passive investments, a partnership providing $15,000 in income and a real estate investment providing $25,000 in losses, only the net loss of $10,000 may be used to offset other income, not the entire $25,000 real estate loss. (See Exhibit 16.2.)

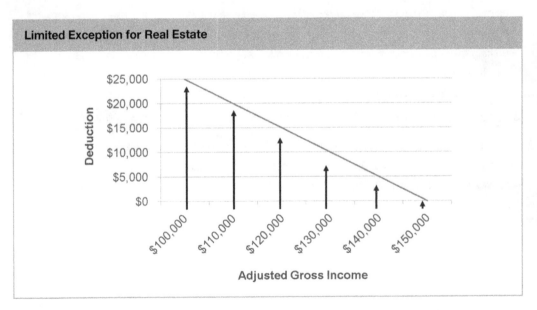

Exhibit 16.2   **Limited Exception for Real Estate**

Income Tax Savings/Payable Steps

The following outlines the income tax savings/payable steps.

1 • Determine NOI

2 • Subtract Mortgage Interest

3 • Subtract Cost Recovery

4 • Taxable Icome

5 • Other Passive Losses to Offset?

6 • Exemptions or Exceptions?

7 • Multiply by Tax Bracket

Example: Applying Tax Savings/Payable Steps

Recall the Mayfair Property from the before-tax cash flow example earlier in this publication.

The Mayfair property was purchased by your client for $6,000,000 with a $1,500,000 down payment and a 30-year $4,500,000 mortgage with a 7% rate (assume monthly payments). No points or fees were charged.

Gross potential income (GPI) is expected to be $775,000 in Year 1. Operating expenses are expected to be $300,000 in Year 1. Both are expected to increase by 2% each year. The property is expected to sell at the end of Year 5 at an 8% going-out capitalization rate. The costs of sale are expected to be 5%. The owner's required return is 10%.

This is an apartment community with land allocation of 20% and improvements of 80%. The owner is in a 30% income tax bracket. She has also hired a professional real estate management firm.

Step 1: Determine NOI

	A	B	C	D	E	F	G	H	I	J
1	Pro Forma Statement						By:			Clear Pro Forma Statem
2	*Instructions: Enter data in the yellow cells only.*									
3										
4	Site:		For:				By:			
5			(Per Square Foot)		Annual %					
6	Income	Actual	Budget	Varianc	Increas	Year 1	Year 2	Year 3	Year 4	Year 5
7	Gross Potential Income (GPI)			0.00%	2.00%	$775,000	$790,500	$806,310	$822,436	$838,885
8	- Loss to Lease			0.00%			$0	$0	$0	$0
9	- Vacancy and Collection Loss			0.00%			$0	$0	$0	$0
10	= Net Rent Revenue	$0	$0	0.00%		$775,000	$790,500	$806,310	$822,436	$838,885
11	+ Miscellaneous Income			0.00%			$0	$0	$0	$0
12	+ Expense Reimbursements			0.00%			$0	$0	$0	$0
13	= Effective Gross Income (EGI)	$0	$0	0.00%		$775,000	$790,500	$806,310	$822,436	$838,885
14										
15	**Operating Expenses**									
16	*Utilities*									
17	Heat			0.00%	2.00%	$300,000	$306,000	$312,120	$318,362	$324,730
18	Electric			0.00%			$0	$0	$0	$0
19	Water and Sewer			0.00%			$0	$0	$0	$0
20	Total Utilities	$0	$0	0.00%		$300,000	$306,000	$312,120	$318,362	$324,730
21	*Maintenance*									
43										
44	- Total Operating Expenses	$0	$0			$300,000	$306,000	$312,120	$318,362	$324,730
45	**(NOI)**	**$0**	**$0**			**$475,000**	**$484,500**	**$494,190**	**$504,074**	**$514,155**

Step 2: Subtract Mortgage Interest

	A	B	C
1	**After-Tax Cash Flow Analysis**		
2	*Instructions: Enter data in the yellow cells only*		
3			
4	Site:		For:
5			
6		ANALYSIS VARIABLES	
7	LOAN 1		
8	Loan Amount		$4,500,000
9	Loan Interest Rate		7.00%
10	Loan Amortization Period (years)		30
11	Analysis Begin Month		1
12	LOAN 2		
13	Loan Amount		$0
14	Loan Interest Rate		
15	Loan Amortization Period (years)		
16	Analysis Begin Month		
17	Owner's Required Return		10.00%
18	Going-Out Capitalization Rate		
19	Cost of Sale		5.00%
20	Income Tax Rate		30%
21	Recapture Rate		
22	Capital Gains Rate		
23			
24	INITIAL ANALYSIS		
25		Initial Value	
26	Purchase Price	$6,000,000	
27	+ Acquisition Exp.	0	
28	+ Points, Fees	0	
29	= Original Basis	$6,000,000	
30	- Loan Amount	4,500,000	
31	= Initial Equity	$1,500,000	

Step 3: Subtract Cost Recovery

Mayfair is a residential property and allowed cost recovery over 27.5 year.

COST RECOVERY			
	Amount	÷ Recovery Per.	= Cost Recovery
Purchase Price + Acq. Exp.	6,000,000		
Land Allocation	1,200,000	N/A	N/A
Building Allocation	4,800,000	27.5	174,545
Personal Property	0	0	0
Loan 1 Points, Fees	0	0	0
Capital Improvements	0	0	0
Loan 2 Points, Fees			0
Annual Total			174,545

Step 4: Result Is Taxable Income

Taxable Income = NOI – Mortgage Interest – Cost Recovery

	Year 1	Year 2	Year 3	Year 4	Year 5
NOI	475,000	484,500	494,190	504,074	514,155
– Interest Deduction	-313,552	-310,247	-306,704	-302,905	-298,830
– Cost Recovery	-174,545	-174,545	-174,545	-174,545	-174,545
– Taxable Income	*(13,097)*	*(293)*	*12,940*	*26,624*	*40,779*

Step 5: Determine if Tax Savings Are Offset by Passive Losses

Passive income in the amount of $25,000 is available each year from another real estate venture. Therefore, the entire Taxable Income is multiplied by 30% to create a Tax Savings in Years 1 to 3. This reduces the Tax Payable in Years 4 to 5.

If there wasn't an income from another venture available to offset the losses, the negative Taxable Income would be suspended for use in future years.

Prior suspended losses may also be used to reduce income and the tax payable.

	Year 1	Year 2	Year 3	Year 4	Year 5
				CASH FLOW AND TAXABLE IN
NOI	475,000	484,500	494,190	504,074	514,155
Loan Principal	45,711	49,016	52,559	56,359	60,433
Loan Interest	313,552	310,247	306,704	302,905	298,830
BTCF	115,737	125,237	134,927	144,810	154,892
Cost Recovery	174,545	174,545	174,545	174,545	174,545
Tax Deduction	488,097	484,793	481,250	477,450	473,376
Taxable Income	(13,097)	(293)	12,940	26,624	40,779
Prev. Susp. Loss		0	0	0	0
Passive Income Avail.	25,000	25,000	25,000	25,000	25,000
Passive Losses Used	13,097	293	0	0	0
Tax Savings/Payable	3,929	88	(3,882)	(7,987)	(12,234)
ATCF	$119,666	$125,325	$131,045	$136,823	$142,658

Step 6: Determine any Exemptions or Exceptions

Because the owner is in a 30% income tax bracket and exceeds the $150,000 ceiling and has hired a highly respected real estate management firm to manage the day-to-day operation, she does not qualify for any exemptions or exceptions.

Step 7: Multiply by the Tax Bracket

	Year 1	Year 2	Year 3	Year 4	Year 5
Taxable Income	(13,097)	(293)	12,940	26,624	40,779
Passive Income Avail	25,000	25,000	25,000	25,000	25,000
30% Tax Savings/Payable	3,929	88	(3,882)	(7,987)	(12,234)

The tax savings is added to the before-tax cash flow to determine the after-tax cash flow.

If the taxable income is positive and there isn't a loss to offset, it is multiplied by the tax rate and becomes a tax payable. A tax payable will reduce the after-tax cash flow.

	Year 1	Year 2	Year 3	Year 4	Year 5
Before-Tax Cash Flow	115,737	125,237	134,927	144,810	154,892
+ Tax Savings Payable	3,929	88	(3,882)	(7,987)	(12,234)
= After-Tax Cash Flow	$119,666	$125,325	$131,045	$136,823	$142,658

CAPITAL GAINS TAX

Capital appreciation results from an increase in the value of a property and is subject to *capital gains tax* (rather than income tax). Taxes on this equity appreciation, however, are not paid unless the property, or interest in the property, is sold. Capital gains tax is paid not only on the equity appreciation but also on **recapture** of cost recovery written off during the holding period.

The capital gains tax rate is subject to frequent and abrupt revision by Congress. The capital gains rate influences investor willingness to buy and sell property. The higher the tax, the less likely an owner with equity appreciation is to sell. The reverse motivation exists with lower capital gains taxes.

Basis

Basis for a purchased property equals the total purchase price of the property. The amount of financing is also included in the property's basis. Basis increases with any capital improvements to the property and decreases by the cost recovery deductions taken. An understanding of basis is necessary to determine cost recovery, gain or loss upon the sale of a property, and amortization deductions. This discussion covers three kinds of basis:

Factor	Description
Original	• Original basis (at acquisition) of a property for tax purposes is the purchase price plus any other costs of acquisition that are capitalized. • Generally all costs of acquisition are added to the basis except deductible income and expense prorations (property taxes, insurance, etc.).
Recoverable	• Includes the value of improvements only. Land is not depreciable for tax purposes. The original basis must be allocated between land and improvements to determine recoverable basis. • Many investors prefer to allocate as much of the original basis as is legally defensible to improvements to maximize cost recovery deductions and shelter as much income as possible.
Adjusted	• Calculated by adjusting the original basis upward or downward over the holding period of the asset to reflect added capital improvements and subtracted cost recovery.

Allocating Basis

Basis is used to determine cost recovery by allocating the total basis of the property between land, improvements, and personal property. This allocation is done because improvements and personal property are subject to cost recovery; land is not. The amount of basis allocated to improvements and personal property is thus called depreciable basis.

For the purposes of discussion here, basis will be allocated between land and improvements. (Personal property includes items such as furniture, computer systems, and appliances.) Basis can be allocated using any defensible, reasonable method, including professional appraisal or tax assessment. Taxpayers should use a method that provides the maximum basis and thus, the maximum financial benefit.

The *Modified Accelerated Cost Recovery System* (MACRS) was introduced by the Economic Recovery Tax Act of 1981 and modified by the Deficit Reduction Tax Act of 1984 and the Tax Reform Act of 1986. Under the MACRS, deductions are greater in the early years of ownership and decrease in later years. The same amount of tax is paid over any selected cost recovery method; however, the MACRS generally allows greater tax savings in earlier years, which is beneficial due to the time value of money. Cost recovery allowances convert to straight-line percentages when straight-line deductions begin to exceed the accelerated deductions. The present tax law includes penalties (recapture) for using the MACRS on real estate; it taxes part or all of the capital gain as ordinary income when the property is sold.

In the straight-line method, deductions for cost recovery remain the same for each year of ownership. Rental real estate placed in use after 1986 must use the straight-line method. Straight-line cost recovery may also be elected for other types of property.

1031 Exchanges

A *1031 Exchange,* also known as a *Like-Kind Exchange,* is a way of structuring a sale of certain kinds of property pursuant to Internal Revenue Code (IRC) Section 1031 so that the seller's profit or gain is not taxed at the time of sale. The condition for this benefit is that the property that is sold be replaced with another "like-kind" property. If the transaction is properly structured, the seller's profit or gain is deferred to a future date.

This allows an investor to sell the property and effectively transfer the gain to another property; thereby allowing one to realize profits, yet not pay the tax due—at least for now. The transfer reduces the basis of the new property purchased by an amount equal to the gain. When the second property is sold, it will thereby produce a correspondingly higher gain than it would have otherwise and that new higher amount will then be subject to taxation. The exchange does *not reduce the taxes,* but rather defers them to a later date. An investor could gauge the decision on when to sell based on a determination of whether the current capital gains rate is advantageous, or whether it is better to transfer the gain to another property. There is no current limit to the number of times the investor can exchange, so a second sale can be exchanged into a third and so on, as long as the basis remains a positive number.

The sale of the relinquished property and the acquisition of the replacement property do not have to be simultaneous. A nonsimultaneous exchange is sometimes called a Starker Tax Deferred Exchange (named for an investor who challenged and won a case against the IRS). For a non-simultaneous exchange, the taxpayer must use a qualified intermediary, follow guidelines of the IRS, and use the proceeds of the sale to buy more qualifying, like-kind property. Most title companies provide intermediary services for an additional fee. The replacement property must be identified within 45 days after the sale of the old property, and the acquisition of the replacement property must be closed within 180 days of the sale of the old property. In addition, the investor cannot receive the money in the interim; it must be held by the intermediary.

Tenants in Common Exchanges

Tenants in Common (TIC) ownership is a form of real estate ownership in which two or more persons have an undivided, fractional interest in the asset, where ownership shares are not required to be equal, and where ownership interests can be inherited. Each co-owner receives an individual deed at closing for his or her undivided percentage interest in the entire property. Although the TIC ownership form has been used for many years, its popularity has been increasing dramatically due to a 2002 IRS ruling that greatly expanded the pool of available properties. Exchangers often have difficulty locating and closing suitable replacement property within the 45-day identification period and the 180-day closing period. An exchange into a TIC interest can address these issues. In addition, a 1031 TIC structure can allow investors to pool their resources and purchase larger, higher-valued and better-positioned properties than they might otherwise be able to acquire. Typically these more prestigious properties can also open doors to high-quality tenants, such as Fortune 500 companies and government entities, reducing tenant credit risk. Real estate firms (sponsors) organize the TIC-owned properties with professional management, removing day-to-day ownership concerns.

Calculating Capital Gains Tax

Capital gains tax is based on the adjusted basis in the property. The taxable gain or loss from the sale of the property is the difference between the net sale price and the adjusted basis of the property.

Therefore, anything that increases adjusted basis reduces the taxable gain on a sale, and anything that reduces adjusted basis increases the taxable gain on a sale.

Under current law, real estate gains are taxed at two different capital gain rates when a property sells for more than its original purchase price plus any capital improvements:

1. All of the capital gain attributable to cost recovery deductions is taxed at 25%. For most real estate, the adjusted basis plus cost recovery equals original purchase price.

2. Any remaining gain, that is, everything above the original purchase price, is taxed like other long-term capital gains at a 5% or 15% rate, depending on the taxpayer's income bracket.

The tax liability upon sale must be determined to calculate the Net Sales Proceeds.

   Sale Price
− Cost of Sale
− Mortgage Balance
_____
= Before Tax Sales Proceeds
− Tax Liability
_____
= After-Tax Net Sales Proceeds

To calculate tax due on sale follow these steps:

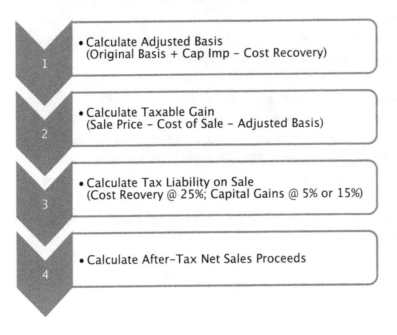

1 • Calculate Adjusted Basis
(Original Basis + Cap Imp − Cost Recovery)

2 • Calculate Taxable Gain
(Sale Price − Cost of Sale − Adjusted Basis)

3 • Calculate Tax Liability on Sale
(Cost Reovery @ 25%; Capital Gains @ 5% or 15%)

4 • Calculate After–Tax Net Sales Proceeds

Example: Applying Tax Due on Sale

Recall again the Mayfair Property from the previous examples.

The Mayfair property was purchased by the owner for $6,000,000 with a $1,500,000 down payment and a 30-year $4,500,000 mortgage with a 7% rate (assume monthly payments). No points or fees were charged.

Gross potential income (GPI) is expected to be $775,000 in Year 1. Operating expenses are expected to be $300,000 in Year 1. Both are expected to increase by 2% each year. The property is expected to sell at the end of Year 5 at an 8% going-out capitalization rate. The costs of sale are expected to be 5%. The owner's required return is 10%.

It is an apartment community with land allocation of 20% and improvements of 80%. The owner is in a 30% income tax bracket. The owner also owns an office building that provides a $25,000 passive income annually. After 5 years of ownership, the sale price of Mayfair is $6,555,480.

Step 1: Calculate Adjusted Basis

Original Basis	$6,000,000
− Land	-1,200,000
= Recoverable Basis	$4,800,000

Calculate total cost recovery.

Cost Recovery 1st year	$174,545
+ Cost Recovery 2nd year	+174,545
+ Cost Recovery 3rd year	+174,545
+ Cost Recovery 4th year	+174,545
+ Cost Recovery 5th year	+174,545
= Total Cost Recovery	=$872,727

Calculate adjusted basis.

Original Basis	$6,000,000
+ Capital Improvements	+0
− Cost Recovery	-872,727
= Adjusted Basis	$5,127,273

Step 2: Calculate Taxable Gain

Sale Price	$6,555,480
–Costs of Sale (5%)	– 327,774
–Adjusted Basis	– 5,127,273
=Taxable Gain on Sale	$1,100,433

Step 3: Calculate Total Tax Liability

Taxable Gain on Sale	$1,100,433
– Cost Recovery	– 872,727
= Capital Gain	$227,706
Capital Gain Due to Cost Recovery	$872,727 x 25% = $218,182
Remaining Capital Gain	$227,706 x 15% = $34,156
Total Capital Gains Tax	$252,338

Step 4: Calculate the After-Tax Net Sales Proceeds

Sale Price	$6,555,480
– Costs of Sale (5%)	– 327,774
– Mortgage Balance	– 4,235,922
= Before-Tax Sales Proceeds	$1,991,784
– Tax Liability	– 252,338
= After-Tax Net Sales Proceeds	$1,739,446

	A	B	C
1	**After-Tax Cash Flow Analysis**		
2	*Instructions: Enter data in the yellow cells onl*		
3			
4	Site:	For:	
5			
6	ANALYSIS VARIABLES		
7	LOAN 1		
8	Loan Amount		$4,500,000
9	Loan Interest Rate		7.00%
10	Loan Amortization Period (years)		30
11	Analysis Begin Month		1
12	LOAN 2		
13	Loan Amount		$0
14	Loan Interest Rate		
15	Loan Amortization Period (years)		
16	Analysis Begin Month		
17	Owner's Required Return		10.00%
18	Going-Out Capitalization Rate		
19	Cost of Sale		5.00%
20	Income Tax Rate		30%
21	Recapture Rate		25%
22	Capital Gains Rate		15%
23			

				PROCEEDS OF SALE ANAL
	Year 1	Year 2	Year 3	Year 4	Year 5
Original Basis	$6,000,000	$6,000,000	$6,000,000	$6,000,000	$6,000,000
+ Capital Imp.	$0	$0	$0	$0	$0
− Cost Recovery	$174,545	$349,091	$523,636	$698,182	$872,727
= Adjusted Basis	$5,825,455	$5,650,909	$5,476,364	$5,301,818	$5,127,273
Sale Price	$6,000,000	-	-	-	$6,555,480
− Cost of Sale	$300,000	-	-	-	$327,774
− Adjusted Basis	$5,825,455	$5,650,909	$5,476,364	$5,301,818	$5,127,273
= Gain	($125,455)	-	-	-	$1,100,433
− Suspended Losses	$0	$0	$0	$0	$0
= Net Gain	($125,455)	$0	$0	$0	$1,100,433
Recapture	$43,636	$87,273	$130,909	$174,545	$218,182
Additional Gain	($45,000)	($52,364)	($78,545)	($104,727)	$34,156
= Tax on Sale	($1,364)	$34,909	$52,364	$69,818	$252,338
Sale Price	$6,000,000	-	-	-	$6,555,480
− Cost of Sale	$300,000	-	-	-	$327,774
− Loan Balance	$4,454,289	$4,405,273	$4,352,713	$4,296,355	$4,235,922
= Before-Tax Procee	$1,245,711	-	-	-	$1,991,784
− Tax on Sale	($1,364)	$34,909	$52,364	$69,818	$252,338
= Net Sales Proceeds	$1,247,075	($34,909)	($52,364)	($69,818)	$1,739,447

With the calculation of the recapture, this makes the actual capital gain tax approximately 22.9% of the gain.

Standalone DCF Analysis: Before-Tax and After-Tax T-Bar

	Before Tax				After Tax		
	Owner's Required Return:	10.00%			Owner's Required Return:	10.00%	
N	$	NSP	Total Cash Flows	N	$	NSP	Total Cash Flows
0	($1,500,000.00)		($1,500,000.00)	0	($1,500,000.00)		($1,500,000.00)
1	$115,736.65		$115,736.65	1	$119,665.86		$119,665.86
2	$125,236.65		$125,236.65	2	$125,324.52		$125,324.52
3	$134,926.65		$134,926.65	3	$131,044.51		$131,044.51
4	$144,810.45		$144,810.45	4	$136,823.31		$136,823.31
5	$154,891.93	$1,991,784.24	$2,146,676.17	5	$142,658.09	$1,739,446.55	$1,882,104.64

NPV	IRR	Price to pay to achieve desired discount rate		NPV	IRR	Price to pay to achieve desired discount rate
$241,913.39	13.82%	$1,741,913.39		$72,907.87	11.21%	$1,572,907.87

Financial Measures

	Before-Tax	After-Tax
$/$%	7.72%	7.98%
Value Enhancement	$555,480	$555,480
IRR	13.82%	11.21%
NPV	$241,913	$72,908

EXAMPLE: AFTER-TAX CASH FLOW ANALYSIS

Taxation can have a significant impact on the cash return investment real estate produces, both during ownership and at sale. A real estate manager has a responsibility to help the owner achieve financial goals for the property. Thus, awareness of the tax laws that affect real estate is important. Real estate managers must direct their clients to their tax accountant or tax attorney for guidance in this area.

Consider Mr. Johnson's property. The purchase price is $800,000 with a 30-year, $700,000 loan at 10.5%. GPI and operating expenses for the first year are expected to be $134,000 and $64,000, respectively. Both are predicted to rise at 8% annually. Going-out cap rate is 9%, cost of sale is 6%, and the required rate of return is 12% for this five-year hold.

Account for the tax consequences in order to calculate after-tax cash flow and after-tax measures of performance.

The tax assessor set Mr. Johnson's land value at $100,000 and the improvement value at $400,000 (20% to 80% land-to-improvement ratio). Mr. Johnson expects to have $40,000 in passive income each year from another venture. He is in the 35% ordinary income tax bracket. There are no previous suspended losses. The property is classified as multi-family residential.

1. Using the tax assessor's land-to-improvement ratio, calculate the basis for depreciation.

Total Cost = $1,000,000
Land (20%) = $1,000,000 × 20% = $200,000
Improvements (80%) = $1,000,000 × 80% = $800,000
Basis for depreciation = $800,000

2. What is the cost recovery for each year?

$800,000 Recoverable Basis ÷ 27.5 Year Recovery Period = $29,091 Annual Cost Recovery

3. What is the taxable income for each year?

	Year 1	Year 2	Year 3	Year 4	Year 5
NOI	82,000	85,260	88,626	92,101	95,688
– Interest Deduction	63,622	62,752	61,811	60,791	59,687
– Cost Recovery	29,091	29,091	29,091	29,091	29,091
= Taxable Income	(10,712)	(6,583)	(2,276)	2,218	6,910

4. What are the tax payable/tax savings and after-tax cash flow for each year?

	Year 1	Year 2	Year 3	Year 4	Year 5
Taxable Income	(10,712)	(6,583)	(2,276)	2,218	6,910
Passive Income Avail	40,000	40,000	40,000	40,000	40,000
– 35% Tax Savings Payable	3,749	2,304	797	(776)	(2,418)
= After-Tax Cash Flow	$11,655	$13,470	$15,328	$17,230	$19,175

5. What is the net gain if the property is sold at the end of Year 5?

Original basis	$1,000,000
+ Capital improvements	+ 0
− Total cost recovery	− $145,455
= Adjusted basis	= $$854,545
Sale price	$$1,325,214
− Cost of sale	− 79,513
− Adjusted basis	− 854,545
= Gain	= $391,156
− Suspended losses	− 0
= Net Gain	= $391,156

6. What is the capital gain on the sale?

Net Gain	$391,156
− Recapture (Cost Recovery x 5)	− 145,455
= Additional Gain	$245,701

7. What is the tax due on sale?

$145,455 Recapture x 25% =	$36,354
+ $245,455 Additional gain x 15% =	+ 36,855
= Tax on sale	$73,219

8. What is the after-tax net sales proceeds?

Sale price	$1,325,214
− Cost of sale @ 6%	− 79,513
− Loan balance	− 738,192
= Before-tax proceeds	= $507,509
− Tax on sale	− 73,219
= Net sales proceeds	$434,291

9. How do the four financial measures compare Before Tax and After Tax?

(Note that the IREM® Financial Analysis Spreadsheet is used here to apply the four financial measures, but any financial analysis tool could be used.)

	A	B	C	D	E	F	G	H	I	J
1	**Pro Forma Statement**									
2	Instructions: Enter data in the yellow cells only.								Clear Pro Forma Statem	
3										
4	Site:		For:				By:			
5			(Per Square Foot)		Annual %					
6	Income	Actual	Budget	Variance	Increase	Year 1	Year 2	Year 3	Year 4	Year 5
7	Gross Potential Income (GPI)			0.00%	3.00%	$122,000	$125,660	$129,430	$133,313	$137,312
8	- Loss to Lease			0.00%			$0	$0	$0	$0
9	- Vacancy and Collection Loss			0.00%			$0	$0	$0	$0
10	= Net Rent Revenue	$0	$0	0.00%		$122,000	$125,660	$129,430	$133,313	$137,312
11	+ Miscellaneous Income			0.00%			$0	$0	$0	$0
12	+ Expense Reimbursements			0.00%			$0	$0	$0	$0
13	= Effective Gross Income (EGI)	$0	$0	0.00%		$122,000	$125,660	$129,430	$133,313	$137,312
14										
15	**Operating Expenses**									
16	Utilities									
17	Heat			0.00%	1.00%	$40,000	$40,400	$40,804	$41,212	$41,624
18	Electric			0.00%			$0	$0	$0	$0
19	Water and Sewer			0.00%			$0	$0	$0	$0
20	Total Utilities	$0	$0	0.00%		$40,000	$40,400	$40,804	$41,212	$41,624
21	Maintenance									
43										
44	- Total Operating Expenses	$0	$0			$40,000	$40,400	$40,804	$41,212	$41,624
45	= Net Operating Income (NOI)	$0	$0			$82,000	$85,260	$88,626	$92,101	$95,688
46										

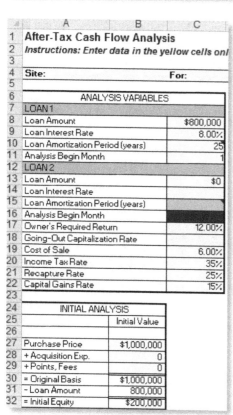

	A	B	C
1	**After-Tax Cash Flow Analysis**		
2	**Instructions: Enter data in the yellow cells on/**		
3			
4	Site:	For:	
5			
6	ANALYSIS VARIABLES		
7	LOAN 1		
8	Loan Amount	$800,000	
9	Loan Interest Rate	8.00%	
10	Loan Amortization Period (years)	25	
11	Analysis Begin Month	1	
12	LOAN 2		
13	Loan Amount	$0	
14	Loan Interest Rate		
15	Loan Amortization Period (years)		
16	Analysis Begin Month		
17	Owner's Required Return	12.00%	
18	Going-Out Capitalization Rate		
19	Cost of Sale	6.00%	
20	Income Tax Rate	35%	
21	Recapture Rate	25%	
22	Capital Gains Rate	15%	
23			
24	INITIAL ANALYSIS		
25		Initial Value	
26			
27	Purchase Price	$1,000,000	
28	+ Acquisition Exp.	0	
29	+ Points, Fees	0	
30	= Original Basis	$1,000,000	
31	- Loan Amount	800,000	
32	= Initial Equity	$200,000	

COST RECOVERY			
	Amount	÷ Recovery Per.	= Cost Recovery
Purchase Price + Acq. Exp.	1,000,000		
Land Allocation	200,000	N/A	N/A
Building Allocation	800,000	27.5	29,091 Residential Prope
Personal Property	0	0	0
Loan 1 Points, Fees	0	0	0
Capital Improvements	0	0	0
Loan 2 Points, Fees			0
Annual Total			29,091

Input Year 1 NOI from Pro Forma Statement Sheet

CASH FLOW AND TAXABLE IN					
	Year 1	Year 2	Year 3	Year 4	Year 5
NOI	82,000	85,260	88,626	92,101	95,688
Loan Principal	10,473	11,342	12,283	13,303	14,407
Loan Interest	63,622	62,752	61,811	60,791	59,687
BTCF	7,906	11,166	14,531	18,006	21,594
Cost Recovery	29,091	29,091	29,091	29,091	29,091
Tax Deduction	92,712	91,843	90,902	89,882	88,778
Taxable Income	(10,712)	(6,583)	(2,276)	2,218	6,910
Prev. Susp. Loss		0	0	0	0
Passive Income Avail.	40,000	40,000	40,000	40,000	40,000
Passive Losses Used	10,712	6,583	2,276	0	0
Tax Savings/Payable	3,749	2,304	797	(776)	(2,418)
ATCF	$11,655	$13,470	$15,328	$17,230	$19,175

	Year 1	Year 2	Year 3	Year 4	Year 5
Original Basis	$1,000,000	$1,000,000	$1,000,000	$1,000,000	$1,000,000
+ Capital Imp.	$0	$0	$0	$0	$0
- Cost Recovery	$29,091	$58,182	$87,273	$116,364	$145,455
= Adjusted Basis	$970,909	$941,818	$912,727	$883,636	$854,545
Sale Price	$1,000,000	-	-	-	$1,325,214
- Cost of Sale	$60,000	-	-	-	$79,513
- Adjusted Basis	$970,909	$941,818	$912,727	$883,636	$854,545
= Gain	($30,909)	-	-	-	$391,156
- Suspended Losses	$0	$0	$0	$0	$0
= Net Gain	($30,909)	$0	$0	$0	$391,156
Recapture	$7,273	$14,545	$21,818	$29,091	$36,364
Additional Gain	($9,000)	($8,727)	($13,091)	($17,455)	$36,855
= Tax on Sale	($1,727)	$5,818	$8,727	$11,636	$73,219
Sale Price	$1,000,000	-	-	-	$1,325,214
- Cost of Sale	$60,000	-	-	-	$79,513
- Loan Balance	$789,527	$778,185	$765,902	$752,599	$738,192
= Before-Tax Procee	$150,473	-	-	-	$507,509
- Tax on Sale	($1,727)	$5,818	$8,727	$11,636	$73,219
= Net Sales Proceeds	$152,200	($5,818)	($8,727)	($11,636)	$434,291

<!-- After Tax section -->

		Year 1	Year 2	Year 3	Year 4	Year 5
$ / $%		5.83%	6.73%	7.66%	8.61%	9.59%
Value Enhancement			-$1,000,000	-$1,000,000	-$1,000,000	$325,214
IRR			-	-	-	22.35%
NPV			($183,493.96)	($174,157.44)	($164,391)	$100,313

5 Year T-BAR	
N	$
Current Equity	(200,000)
BTCF Year 1	7,906
BTCF Year 2	11,166
BTCF Year 3	14,531
BTCF Year 4	18,006
BTCF Year 5 + NSP	529,103

	Year 5 BTCF	Sales Proceeds
	21,594	507,509

N	$	NSP	Total Cash Flows
0	($200,000.00)		($200,000.00)
1	$11,654.99		$11,654.99
2	$13,469.76		$13,469.76
3	$15,328.05		$15,328.05
4	$17,229.87		$17,229.87
5	$19,175.14	$434,290.66	$453,465.80

Before Tax

Owner's Required Return: 12.00%

N	$	NSP	Total Cash Flows
0	($200,000.00)		($200,000.00)
1	$7,905.64		$7,905.64
2	$11,165.64		$11,165.64
3	$14,531.44		$14,531.44
4	$18,006.30		$18,006.30
5	$21,593.56	$507,509.44	$529,103.00

NPV	IRR	Price to pay to achieve desired discount rate
$137,973.56	25.22%	$337,973.56

After Tax

Owner's Required Return: 12.00%

N	$	NSP	Total Cash Flows
0	($200,000.00)		($200,000.00)
1	$11,654.99		$11,654.99
2	$13,469.76		$13,469.76
3	$15,328.05		$15,328.05
4	$17,229.87		$17,229.87
5	$19,175.14	$434,290.66	$453,465.80

NPV	IRR	Price to pay to achieve desired discount rate
$100,313.02	22.35%	$300,313.02

	Before-Tax	After-Tax
$/$%	3.95%	5.83%
Value Enhancement	$325,214	$325,214
IRR	25.22%	22.35%
NPV	$137,974	$100,313

REVIEW QUESTIONS

- How does income tax impact an owner's return on investment?

- What are the two forms of federal tax to which property owners are subject?

- Whom should a real estate manager consult for questions regarding tax codes and tax advice?

- What is taxable income, and how is it derived?

- What deductions from income to determine taxable income does the tax code specify?

- Describe the three income-producing activities that comprise total income.

- What are the seven income tax savings/payable steps?

- What category of income is most rental activity considered to be?

- Which type of basis is used to calculate capital gains tax?

- What are the four steps used to calculate tax due on sale?

Appendix: Annual Compound Interest Tables

3% ANNUAL COMPOUND INTEREST RATE

3% RATE i n	1 AMOUNT OF $1 The amount to which $1 will grow with compound interest	2 AMOUNT OF $1 PER PERIOD The amount to which $1 per period will grow with compound interest	3 SINKING FUND FACTOR The amount per period which will grow with compound interest to $1	4 PRESENT WORTH OF $1 What $1 due in the future is worth today	5 PRESENT WORTH OF $1 PER PERIOD What $1 payable periodically is worth today	6 PARTIAL PAYMENT The installment to repay $1 with interest	3% RATE i n
1	1.030 000	1.000 000	1.000 000	.970 874	.970 874	1.030 000	1
2	1.060 900	2.030 000	.492 611	.942 596	1.913 470	.522 611	2
3	1.092 727	3.090 900	.323 530	.915 142	2.828 611	.353 530	3
4	1.125 509	4.183 627	.239 027	.888 487	3.717 098	.269 027	4
5	1.159 274	5.309 136	.188 355	.862 609	4.579 707	.218 355	5
6	1.194 052	6.468 410	.154 598	.837 484	5.417 191	.184 598	6
7	1.229 874	7.662 462	.130 506	.813 092	6.230 283	.160 506	7
8	1.266 770	8.892 336	.112 456	.789 409	7.019 692	.142 456	8
9	1.304 773	10.159 106	.098 434	.766 417	7.786 109	.128 434	9
10	1.343 916	11.463 879	.087 231	.744 094	8.530 203	.117 231	10
11	1.384 234	12.807 796	.078 077	.722 421	9.252 624	.108 077	11
12	1.425 761	14.192 030	.070 462	.701 380	9.954 004	.100 462	12
13	1.468 534	15.617 790	.064 030	.680 951	10.634 955	.094 030	13
14	1.512 590	17.086 324	.058 526	.661 118	11.296 073	.088 526	14
15	1.557 967	18.598 914	.053 767	.641 862	11.937 935	.083 767	15
16	1.604 706	20.156 881	.049 611	.623 167	12.561 102	.079 611	16
17	1.652 848	21.761 588	.045 953	.605 016	13.166 118	.075 953	17
18	1.702 433	23.414 435	.042 709	.587 395	13.753 513	.072 709	18
19	1.753 506	25.116 868	.039 814	.570 286	14.323 799	.069 814	19
20	1.806 111	26.870 374	.037 216	.553 676	14.877 475	.067 216	20
21	1.860 295	28.676 486	.034 872	.537 549	15.415 024	.064 872	21
22	1.916 103	30.536 780	.032 747	.521 893	15.936 917	.062 747	22
23	1.973 587	32.452 884	.030 814	.506 692	16.443 608	.060 814	23
24	2.032 794	34.426 470	.029 047	.491 934	16.935 542	.059 047	24
25	2.093 778	36.459 264	.027 428	.477 606	17.413 148	.057 428	25
26	2.156 591	38.553 042	.025 938	.463 695	17.876 842	.055 938	26
27	2.221 289	40.709 634	.024 564	.450 189	18.327 031	.054 564	27
28	2.287 928	42.930 923	.023 293	.437 077	18.764 108	.053 293	28
29	2.356 566	45.218 850	.022 115	.424 346	19.188 455	.052 115	29
30	2.427 262	47.575 416	.021 019	.411 987	19.600 441	.051 019	30
31	2.500 080	50.002 678	.019 999	.399 987	20.000 428	.049 999	31
32	2.575 083	52.502 759	.019 047	.388 337	20.388 766	.049 047	32
33	2.652 335	55.077 841	.018 156	.377 026	20.765 792	.048 156	33
34	2.731 905	57.730 177	.017 322	.366 045	21.131 837	.047 322	34
35	2.813 862	60.462 082	.016 539	.355 383	21.487 220	.046 539	35
36	2.898 278	63.275 944	.015 804	.345 032	21.832 252	.045 804	36
37	2.985 227	66.174 223	.015 112	.334 983	22.167 235	.045 112	37
38	3.074 783	69.159 449	.014 459	.325 226	22.492 462	.044 459	38
39	3.167 027	72.234 233	.013 844	.315 754	22.808 215	.043 844	39
40	3.262 038	75.401 260	.013 262	.306 557	23.114 772	.043 262	40
41	3.359 899	78.663 298	.012 712	.297 628	23.412 400	.042 712	41
42	3.460 696	82.023 196	.012 192	.288 959	23.701 359	.042 192	42
43	3.564 517	85.483 892	.011 698	.280 543	23.981 902	.041 698	43
44	3.671 452	89.048 409	.011 230	.272 372	24.254 274	.041 230	44
45	3.781 596	92.719 861	.010 785	.264 439	24.518 713	.040 785	45
46	3.895 044	96.501 457	.010 363	.256 737	24.775 449	.040 363	46
47	4.011 895	100.396 501	.009 961	.249 259	25.024 708	.039 961	47
48	4.132 252	104.408 396	.009 578	.241 999	25.266 707	.039 578	48
49	4.256 219	108.540 648	.009 213	.234 950	25.501 657	.039 213	49
50	4.383 906	112.796 867	.008 865	.228 107	25.729 764	.038 865	50
51	4.515 423	117.180 773	.008 534	.221 463	25.951 227	.038 534	51
52	4.650 886	121.696 197	.008 217	.215 013	26.166 240	.038 217	52
53	4.790 412	126.347 082	.007 915	.208 750	26.374 990	.037 915	53
54	4.934 125	131.137 495	.007 626	.202 670	26.577 660	.037 626	54
55	5.082 149	136.071 620	.007 349	.196 767	26.774 428	.037 349	55
56	5.234 613	141.153 768	.007 084	.191 036	26.965 464	.037 084	56
57	5.391 651	146.388 381	.006 831	.185 472	27.150 936	.036 831	57
58	5.553 401	151.780 033	.006 588	.180 070	27.331 005	.036 588	58
59	5.720 003	157.333 434	.006 356	.174 825	27.505 831	.036 356	59
60	5.891 603	163.053 437	.006 133	.169 733	27.674 428	.036 133	60
n	$S^n=(1+i)^n$	$S_{\overline{n}|}=\dfrac{S^n-1}{i}$	$\dfrac{1}{S_{\overline{n}|}}=\dfrac{i}{S^n-1}$	$\dfrac{1}{S^n}=\dfrac{1}{(1+i)^n}$	$a_{\overline{n}|}=\dfrac{1-1/S^n}{i}$	$\dfrac{1}{a_{\overline{n}|}}=\dfrac{i}{1-1/S^n}$	n

$$S=1+i$$

5% ANNUAL COMPOUND INTEREST RATE

5% RATE i	1 AMOUNT OF $1	2 AMOUNT OF $1 PER PERIOD	3 SINKING FUND FACTOR	4 PRESENT WORTH OF $1	5 PRESENT WORTH OF $1 PER PERIOD	6 PARTIAL PAYMENT	5% RATE i
n	The amount to which $1 will grow with compound interest	The amount to which $1 per period will grow with compound interest	The amount per period which will grow with compound interest to $1	What $1 due in the future is worth today	What $1 payable periodically is worth today	The installment to repay $1 with interest	n
1	1.050 000	1.000 000	1.000 000	.952 381	.952 381	1.050 000	1
2	1.102 500	2.050 000	.487 805	.907 029	1.859 410	.537 805	2
3	1.157 625	3.152 500	.317 209	.863 838	2.723 248	.367 209	3
4	1.215 506	4.310 125	.232 012	.822 702	3.545 951	.282 012	4
5	1.276 282	5.525 631	.180 975	.783 526	4.329 477	.230 975	5
6	1.340 096	6.801 913	.147 017	.746 215	5.075 692	.197 017	6
7	1.407 100	8.142 008	.122 820	.710 681	5.786 373	.172 820	7
8	1.477 455	9.549 109	.104 722	.676 839	6.463 213	.154 722	8
9	1.551 328	11.026 564	.090 690	.644 609	7.107 822	.140 690	9
10	1.628 895	12.577 893	.079 505	.613 913	7.721 735	.129 505	10
11	1.710 339	14.206 787	.070 389	.584 679	8.306 414	.120 389	11
12	1.795 856	15.917 127	.062 825	.556 837	8.863 252	.112 825	12
13	1.885 649	17.712 983	.056 456	.530 321	9.393 573	.106 456	13
14	1.979 932	19.598 632	.051 024	.505 068	9.898 641	.101 024	14
15	2.078 928	21.578 564	.046 342	.481 017	10.379 658	.096 342	15
16	2.182 875	23.657 492	.042 270	.458 112	10.837 770	.092 270	16
17	2.292 018	25.840 366	.038 699	.436 297	11.274 066	.088 699	17
18	2.406 619	28.132 385	.035 546	.415 521	11.689 587	.085 546	18
19	2.526 950	30.539 004	.032 745	.395 734	12.085 321	.082 745	19
20	2.653 298	33.065 954	.030 243	.376 889	12.462 210	.080 243	20
21	2.785 963	35.719 252	.027 996	.358 942	12.821 153	.077 996	21
22	2.925 261	38.505 214	.025 971	.341 850	13.163 003	.075 971	22
23	3.071 524	41.430 475	.024 137	.325 571	13.488 574	.074 137	23
24	3.225 100	44.501 999	.022 471	.310 068	13.798 642	.072 471	24
25	3.386 355	47.727 099	.020 952	.295 303	14.093 945	.070 952	25
26	3.555 673	51.113 454	.019 564	.281 241	14.375 185	.069 564	26
27	3.733 456	54.669 126	.018 292	.267 848	14.643 034	.068 292	27
28	3.920 129	58.402 583	.017 123	.255 094	14.898 127	.067 123	28
29	4.116 136	62.322 712	.016 046	.242 946	15.141 074	.066 046	29
30	4.321 942	66.438 848	.015 051	.231 377	15.372 451	.065 051	30
31	4.538 039	70.760 790	.014 132	.220 359	15.592 811	.064 132	31
32	4.764 941	75.298 829	.013 280	.209 866	15.802 677	.063 280	32
33	5.003 189	80.063 771	.012 490	.199 873	16.002 549	.062 490	33
34	5.253 348	85.066 959	.011 755	.190 355	16.192 904	.061 755	34
35	5.516 015	90.320 307	.011 072	.181 290	16.374 194	.061 072	35
36	5.791 816	95.836 323	.010 434	.172 657	16.546 852	.060 434	36
37	6.081 407	101.628 139	.009 840	.164 436	16.711 287	.059 840	37
38	6.385 477	107.709 546	.009 284	.156 605	16.867 893	.059 284	38
39	6.704 751	114.095 023	.008 765	.149 148	17.017 041	.058 765	39
40	7.039 989	120.799 774	.008 278	.142 046	17.159 086	.058 278	40
41	7.391 988	127.839 763	.007 822	.135 282	17.294 368	.057 822	41
42	7.761 588	135.231 751	.007 395	.128 840	17.423 208	.057 395	42
43	8.149 667	142.993 339	.006 993	.122 704	17.545 912	.056 993	43
44	8.557 150	151.143 006	.006 616	.116 861	17.662 773	.056 616	44
45	8.985 008	159.700 156	.006 262	.111 297	17.774 070	.056 262	45
46	9.434 258	168.685 164	.005 928	.105 997	17.880 066	.055 928	46
47	9.905 971	178.119 422	.005 614	.100 949	17.981 016	.055 614	47
48	10.401 270	188.025 393	.005 318	.096 142	18.077 158	.055 318	48
49	10.921 333	198.426 663	.005 040	.091 564	18.168 722	.055 040	49
50	11.467 400	209.347 996	.004 777	.087 204	18.255 925	.054 777	50
51	12.040 770	220.815 396	.004 529	.083 051	18.338 977	.054 529	51
52	12.642 808	232.856 165	.004 294	.079 096	18.418 073	.054 294	52
53	13.274 949	245.498 974	.004 073	.075 330	18.493 403	.054 073	53
54	13.938 696	258.773 922	.003 864	.071 743	18.565 146	.053 864	54
55	14.635 631	272.712 618	.003 667	.068 326	18.633 472	.053 667	55
56	15.367 412	287.348 249	.003 480	.065 073	18.698 545	.053 480	56
57	16.135 783	302.715 662	.003 303	.061 974	18.760 519	.053 303	57
58	16.942 572	318.851 445	.003 136	.059 023	18.819 542	.053 136	58
59	17.789 701	335.794 017	.002 978	.056 212	18.875 754	.052 978	59
60	18.679 186	353.583 718	.002 828	.053 536	18.929 290	.052 828	60
n	$S^n=(1+i)^n$	$S_{\overline{n}|}=\dfrac{S^n-1}{i}$	$\dfrac{1}{S_{\overline{n}|}}=\dfrac{i}{S^n-1}$	$\dfrac{1}{S^n}=\dfrac{1}{(1+i)^n}$	$a_{\overline{n}|}=\dfrac{1-1/S^n}{i}$	$\dfrac{1}{a_{\overline{n}|}}=\dfrac{i}{1-1/S^n}$	n

$$S=1+i$$

10% ANNUAL COMPOUND INTEREST RATE

10% RATE i	1 AMOUNT OF $1	2 AMOUNT OF $1 PER PERIOD	3 SINKING FUND FACTOR	4 PRESENT WORTH OF $1	5 PRESENT WORTH OF $1 PER PERIOD	6 PARTIAL PAYMENT	10% RATE i
n	The amount to which $1 will grow with compound interest	The amount to which $1 per period will grow with compound interest	The amount per period which will grow with compound interest to $1	What $1 due in the future is worth today	What $1 payable periodically is worth today	The installment to repay $1 with interest	n
1	1.100 000	1.000 000	1.000 000	.909 091	.909 091	1.100 000	1
2	1.210 000	2.100 000	.476 190	.826 446	1.735 537	.576 190	2
3	1.331 000	3.310 000	.302 115	.751 315	2.486 852	.402 115	3
4	1.464 100	4.641 000	.215 471	.683 013	3.169 865	.315 471	4
5	1.610 510	6.105 100	.163 797	.620 921	3.790 787	.263 797	5
6	1.771 561	7.715 610	.129 607	.564 474	4.355 261	.229 607	6
7	1.948 717	9.487 171	.105 405	.513 158	4.868 419	.205 405	7
8	2.143 589	11.435 888	.087 444	.466 507	5.334 926	.187 444	8
9	2.357 948	13.579 477	.073 641	.424 098	5.759 024	.173 641	9
10	2.593 742	15.937 425	.062 745	.385 543	6.144 567	.162 745	10
11	2.853 117	18.531 167	.053 963	.350 494	6.495 061	.153 963	11
12	3.138 428	21.384 284	.046 763	.318 631	6.813 692	.146 763	12
13	3.452 271	24.522 712	.040 779	.289 664	7.103 356	.140 779	13
14	3.797 498	27.974 983	.035 746	.263 331	7.366 687	.135 746	14
15	4.177 248	31.772 482	.031 474	.239 392	7.606 080	.131 474	15
16	4.594 973	35.949 730	.027 817	.217 629	7.823 709	.127 817	16
17	5.054 470	40.544 703	.024 664	.197 845	8.021 553	.124 664	17
18	5.559 917	45.599 173	.021 930	.179 859	8.201 412	.121 930	18
19	6.115 909	51.159 090	.019 547	.163 508	8.364 920	.119 547	19
20	6.727 500	57.274 999	.017 460	.148 644	8.513 564	.117 460	20
21	7.400 250	64.002 499	.015 624	.135 131	8.648 694	.115 624	21
22	8.140 275	71.402 749	.014 005	.122 846	8.771 540	.114 005	22
23	8.954 302	79.543 024	.012 572	.111 678	8.883 218	.112 572	23
24	9.849 733	88.497 327	.011 300	.101 526	8.984 744	.111 300	24
25	10.834 706	98.347 059	.010 168	.092 296	9.077 040	.110 168	25
26	11.918 177	109.181 765	.009 159	.083 905	9.160 945	.109 159	26
27	13.109 994	121.099 942	.008 258	.076 278	9.237 223	.108 258	27
28	14.420 994	134.209 936	.007 451	.069 343	9.306 567	.107 451	28
29	15.863 093	148.630 930	.006 728	.063 039	9.369 606	.106 728	29
30	17.449 402	164.494 023	.006 079	.057 309	9.426 914	.106 079	30
31	19.194 342	181.943 425	.005 496	.052 099	9.479 013	.105 496	31
32	21.113 777	201.137 767	.004 972	.047 362	9.526 376	.104 972	32
33	23.225 154	222.251 544	.004 499	.043 057	9.569 432	.104 499	33
34	25.547 670	245.476 699	.004 074	.039 143	9.608 575	.104 074	34
35	28.102 437	271.024 368	.003 690	.035 584	9.644 159	.103 690	35
36	30.912 681	299.126 805	.003 343	.032 349	9.676 508	.103 343	36
37	34.003 949	330.039 486	.003 030	.029 408	9.705 917	.103 030	37
38	37.404 343	364.043 434	.002 747	.026 735	9.732 651	.102 747	38
39	41.144 778	401.447 778	.002 491	.024 304	9.756 956	.102 491	39
40	45.259 256	442.592 556	.002 259	.022 095	9.779 051	.102 259	40
41	49.785 181	487.851 811	.002 050	.020 086	9.799 137	.102 050	41
42	54.763 699	537.636 992	.001 860	.018 260	9.817 397	.101 860	42
43	60.240 069	592.400 692	.001 688	.016 600	9.833 998	.101 688	43
44	66.264 076	652.640 761	.001 532	.015 091	9.849 089	.101 532	44
45	72.890 484	718.904 837	.001 391	.013 719	9.862 808	.101 391	45
46	80.179 532	791.795 321	.001 263	.012 472	9.875 280	.101 263	46
47	88.197 485	871.974 853	.001 147	.011 338	9.886 618	.101 147	47
48	97.017 234	960.172 338	.001 041	.010 307	9.896 926	.101 041	48
49	106.718 957	1057.189 572	.000 946	.009 370	9.906 296	.100 946	49
50	117.390 853	1163.908 529	.000 859	.008 519	9.914 814	.100 859	50
51	129.129 938	1281.299 382	.000 780	.007 744	9.922 559	.100 780	51
52	142.042 932	1410.429 320	.000 709	.007 040	9.929 599	.100 709	52
53	156.247 225	1552.472 252	.000 644	.006 400	9.935 999	.100 644	53
54	171.871 948	1708.719 477	.000 585	.005 818	9.941 817	.100 585	54
55	189.059 142	1880.591 425	.000 532	.005 289	9.947 106	.100 532	55
56	207.965 057	2069.650 567	.000 483	.004 809	9.951 915	.100 483	56
57	228.761 562	2277.615 624	.000 439	.004 371	9.956 286	.100 439	57
58	251.637 719	2506.377 186	.000 399	.003 974	9.960 260	.100 399	58
59	276.801 490	2758.014 905	.000 363	.003 613	9.963 873	.100 363	59
60	304.481 640	3034.816 395	.000 330	.003 284	9.967 157	.100 330	60

| n | $S^n = (1+i)^n$ | $S_{\overline{n}} = \dfrac{S^n - 1}{i}$ | $\dfrac{1}{S_{\overline{n}}} = \dfrac{i}{S^n - 1}$ | $\dfrac{1}{S^n} = \dfrac{1}{(1+i)^n}$ | $a_{\overline{n}} = \dfrac{1 - 1/S^n}{i}$ | $\dfrac{1}{a_{\overline{n}}} = \dfrac{i}{1 - 1/S^n}$ | n |

$$S = 1 + i$$

References

Akerson, Charles B. *Capitalization Theory and Techniques Study Guide, 3rd ed.* Chicago: Appraisal Institute, 2009.

Alexander, Alan and Richard Muhlebach. *Managing and Leasing Commercial Properties, Volumes 1 and 2.* Chicago: Institute of Real Estate Management, 2007.

Appraisal Institute. *The Appraisal of Real Estate, 13th ed.* Chicago: Appraisal Institute, 2008.

Droms, William G. *Finance and Accounting for Nonfinancial Mangers.* Boston: Addison-Wesley Publishing Company, Inc., 1990.

Fanning, Stephen F., Terry V. Grissom, and Thomas D. Pearson. *Market Analysis for Valuation Appraisals.* Chicago: Appraisal Institute, 1994.

Institute of Real Estate Management. *Income/Expense Analysis®: Condos, Cooperatives, PUDs.* Chicago: Institute of Real Estate Management, published annually.

Institute of Real Estate Management. *Income/Expense Analysis®: Conventional Apartments.* Chicago: Institute of Real Estate Management, published annually.

Institute of Real Estate Management. *Income/Expense Analysis®: Federally Assisted Apartments.* Chicago: Institute of Real Estate Management, published annually.

Institute of Real Estate Management. *Income/Expense Analysis®: Office Buildings.* Chicago: Institute of Real Estate Management, published annually.

Institute of Real Estate Management. *Income/Expense Analysis®: Shopping Centers.* Chicago: Institute of Real Estate Management, published annually.

Institute of Real Estate Management. *Investment Real Estate Financial Tools (FIN402).* Chicago: Institute of Real Estate Management, 2012. Course.

Institute of Real Estate Management. *Investment Real Estate: Financing & Valuation, Part One (ASM603).* Chicago: Institute of Real Estate Management, 2012. Course.

Institute of Real Estate Management. *Investment Real Estate: Financing & Valuation, Part Two (ASM604).* Chicago: Institute of Real Estate Management, 2012. Course.

Institute of Real Estate Management. *Investment Real Estate: Financing & Valuation, Part Three (ASM605).* Chicago: Institute of Real Estate Management, 2012. Course.

Institute of Real Estate Management. *IREM Financial Analysis Spreadsheet.*® Chicago: Institute of Real Estate Management, 2012. Microsoft Excel® spreadsheet tool.

Institute of Real Estate Management. *Principles of Real Estate Management, 16th ed.* Chicago: Institute of Real Estate Management, 2011.

Kolb, Burton A. and Richard F. Demong. *Principles of Financial Management.* C: Business Publications Inc. 1988.

Kolbe, Phillip T. and Gaylon E. Greer. *Investment Analysis for Real Estate Decisions, 7th ed.* Chicago: Dearborn Financial Publishing, Inc., 2009.

Kolbe, Phillip T., Gaylon E. Greer, and Henry G. Rudner III. *Real Estate Finance.* Chicago: Kaplan Publishing for Dearborn Real Estate Education, 2008.

Rattermann, Mark. *The Student Handbook to the Appraisal of Real Estate, 13th ed.* Chicago: Appraisal Institute, 2009.

Woverton, Marvin. *An Introduction to Statistics for Appraisers.* Chicago: Appraisal Institute, 2009.

Glossary

A

Abstract: The most important terms and financial clauses of a lease condensed into a form that is more easily accessible and understandable.

Accelerate: Action taken by a lender during foreclosure wherein immediate payment of the entire loan balance is required, which includes the entire amount due (delinquent mortgage payments, outstanding interest and principle, taxes, penalty fees, collection fees).

Account payable: Monies due to others for services rendered or goods ordered and received.

Account receivable: Monies due from others for services rendered or goods ordered and delivered.

Accrual-basis accounting: The method of accounting that involves entering amounts of income when they are earned and amounts of expense when they are incurred, even though the cash may not be received or paid; also called accrual accounting. All certified audits must use accrual accounting. Compare *cash-basis accounting.*

Accrue: To accumulate growth or value to an asset over a period of time.

Adjusted funds from operations (AFFO): AFFO is equivalent to funds from operations (FFO) less an allowance for maintenance capital expenditures and leasing costs to reflect the cash a REIT spends to maintain its buildings. *(See funds from operations.)*

Adjustment: A component of the real estate cycle. A period when demand declines, occupancy diminishes, and rent concessions become widespread, usually in conjunction with a period of recession or depression. In accounting, modification of account records to reflect actual conditions at the close of a given period (e.g., by adjustment of journal records for accruals, corrections, and depreciation). In employment, an increase (or decrease) of an individual's wages or salary. In insurance, agreement on the amount to be paid to the insured.

After-tax cash flow (ATCF): The money remaining for an investor after income taxes have been deducted; a real estate owner's net profit.

Agency account: An account in which the real estate manager acts for the owner but without acquiring title to assets. The agent (real estate manager) acts for a principal (owner) and agrees to carry out certain duties with respect to the principal's (owner's) property. Serves a similar purpose as a trust account.

Allowance for doubtful accounts: Method used for budget forecasting based on the assumption that there is no way to know which tenant account may become delinquent.

Amortization: Gradual reduction of a debt by periodic payments that include interest and a portion of the principal over the term of the loan.

Amortization schedule/table: A table which separates a loan into its components of principal and interest across the life of the loan.

Anchor: A major shopping center tenant that will draw the majority of customers to the site. Normally an anchor tenant occupies a large space in a desirable location in the shopping center. Often there are two or more anchor tenants, depending on the type of center.

Annual budget: A twelve-month estimate of income and expenses for a property.

Annual debt service (ADS): Total payments, of both principal and interest, per year to one or more lenders.

Annual interest rate (I/YR): The rate of return, or the discount rate, on an investment. For a loan, it is the interest rate charged.

Annuity: An amount to be paid yearly or at other regular intervals, often on a guaranteed dollar basis. An insurance contract that provides a lump sum payout or makes a periodic payment for a specified period or for the life of the insured, beginning at a predetermined date. Money is paid into the fund in a lump sum or in the form of premiums until maturity. Payouts include a portion of the capital (premiums) plus accrued interest. The policy is designed to liquidate funds rather than accumulate them.

Appraisal: An opinion or estimate of the value of a property. An estimate of value that is (usually) prepared by a certified or accredited appraiser. Four methods of appraisal are common—the cost approach, based on the estimated value of the land plus the estimated cost of replacing the improvements on it less depreciation; the market approach (also called sales approach), based on a comparison to similar properties in the market that have been sold recently; the income capitalization approach, based on the net operating income of the property; and the discounted cash flow method, which discounts all future fiscal benefits of an investment property over a predetermined holding period. All four are used to estimate value if sufficient information is gathered in each approach to do so.

Appraised value: Estimate of market value of a property as of the date of an appraiser's appraisal report. Sometimes referred to as final value estimate.

Appraiser: One who performs a formal, detailed estimate of a property's value. An individual who is qualified to estimate the value of real property.

Appreciation: An increase in exchangeable value, as of money, goods, or property. Compare depreciation.

As-is analysis: An analysis of the impact of continuing to operate the property under the same or similar circumstances.

Asset manager: One who is charged with supervising an owner's real estate assets at the investment level. In addition to real estate management responsibilities that include maximizing net operating income and property value, an asset manager may recommend or be responsible for or participate in property acquisition, development, and divestiture. An asset manager may have only superficial involvement with day-to-day operations at the site (e.g., supervision of personnel, property maintenance, tenant relations).

B

Back office: Accounting functions that do not require interaction with tenants. These may include preparation of historical operating data after an accounting period is closed, payment of operating expenses for properties, and operation of the management company.

Balance sheet: A statement of the financial position of a person or a business (or investment property) at a particular time, indicating assets, liabilities, and owner equity.

Balanced portfolio: A portfolio consisting of a variety of properties and risk levels, the intent being that the "safe" investments will provide returns only as expected and some of the higher-risk items will be more financially successful, resulting in a higher overall return for the portfolio.

Balloon loan: Action occurring during the final stages of a loan wherein the last payment of a loan is larger than the previous monthly payments in order to fully repay the outstanding principal balance.

Base-year method: Method of calculating pass through expenses that requires tenants to pay a particular percentage of operating costs above those incurred in the base year.

Before-tax cash flow (BTCF): Amount of money remaining after operating expenses (including real estate taxes and debt service) have been bumped out before income taxes are considered.

Best practices: Norms for operation used by the most ethical and honest companies established by industry practitioners, professional associations, and amongst firms.

Book value: The value of an item, such as real property, as stated in books of account and differentiated from its market value. Calculated as the cost of a property, plus capital additions, less accrued depreciation (cost recovery) that has been charged off for income tax purposes and partial sales. Compare market value. Also, the value of capital stock (as of a corporation) based on the excess of assets over liabilities.

Broker: An agent with a real estate license who acts as a representative for an owner or tenant, within specific limits of authority. Also, an agent who buys, sells, or leases for a principal on a commission basis without having title to the property.

Bundle of rights: Limited rights included with a property to surface area of the property above and below the property itself. These rights are limited by public and private restrictions based on local law.

C

CAM budget: Estimates the funds that will be needed for the coming year's operating expenses for areas not owned by any one tenant in an office or retail building.

Capital budget: An estimate of costs of major improvements or replacements; generally a long-range plan for improvements to a property. Also used in referring to a long-range financial plan for acquiring and financing capital assets.

Capital expenditure(s): Spending on capital assets, such as major improvements, large equipment, additions to buildings, buildings themselves, and land.

Capitalization: The treatment of future income as part of a firm's capital. In appraisal, the process employed in estimating the market value of real property by applying a proper investment rate of return to the annual net operating income expected to be produced by the property, the formula being: Income (I) divided by Rate (R) equals Value (V), or $I \div R = V$—the IRV formula.

Capitalization rate: A single rate that converts a single year's income into value. It is the rate of return to estimate the property's value. The capitalization rate formula is: Net Operating Income (NOI) $\div$ Property Value (or sales price).

Cash-basis accounting: The method of accounting that recognizes income and expenses when money is actually received or paid; also called cash accounting. Compare *accrual-basis accounting.*

Cash flow: The amount of spendable income from a real estate investment. The amount of cash available after all payments have been made for operating expenses, debt service (mortgage principal and interest), and capital reserve funds; also called pre-tax cash flow to indicate that income taxes have not been deducted.

Cash flow analysis worksheet: Forms used to organize financial analyses. These worksheets can be titled in many different ways, such as annual operating data and multi-year operating data.

Cash flow budget: Monthly or other projection of the cash position of a business (or investment property) accounting for all sources of income and all expected expenditures, including debt service and monies contributed to capital reserves as well as ordinary operating expenses, but excluding income taxes.

Cash flow statements: Reports of the actual inflow and outflow of cash and its related sources and uses in a given accounting period.

Cash-on-cash rate of return: Measures an investor's rate of return on the capital invested, compares the equity invested with the before-tax cash flow for one year. The formula is: BTCF ÷ Initial Equity = Cash-on-Cash Rate of Return.

Chart of accounts: A classification or arrangement of account items by type of income or expense (e.g., rent, advertising, insurance, maintenance), as well as assets and liabilities, accounts receivable, and accounts payable.

Closing: In salesmanship, persuading the customer to buy the product after the product has been explained and demonstrated; the last step in the sales process. The signing of a lease after negotiations have concluded. Used in apartment leasing to refer to the point at which the leasing agent's efforts have resulted in a prospective resident agreeing to sign a lease. More commonly in real estate, closing refers to the final transaction session at which the mortgage is secured (unless the sale is all cash), possession (title) of the real estate is transferred, and the money (consideration) changes hands.

Collection loss: Revenue loss consisting of bad debts, rents that may not be collected, and concessions.

Commercial mortgage-backed security (CMBS): The secondary market for commercial mortgages, in which commercial mortgages are bundled and securitized.

Commingling: To mix or combine; a prohibited practice in real estate wherein the money of more than one person or entity is combined into a common fund.

Common area maintenance (CAM): Upkeep of areas not owned by any one tenant in an office or retail building.

Comparable sales approach: (See market data approach.)

Compounding: In banking, calculation and payment of interest on the principal and on any previous interest.

Concessions: Revenue loss used to attract tenants (e.g., reductions to rent).

Conformity: Concept that maintains that maximum value will be derived by a product that adheres to the demands of the widest part of the market.

Consumer Price Index (CPI): A way of measuring consumer purchasing power by comparing the current costs of goods and services to those of a selected base period; formerly cost-of-living index. Sometimes used as a reference point for rent escalations in commercial leases (i.e., as a measure of inflation). The CPI is published monthly by the U.S. Department of Labor, Bureau of Labor Statistics.

Contract rent: The rent stipulated in an existing lease, which may differ from the economic or market rent. In government-assisted housing, the total rent HUD (or the contract administrator) authorizes an owner to collect from all sources for a unit occupied by a family receiving assistance.

Controllable expenses: An operating expense for which management has defined responsibility and over which it has control (e.g., advertising, energy consumption, maintenance and repairs, and purchase of supplies).

Cost approach: A method of appraising real property in which the value of the improvements is estimated on the basis of the cost to reproduce them minus accrued depreciation; also called summation approach.

Cost recovery: A tax deduction allowed by the Internal Revenue Service to recover the cost of a depreciable asset.

Curb appeal: General cleanliness, neatness, and attractiveness of a building as exemplified by the appearance of the exterior and grounds and the general level of housekeeping. The aesthetic image and appearance projected by a property; the first impression it creates.

D

Debt coverage ratio (DCR): A lender's ratio that compares the annual net operating income (NOI) to the annual debt service of the loan and expresses the ability of the property to pay back the loan. The formula is: NOI ÷ ADS = DCR.

Debt financing: Use of borrowed funds to invest in real estate.

Debt investment: A form of real estate investment where funds are loaned to property owners in exchange for a payment of interest (i.e., lender).

Defeasance: Act of using substitute collateral to satisfy a borrower's loan and allowing a property to then be sold or refinanced. This is typically achieved by using government-backed securities to substitute for the cash flow that the original loan guaranteed. Defeasance does not prepay the loan; rather, it substitutes a specific set of securities that produce the same income over the same time frame.

Default: Failure to fulfill an obligation (as a mortgage or other contracted payment) when it is due. The nonperformance of a duty, such as those required in a lease or other contract. Sometimes called breach of contract.

Deferred maintenance: Ordinary maintenance of a building that, because it has not been performed, negatively affects the use, occupancy, and value of the property. Also, an amount needed for repairs, restoration, or rehabilitation of an asset (e.g., real property) but not yet expended.

Delinquency report: Failure to make payment on a debt or obligation when due. A report that states being overdue. A debt on which payment is in arrears, as of mortgage principal or interest or rent under a lease.

Deposit account: One of two types of accounts frequently kept for each client in a property. Specifically, a deposit account is an interest-bearing account frequently used as a repository for all income.

Depreciation: Loss of value. In real estate, decline in value of a property resulting from physical deterioration (ordinary wear and tear), functional obsolescence (out-of-date systems and/or equipment), and/or economic obsolescence (market changes). See also obsolescence. In accounting, the gradual process of converting a fixed asset into an expense. Also, the tax deduction that allows for recovery of the investment in certain types of property by allocation of the cost over the estimated useful life of the property; also called cost recovery. In real estate, depreciation (and cost recovery) applies to the cost of improvements to land; the land itself is not depreciated.

Depression: Part of the business cycle, a period of low economic activity characterized by high unemployment, low levels of investment, falling prices (including rents), reduced purchasing power, decreasing use of resources, and currency deflation.

Development: A component of the real estate cycle. A period when occupancy is high, rents are rising, and absorption levels are high, usually coincident with increasing prosperity and leading to new construction to meet demand for housing and commercial space that exceeds the available supply. Also used in referring to developed real estate, as a large-scale or multi-building residential or commercial project that may be built in phases.

Direct write-off: Method of dealing with delinquent accounts wherein tenants are evicted when their debt becomes uncollectable.

Disbursement account: One of two types of accounts frequently kept for each client in a property. A disbursement account is often used to pay expenses relevant to the client and/or property.

Discount: A reduction in price, usually as a reward for paying a charge prior to the date of delinquency or for buying in quantity.

Discount rate: Any rate used to translate a future dollar amount into an equivalent present value. Also, the interest rate the Federal Reserve Bank charges commercial banks.

Discounted cash flow (DCF): Financial analysis using the time value of money to determine how much an investment held for several years into the future would be worth in present dollars.

Discounted cash flow (DCF) analysis/method: A method of valuation that discounts all future fiscal benefits of an investment property over a predetermined holding period. See also *appraisal*.

Discounting: Calculating how much a future sum of money would be worth at present.

Due diligence: The duty of a seller to ensure that the offering statement does not misstate or omit pertinent information. The appropriate or sufficient level of care and attention that should be given during the examination or evaluation of a property, either as preparation for financing or refinancing or in an effort to identify environmental problems that must be addressed.

E

Economic obsolescence: Impairment of desirability or useful life of property, or its loss in use and value, arising from economic forces outside of the building or property, such as changes in optimum land use, legislative enactments that restrict or impair property rights, and changes in market conditions (e.g., supply-demand relationships).

Economic vacancy: Commonly used in rental housing to mean all vacant units that are not producing income. In addition to physical vacancies, this includes units that are not available for lease (e.g., apartments used as models or offices, staff apartments, cannibalized units) as well as leased units that are not yet occupied and occupied units that are not producing rent (i.e., delinquencies); usually expressed as a percentage of the total number of units. (In other words, the number of unoccupied units may not always be an accurate reflection of the impact of vacancies.) A similar determination may be made for commercial properties based on unoccupied square footage. In economic terms, the rent dollars lost from such vacancies, expressed as a percentage of the gross potential income of the property.

Effective Age: The estimated age of a structure based on its utility, observed deterioration, and obsolescence.

Effective gross income (EGI): The total amount of income actually collected during a reporting period; the gross receipts of a property. Gross potential rental income, less vacancy, and collection losses plus miscellaneous or unscheduled income.

Effective interest rate: The actual rate of interest paid on a loan, which may include adjustments.

Eminent domain: The right of a government or municipal quasi-public body to acquire private property for public use through a court action called condemnation in which the court determines that the use is a public use and determines the price or compensation to be paid to the owner. (The owner of the property must be fairly compensated, usually based on an appraisal of the fair market value.)

Equity: The value of real property in excess of debt. The interest or value that an owner has in real estate over and above the mortgage and other financial liens against it; outright ownership. In accounting, the excess of a firm's assets over its liabilities.

Equity investment: Investment in the form of a down payment made by a property owner when purchasing a new property.

Equity ownership: Legal right of possession. The owner or owners of a rental (apartment, office, retail, or industrial) building who contract for professional property management and/or employ a leasing agent(s).

Equity REIT: A real estate investment trust that owns or has an equity interest in rental real estate (rather than making loans secured by real estate collateral).

Expense stops: Costs paid by the owner of an office or retail property to cover operating expenses of the building.

Expense-stop method: In an office lease, a clause obligating the property owner to pay operating costs up to a certain amount per square foot per year; tenants pay their pro rata share of any costs in excess of that amount. When used in a retail lease, a clause obligating the tenants to pay a pro rata share of operating expenses up to a certain amount per year (expense cap); the owner pays any costs in excess of that amount.

Explanation of accounts: A guide or legend that details which category to use for each instance of cash inflow, cash outflow, and expense accrual. Sometimes referred to as manual of accounts.

F

Fair market value: The price paid, or one that might be anticipated as necessarily payable, by a willing and informed buyer to a willing and informed seller (neither of whom is under any compulsion to act), if the object sold has been reasonably exposed to the market. In real estate, the price at which a property is sold to a willing buyer by a willing seller.

Fee management firm: Firms that charge a fee to manage their properties.

Fee simple ownership: The most complete type of private ownership of real estate which gives the titleholder the right to possess, control, use, and dispose of the property without time limitation, including the unlimited right to divide the property among one's heirs. Sometimes called fee simple *absolute.*

Fidelity bond: A contract issued by a third party (usually an insurance company) that protects one individual against financial loss that might result from dishonest acts of another specific individual. A bond obtained by an employer to protect against the loss of money or property sustained because of the dishonesty of an employee.

Fiduciary: One charged with a relationship of trust and confidence, as between a principal and agent, trustee and beneficiary, or attorney and client, when one party is legally empowered to act on behalf of another.

Financial accounting: A system of classifying financial transactions that documents a company's financial position in the form of a balance sheet and an income statement (external reports).

Financial Accounting Standards Board: Independent agency responsible for setting Generally Accepted Accounting Principles (GAAP).

Financial Institution Reform, Recovery, and Enforcement Act: A U.S. federal law enacted on August 9, 1989 in the wake of the savings and loan crisis of the 1980s. It established the Resolution Trust Corporation (RTC) to close hundreds of insolvent thrifts and provided funds to pay out insurance to their depositors. It transferred thrift regulatory authority from the Federal Home Loan Bank Board to the Office of Thrift Supervision, and dramatically changed the savings and loan industry and its federal regulation to encourage loan origination.

Financial management rate of return (FMRR): A method that relies on investor selected rates of return in calculating positive cash flow as a basis for decision-making. FMRR varies from *internal rate of return (IRR)* with regard to reinvestment rates and tends to project a more market-driven return.

Fixed cost: Costs that do not change as occupancy rates change and are generally stable during a budget period. Fixed costs also include insurance costs and real estate taxes.

Forbearance: Property workout in the form of a temporary period during which the lender of a defaulted loan withholds legal action so as to allow the property owner time to make the loan current.

Foreclose / foreclosure: A court action initiated by the mortgagee, or a lienor, for the purpose of having the court order the debtor's real estate sold to pay the mortgage or lien (e.g., a mechanic's lien or court judgment).

Free-and-clear rate of return: A ratio that measures the return potential of a property that is free of debt, compares net operating income (NOI) with the total property value. The formula is: NOI ÷ Property Value = Free-and-Clear Rate of Return.

Front office: The real-time accounting functions that require interaction with tenants or residents, including lease administration and enforcement and rent collection.

Functional obsolescence: A condition of obsolete design or use of a property. Defects in a building or structure that detract from its value or marketability. Such defects may be curable or incurable.

Funds from operations (FFO): A measure used by real estate investment trusts (REITs) in referring to operationally derived funds (as opposed to investment capital). Also used in referring to property income collected before payment of any expenses or debt service has been made. *(See adjusted funds from operations.)*

Future value (FV): A concept derived from the *time value of money* that describes how much an investment will be worth after a specified time span at a given rate of interest.

G

Gain: An increase in wealth or resources.

Gain to lease: The amount of money gained due to rental rates being less than the maximum market rents (or GPI).

General ledger: A formal record of all the financial transactions of a business. Accounts are transferred as final entries from the various journals to the general ledger, where they are posted as debits and credits and thus show the accumulated effects of transactions.

Generally Accepted Accounting Principles (GAAP): Professional standards for tax returns and full-accrual financial statements set by the Financial Accounting Standards Board.

Going-in cap rate: The ratio of the first year's net operating income to the acquisition price of an investment property.

Going-out cap rate: The forecast ratio of the next year's operating income to the sales price at the time the property is expected to be resold.

Gross possible income: The total monthly or annual possible income before uncollected income is deducted.

Gross potential income (GPI): The maximum amount of rent a property can produce. The sum of the rental rates of all spaces available to be rented in a property at 100 percent occupancy. In assisted housing, GPI includes payments from governmental agencies as well as tenant payments.

Gross potential rent (GPR): The sum of the rental rates of all spaces available to be rented in a property, regardless of occupancy. The maximum amount of rent a property can produce.

H

High and best use: That use of real property that will produce the highest property value and develop a site to its fullest economic potential. In appraisal, the reasonably probable and legal use of vacant land or an improved property that is physically possible, appropriately supported, financially feasible, and results in the highest value. The four criteria for highest and best use are: physical possibility, legal permissibility, financial feasibility, and maximum profitability.

Hybrid REIT: A real estate investment trust that combines the strategies of an equity REIT and a mortgage REIT. In effect, they may own loans or obligations backed with real estate collateral and own equity or interest in other properties.

I

Income capitalization approach: The process of estimating the value of an income-producing property by capitalization of the annual net income expected to be produced by the property during its remaining useful life.

Inflation: The increase in the average level of prices, or equivalently, the decrease in the value of money.

In-house manager: Management originating from within an organization or company (i.e., by the staff of the corporation owning the property) rather than being contracted with an independent third party (i.e., professional management services).

Interest: The cost of borrowing money, expressed as a percentage of the amount borrowed to be paid in one year. The yield required by lenders on their investment. Also, right, title, or legal share in something, as a share in ownership of a property.

Interest rate: The percentage of an amount of money charged for its use, as of a loan. Also, the rate of return on an investment, as of capital.

Internal rate of return (IRR): The rate of return at which the discounted value of all benefits received during ownership is equal to the value of the owner's equity in the investment. The true annual earnings of an investment expressed as a percentage. A method used by investors to determine cash returns in relation to cash invested. (The calculation assumes that the annual proceeds can be invested at the same rate as the IRR.) In financial analysis, the specific discount rate for which the net present value (NPV) is zero, which gives a percentage that indicates the viability of a project or the profitability of an investment. *See also financial management rate of return (FMRR); modified internal rate of return (MIRR).*

Investment: Expenditure of money to purchase something of intrinsic value or to generate income or profits. Purchase of property that will be held for a relatively long period, during which it is expected to increase in value.

Investment value: The worth of a property to a particular investor based on predetermined criteria. The price that an investor bound by special circumstances and restraints will agree to pay. Investment value relates to equity ownership and is an individualized or personal value as compared to market value, which is impersonal and detached.

IREM® Financial Analysis Spreadsheet: Created by IREM to perform cash flow analyses based on property performance and owners' goals and objectives. The spreadsheet automatically amortizes and analyzes property loans and leverage positions; forecasts net operating income (NOI) based on property income and expenses; calculates cash-on-cash return, value enhancement, net present value (NPV), and internal rate of return (IRR); creates t-bars to visualize income stream.

L

Land economics: The study of the geographic, environmental, legal, economic, and social aspects of the primary units of production addressed in macroeconomics—land, labor, capital, and entrepreneurship.

Leasehold advantage: The positive difference between the then current rental being paid on a property and its *Fair Market Value (FMV)*.

Leasing agent: A person who is directly responsible for renting space in assigned properties.

Lease-up budget: Projection of income and expenses for a newly developed property; also called rent-up budget. Having such a separate budget allows the developer or property manager to account for the wide variances in income and expenses that occur before there is sufficient occupancy to stabilize its financial picture.

Leverage: The use of borrowed funds to increase one's purchasing power. In real estate, use of borrowed funds to purchase investment property with the expectation of realizing a return that exceeds the cost of the borrowed funds. Also used to describe how effectively an investor is using debt. Positive leverage means that debt increases return on equity. Negative leverage decreases such return.

Lien: A claim against property by a creditor under which the property becomes security for the debt owed to the creditor. The legal right of a creditor to have his/her debt paid out of the property of the debtor. Mortgages, mechanic's liens, and tax liens are monetary liens against a property for the satisfaction of debt.

Limited liability company (LLC): Created by state statute, a business ownership form that functions like a corporation—its members are protected from liability—but for income tax purposes is classified as a partnership. Income and expenses flow through to the individual members. The arrangement offers considerable flexibility in its organization and structure.

Liquidity: The ability to convert assets into cash. The ease with which a person or business can meet its obligations without selling fixed assets.

Loan constant: A ratio that represents the current amount paid for each dollar of borrowed funds, a percentage of a loan balance that is required annually to service principal and interest payments on the loan. The formula is: Loan Constant (k%) = Annual Debt Service (ADS) ÷ Loan Amount.

Loan-to-value ratio (LTR): A measure of the lender's risk of loss in making a loan. The relationship between the amount of the principal of a loan and the market value of the real estate securing it; usually expressed as a percentage using the formula: loan amount ÷ property value. The value may be the price being paid for the property or the appraised value. An LTV above 85 percent would be considered high risk.

Long-term budget: A long-range projection that estimates future expenditures and the return period— usually three to five years.

Loss: In accounting, any excess of costs over income. In insurance, the basis of a valid claim for damages or indemnity under the terms of a given policy.

Loss to lease: The amount of money lost due to rental rates being less than the maximum market rents (or GPI).

M

Management agreement: A contractual arrangement between the owner(s) of a property and the designated managing agent, describing the duties and establishing the authority of the agent and detailing the responsibilities, rights, and obligations of both agent and owner(s).

Management plan: The fundamental document for the short-term operation of a property that represents a statement of facts, objectives, and policies and details how the property is to be operated during the coming year. Such a plan usually includes the annual budget.

Managerial accounting: Use of financial information and records to make business planning decisions. A system designed to facilitate decision-making, planning, and control. Because managerial accounting forecasts are not actual transactions, they are not auditable. See also *financial accounting*.

Managerial reporting: Use of financial information and records to make business planning decisions. A system designed to facilitate decision-making, planning, and control. Because managerial reporting forecasts are not actual transactions, they are not auditable.

Manual of accounts: See *explanation of accounts*.

Market data approach: A method of valuation based on a comparison of data from recent sales of similar properties in the market.

Market rent: Rent that a property is capable of yielding if leased under prevailing market conditions; economic rent. Also, the amount that comparable space would command in a competitive market. Often used interchangeably with street rent and contract rent. (By definition, the latter is the rent stated in a specific lease.) For apartments, the basis is unit type and size. For office buildings, the basis would be dollars per rentable square foot; for retail space, it would be dollars per square foot of gross leasable area (GLA). In government-assisted housing, the rent HUD authorizes the owner to collect from families who are ineligible for assistance.

Market value: The price at which a seller would willingly sell an item and a buyer would willingly buy it in an open market if neither were acting under unusual pressure. The price that a piece of property might be expected to bring if offered for sale in an open market comprised of willing buyers and sellers where the property has been available for sale for a reasonable period of time.

Mark to market: An accounting regulation that prevents workouts or refinancing under conditions where the value of property has dropped significantly.

Mezzanine financing: Financing practice which funds the gap between traditional loan-to-value ratios and the desires of investors. Such loans are typically small and for a short term.

Midstream analysis: The part of the cash flow analysis that is prepared after a property is bought, thus allowing new figures to be added and a revised, more accurate investment base to be calculated.

Modified accrual accounting: A method of accounting in which items that repeat at regular intervals are accounted on a cash basis while those requiring accumulation of funds toward a large dollar payout are accounted on an accrual basis; sometimes also called modified cash-accrual system.

Modified internal rate of return (MIRR): In financial analysis, an indicator that uses investor selected rates of return in calculating positive cash flow as a basis for decision-making.

Mortgage broker: A banker looks at a property from the perspective of a lender, which must weigh the risk of an investment package against strategies of institutional investors.

Mortgage REIT: A real estate investment trust that makes or owns loans and other obligations that are secured by real estate collateral.

N

Narrative appraisal report: A report that explains any differences or variances between the actual income and expenses and the amounts projected for them in the budget and also gives a detailed discussion of all factors contributing to the value.

Negative leverage: The use of borrowed funds to purchase investment property with the expectation of realizing a return that exceeds the cost of the borrowed funds. Also used to describe how effectively an investor is using debt. Negative leverage decreases such return.

Net asset value (NAV): One of the valuation indices of real estate investment trusts (REITs); normally quoted per investment unit where the value is divided by the number of total outstanding investment units; an adjusted net asset value reflecting the market values of real estate properties held by an investment corporation.

Net income: An accounting term that represents the profit of an entire business entity from the perspective of the investor for whom a statement is prepared.

Net operating income (NOI): Total collections (gross receipts) less operating expenses; may be calculated on an annual or a monthly basis. More broadly, cash available after all operating expenses have been deducted from collected rental income and before debt service and capital expenses have been deducted.

Net profit: The money remaining for an investor after income taxes have been deducted.

Net rent revenue: Gross Potential Income (GPI) adjusted for loss to lease and for vacancy and collection loss. This adjustment is the first part of the equation for calculating NOI.

Nonrecourse: Having no personal liability. In the case of a loan that is nonrecourse, the lender must rely solely on the property pledged as collateral for payment in the event of default by the borrower; other assets of the borrower cannot be taken.

Nonrecourse loan: Loans in which the investor's risk is limited to their investment.

O

Obsolescence: Generally speaking, a loss of value brought about by a change in design, technology, taste, or demand. *Physical obsolescence* (deterioration) is a result of aging (wear and tear) or deferred maintenance. *Functional obsolescence* is an internal condition of a property related to its design or use. *Economic obsolescence* is an inability to generate enough income to offset operating expenses, usually due to conditions external to the property (changes in populations and/or land uses, legislation, etc.). Also used in referring to the process by which property loses its economic usefulness to the owner/taxpayer due to causes other than physical deterioration (e.g., technological advancements, changes in public taste); an element of *depreciation*.

Operating budget: A listing of all anticipated income from and expenses of operating a property, usually projected on an annual basis. While funds for accumulation of capital reserves would be deducted from net operating income (NOI) in an operating budget (and the accumulated funds would be recorded as a capital or asset item), actual expenditures of such reserve funds would be anticipated in a capital budget.

Operating expenses: The normal costs of running a business. In real estate, the expenditures for real estate taxes, salaries, insurance, maintenance, utilities, and similar items paid in connection with the operation of a rental property that are properly charged against income. More broadly, all expenditures made in connection with operating a property with the exception of debt service, capital reserves (and/or capital expenditures), and income taxes. At commercial properties, increases in operating expenses are often used as a basis for rent increases. Items included for this purpose can vary by property type and geographic location.

Opportunity cost: The cost of not selling and reinvesting the proceeds of an investment, calculated by an investor at a certain time as a measure of performance. The return that could have been earned if the money were available for investment immediately. The monetary or other advantage that is foregone today in order to obtain something that will have value in the future. Investors use the discounted cash flow (DCF) method to determine whether an investment in real estate will have a comparable or better yield than other investments. The discount rate is based on the rate of return on financial assets whose risk is equivalent to the risk of investing in the particular property under consideration. See also internal *rate of return* and *time value of money (TVM)*.

Overbuilding: A component of the real estate cycle. A period when real estate activity is high as a consequence of prosperity. Money is readily available from lenders for development of housing and office, store, and warehouse space to meet pent-up demand. Demand that cannot be sustained or is miscalculated leads to declining real estate values.

P

Pass-through: In commercial leasing, operating expenses of a property that are paid by the tenants, usually on a pro rata basis in addition to base rent, including real estate taxes, insurance on the property, and *common area maintenance (CAM)* costs.

Percentage rent: In retail leasing, rent that is based on a percentage of a tenant's gross sales (or sometimes net income or profits), often compared to the guaranteed minimum or base rent under the lease and paid as overage (i.e., the amount of percentage rent in excess of the minimum or base rent due). See also *breakpoint.* A percentage rent provision may also be written such that the tenant in a shopping center is required to pay a percentage of gross sales in lieu of minimum rent under certain circumstances (e.g., loss of an anchor tenant).

Periodic payment (PMT): A cash flow or benefit that is paid more than once in the same amount. In the case of a loan, it is one payment.

Physical depreciation: The aging or deterioration of the property; these defects may be curable through property maintenance.

Physical vacancy: The number of vacant units in a building or development that are available for rent, usually expressed as a percentage of the total number of units.

Police power: The right of a governmental agency to enact and enforce regulations regarding the health, safety, and general welfare of the population within its jurisdiction.

Portfolio: A selection of assets held by an investor.

Portfolio loan: Loans made that do not qualify to be sold or are not sold to a secondary market and collect payments in the traditional way.

Positive leverage: The use of borrowed funds to purchase investment property with the expectation of realizing a return that exceeds the cost of the borrowed funds. Also used to describe how effectively an investor is using debt. Positive leverage means that debt increases return on equity.

Present value (PV): The current dollar value of a sum of money to be received in the future that has been discounted by a given percentage rate. The amount one would have to invest today at a given rate for the period to yield the future sum.

Price index: A database that traces the changes in prices of a selection of representative commodities over specified time spans.

Principal: In real estate, one who owns property. In real estate management, the property owner who contracts for the services of an agent. In finance, the amount of money that is borrowed in a loan as distinct from the interest on such loan; the original amount or remaining balance of a loan. Also, the original amount of capital invested. In law, the individual being represented in a business transaction by an agent authorized to do so.

Pro forma budget: Budget used to analyze the merits and drawbacks of real estate investments based on projected results. Revenues and expenses are estimated under normal, stable market conditions. It is also used to analyze the effects of major changes to a property.

Pro forma statement: A projection of future earnings and expenses based on specific assumptions.

Prosperity: Part of the business cycle, a period of economic growth characterized by business expansion, increased consumer spending, and low levels of unemployment.

R

Real estate investment trust (REIT): A company which sells publicly traded shares and distributes at least 90 percent of its taxable income to shareholders in the form of dividends. They pass returns through to the investor to be taxed at the individual's tax rate. See also *equity REIT, mortgage REIT,* and *hybrid REIT.*

Recapture: An income tax term describing money taken back or forfeited; a kind of tax penalty. For example, if a tax deduction was taken but does not meet all conditions, the deduction will be disallowed and the taxpayer will be required to pay tax on the income that had been offset by the deduction. This money is said to be recaptured by the taxing body.

Receiver: An individual appointed by a court to manage a property that is the subject of a pending bankruptcy or foreclosure. A receiver's role is to preserve property that has been abandoned or for which there have been allegations of fraud or mismanagement by the owner. In some states, property is assigned to a receiver during the statutory redemption period after a foreclosure sale.

Recession: Part of the business cycle, a period of reduced general economic activity characterized by tightened credit, reduced consumer and business spending, and declining employment, profits, production, and sales that is not as severe or protracted as a depression.

Recovery: Part of the business cycle, a period of economic upturn following a depression characterized by increasing demand for goods and services and rising prices. Also, obtaining something by a court judgment.

Rent-up budget: A variation of an annual operating budget used for new buildings, rehab projects, and properties with abnormal vacancies, estimating income and expenses for the first year of operation or until occupancy is stabilized.

Replacement cost: The estimated cost to replace or restore a building to its pre-existing condition and appearance (and in compliance with applicable current building codes); a common method of determining insurance coverage. In appraisal, the cost at current prices to replace an existing building with one of equal utility. In insurance, replacement cost coverage reimburses the total cost of rebuilding; no deductions are made for depreciation.

Reproduction cost: The cost at current prices to construct an exact duplicate of a building using the same materials. In appraisal, a consideration in regard to historic buildings.

Resolution Trust Corporation (RTC): A governmental agency created to manage and dispose of the assets of thrifts that were in receivership; contracted with real estate management firms to manage and market many of those assets for disposition.

Restrictive covenant: Private restrictions to a bundle of rights which may prohibit certain uses of a property.

Return of investment: Allows the owner to recover a portion of the original cost through deductions for the physical loss in value resulting from a property's aging.

Return on investment: The ratio of net operating income to the total investment amount, for a given time period, which provides a measure of the financial performance of the investment. A measure of profitability expressed as a percentage and calculated by comparing periodic income to the owner's equity in the property (income ÷ equity = % ROI). A measure of cash flow against investment, it can be calculated either before or after deduction of income tax. ROI measures overall effectiveness of management in generating profits from available assets; however, it does not consider the *time value of money.*

Revenue: Total assets returned on an investment.

Reversion value: The value of the property when sold at the end of the investment.

Risk: The likelihood of loss. In insurance, the degree of probability of loss to the insured from the peril or perils specified in an insurance policy. In finance, the probability that an investor will not receive the required or expected rate of return.

S

Sale proceeds: The difference between a sale price and the costs associated with the sale.

Servicing agent: Responsible party for acting on behalf of the end lender in collecting loan payments and taking collection action in case of delinquency.

Short sale: Type of sale with special circumstances in which a sale could be negotiated as fulfillment of a loan.

Speculation: Real estate speculation offers an investor an opportunity to take high risk and potentially receive high reward during a relatively short holding period. The return is typically achieved at the time of sale from the profit made in selling the property.

Stabilization: A component of the real estate cycle, comparable to the recovery period in the business cycle. A period when demand begins to increase and absorb the oversupply, but there is little new construction, and rental increases are asked to keep pace with inflation.

Stabilized NOI: Income of a property adjusted for operating expenses but before considering debt service. See net operating income (NOI).

Sublet space: The leasing of part or all of the premises by a tenant to a third party for part or all of the tenant's remaining term. Under a subletting agreement, the original tenant is responsible for rent not paid or damages committed by the subtenant regardless of his/her agreement with the subtenant.

Syndicator: In the context of a partnership, packages real estate investments as tax shelters with the goal of making ownership of large properties available to numerous small investors desiring an investment with favorable tax treatment.

T

Taxable income: Income for a given period of time against which there is an income tax liability to a municipal, state, or federal income tax agency. Under federal tax law, taxable income is what remains after gross income is reduced by adjustments and allowable deductions.

Tenant improvements: Fixed improvements made to tenants' office space, usually based on specific building standards determined in advance by ownership; specifics are often negotiable, especially in a slow market. In apartment rentals, additions or alterations to the leased premises for the use of the tenant, made at the cost and expense of the tenant and becoming a part of the realty unless otherwise agreed to in writing.

Terminal value: The price a property is expected to sell for at the end of a specified holding period.

Time point zero: The time when a property was valued by the appraiser would be considered the start of a new analysis.

Time value of money (TVM): The assumption that a dollar today is worth more than a dollar at some future date. The basis of compounding to determine future value or discounting to determine present value.

Triple net (NNN): A lease under which the tenant pays a prorated share of some or all operating expenses in addition to base or minimum rent. The terms net-net (or double-net) and net-net-net (or triple-net) are also used, depending on the extent of the costs that are passed through to the tenant. Used most often for commercial tenants, the definitions of the terms vary with location and type of property (e.g., office, retail, industrial). In retail leasing, the tenant pays a prorated share of property taxes under a net lease, prorated shares of both property taxes and insurance under a net-net (or double-net) lease, and prorated shares of all operating expenses (including common area maintenance) under a net-net-net (or triple-net) lease.

Trust account: A fiduciary account established by one person to hold funds that belong to another person. A separate bank account, segregated from an agent's own funds, in which the agent is required to deposit monies collected for the client.

U

Uncontrollable expenses: Operating expense items over which property management has no control (e.g., real estate taxes, insurance premiums, labor-union wages).

Underwrite: Financial backing; an agreement to contribute to a financial venture. In insurance, the process of evaluating an applicant against pre-established criteria of insurability to determine whether the applicant will be accepted for coverage (or rejected) and whether the premiums will be set at standard or modified rates.

Underwriting criteria: Policies set by a lender that limit the percentage of value that can be loaned against a particular property.

Uniform Standards of Appraisal Practice (USPAP): Appraisal standards set by the Appraisal Institute and the National Association of REALTORS.

Upside potential: The possibility for an investment to increase or grow in value.

V

Valuation: An estimation or calculation of the worth of an object; the process of determining an object's worth. The result of the process of appraising property for tax and other purposes. See also *appraisal*. Market value is the price at which a willing seller would sell and a willing buyer would buy—the most likely price that an asset on the open, competitive market will fetch. Investment value is the value of the property according to the specific requirements of the investor and is measured by capitalizing the cash flow. See also market value; investment value.

Variable cost: Costs which change with usage, such as electricity and water charges.

Variance: A difference between what was forecast and documented financial results.

W

Workouts: Arrangements made between a lender and property owner that allows for the owner to retain ownership while a loan is restructured.

Write off: A reduction in recognized value; refers to recognition of the reduced or zero value of an asset.

Y

Yield: The total economic return to an investor. The rate of return on a financial investment usually expressed as a percentage of the original amount invested. From a lender's perspective, the amount of money paid back on a loan over a certain period of time. See also rate of return; return; revenue.

Yield maintenance: Another name for maintenance yield.

Z

Zero-based budgeting: A technique that minimizes the use of historical data and focuses instead on data from outside sources. Zero-based budgeting is always used when no history is available, as in the case of new construction or a property whose historical data is unavailable or unreliable due to changes in ownership or use.

Index

*Page numbers followed by "e," such as 36e, indicate exhibits.